P9-DHQ-258

FOOTSORE 1

Walks & Hikes Around Puget Sound

Second Edition

**By Harvey Manning/Photos by Bob & Ira Spring
Maps by Gary Rands/The Mountaineers • Seattle**

*Seattle • Puget Sound Trail from Tacoma to Everett
• Overlake Highlands and Sammamish Valley
• Issaquah Alps • Cedar River
• Duwamish-Green River • White River*

The Mountaineers: Organized 1906 ". . . to explore, study, preserve and enjoy the natural beauty of the Northwest."

Safety is an important concern in all outdoor activities. No guidebook can alert you to every hazard or anticipate the limitations of every reader, so the descriptions in this book are not representations that a particular trip is safe for your party. When you take a trip, you assume responsibility for your own safety. Some of the trips described in this book may require you to do no more than look both ways before crossing the street; on others, more attention to safety may be required due to terrain, traffic, weather, the capabilities of your party, or other factors. Keeping informed on current conditions and exercising common sense are the keys to a safe, enjoyable outing.

Copyright 1977, 1982 by Harvey Manning
All rights reserved

Published by
The Mountaineers
306 2nd Ave. W., Seattle, Washington 98119

Published simultaneously in Canada by
Douglas & McIntyre, Ltd., 1615 Venables St.,
Vancouver, British Columbia V5L 2H1

Series design by Marge Mueller; layout by Barbara Haner
Cover photo: Footbridge across the Green River in city of Auburn

Manufactured in the United States of America
First edition, December 1977; second printing November 1978
Second edition, February 1982; second printing April 1984;
third printing August 1985; fourth printing June 1986

Library of Congress Cataloging in Publication Data

Manning, Harvey
    Footsore : walks and hikes around Puget Sound.

    Includes index.
    1. Hiking—Washington (State)—Puget Sound
region—Guide-books.   2. Puget Sound region (Wash.)
—Description and travel—Guide-books.   I. Title.
GV199.42.W22P835   1982   917.97′79   82-2100
ISBN 0-89886-065-2   AACR2

INTRODUCTION I

Other guidebooks published by The Mountaineers direct the feet to high or distant areas where, to quote the 1964 Wilderness Act, "the earth and its community of life are untrammeled by man, where man himself is a visitor who does not remain." Quite different is the realm—Puget Sound City and outskirts—of the **Footsore** series. There man definitely does remain. He lives there. Works there. Fools around there. And trammels there—boy does he ever trammel. Yet his creations/destructions are not unrelieved; on the walks described in these pages tree green is more prominent than asphalt black, birdsongs than hornhonks, clean breezes than vile gases. If the routes traverse little pristine wilderness they're wild to a degree. Or wildlike in part. Or anyhow nice.

And they're close to home. Few **Footsore** paths lie more than a going-and-coming total of 2 automobile hours (many are less than 1 hour) from one or another major lump of Puget Sound City population, whether in Everett or Olympia, Bremerton or Bellevue. The Two-Hour Rule derives from this book's philosophical foundation that (1) walking is good-in-itself and good for you; (2) automobile riding in more than modest doses is very bad for you. Walking is medicine for under-exercised bodies and over-stressed minds, but the knitting together of damaged flesh and spirit by a day on the trail can be unraveled by too long an evening battle homeward through the mobs of deranged children whose grim joy is playing war games on freeways and byways. If to gain for a day the sweet balm of Nature a person must suffer more than 2 or 3 hours of automobile trauma, he perhaps is better off spending the re-creation day home in bed.

Automobile ownership continues to be a prerequisite for full American citizenship and all its rights and privileges, including easy transport to trails. On some surveys for this book the thumb was employed, with varying success; other hitchhikers unquestionably would be picked up faster than was the surveyor, but being old, crummy, and poor is not without compensations—a roadside display of youth, beauty, or wealth, particularly by a solitary thumber, is asking for it. Risks aside, hitchhiking nearly always adds time to a trip, maybe a lot. But if you don't get dumped in the ditch it's cheap.

Then there's the bus. The text here notes walking routes reasonably accessible via Metro Transit as of 1981. For precise planning one must obtain current route maps and schedules; the notes are intended mainly to stimulate hikers to think bus—and bus managers to think hikers.

NO MONEYBACK GUARANTEE

The country of **Footsore I** is portrayed here as it was when surveyed during the winter-spring of 1976-77. All trailheads and much of nearly all routes were resurveyed in the summer-fall of 1981; a number of new trips were added from scratch. However, the walking may not be the same when you arrive. This lived-on, worked-on, fooled-around on, trammeled land is ever changing, often radically and without notice.

Volumes in the **Footsore** series are periodically revised, correcting errors, updating information, dropping trips that have been trammeled to death and

Lake Washington and Madison Park

replacing them with new ones. However, the series covers upwards of 3000 miles and the surveyor, who does not walk every step every year, will gladly accept any help anybody cares to offer. And don't bother to be polite. Address diatribes c/o The Mountaineers, 715 Pike Street, Seattle 98101.

Several specific caveats must be made:

1. A great many **Footsore** trips cross private property where trespassing long has been tolerated and was at the time of survey. But a copy of this book in your hot little hand does not serve as a license to infringe on property rights. If the "No Trespassing" signs have gone up, you must obey.

The behavior of you and other **Footsore** readers in many cases will determine whether or not trespassing continues to be tolerated. Obviously you should not foul the path with body wastes or garbage—and in fact the modern thoughtful walker picks up and carries out garbage left by others, gaining a glow of virtue plus whatever cash the glass and metal earn at the recycling station. For further discussion of trespassing see the introduction to "Puget Sound Trail: Seattle to Tacoma."

2. Railroad rights-of-way are private property and the owners do not invite trespassing. Walking tracks can be dangerous, as witness the annual death toll. However, tens of thousands of people annually trespass on Puget Sound train tracks and the trains do not object; occasionally they run over somebody, but it's nothing personal. Just keep an eye over the shoulder.

3. Vast expanses of **Footsore** country are in tree farms managed by the state Department of Natural Resources (DNR) and private landowners. Unlike

national forests, where the Sustained Yield-Multiple Use Act places recreation on a parity with lumber and pulp, the laws of the state on DNR lands and the laws of economics on private lands give short shrift to any statistic not preceded by a $.

Let us remember that you can't get beefsteak without hurting the cow nor boards for houses and paper for guidebooks without letting daylight into the swamp. Tree farms demand some stiffness in the upper lip. A walk described as being through cool depths of a green tunnel may be, when you arrive, in sun-blasted bleakness of a raw new clearcut. You may not be able to find the route at all, out there in the stumps and slash.

4. Not merely man transforms the terrain. Nature, too, runs amok. Many **Footsore** routes are maintained, if at all, solely by the stomping boots and brushcrashing bodies of hikers who, should their attention wander briefly, soon lose the contest to rank greenery.

5. Some trips are so lacking in distinctive landmarks you may be unable to follow the surveyor's confusing directions without map and compass, a higher order of routefinding skill than required in the North Cascades wilderness, and lots of luck.

FOOTROADS (ALL POWER TO THE FEET)

Were **Footsore** confined to protected footpaths the series would boil down to a skinny pamphlet. If you're going to do much walking in and around Puget Sound City you're going to walk a lot of roads. The question is, how much wheeled traffic can a pedestrian accept? The amount varies, of course, from person to person, situation to situation. Strolling the shore of Lake Washington one may be oblivious to a steady stream of Sunday drivers creeping along the adjacent boulevard. Deep in the wildwood a single snarling motorcycle may be a stomach-churning outrage.

The finest footroads have perfect wheelstops that convert them to de facto trails. Generally quite acceptable are ways traveled only by the occasional logging truck or other work machine. Meeting two or three recreation vehicles an hour may not critically aggravate the hypertension. A day-long parade of razzing motorcycles — well, you'd have better stood in bed.

The surveyor sought routes reasonably free of racket most of the time. Some routes were judged too scenicly splendid to be conceded to wheels; labeled "Never on Sunday," they are recommended for, say, stormy winter Wednesdays before school lets out. Some routes found serene by the surveyor may subsequently have been invaded, some perfect wheelstops breached by jeeper engineers, those good-deed-a-weekend latter-day Dan'l Boones.

HOW TO BE FOOTSORE

Outdoor recreation professionals distinguish between "walks," short excursions on easy paths in forgiving terrain, requiring no special clothing or equipment and no experience or training, and "hikes," longer and/or rougher, potentially somewhat dangerous, demanding stout shoes or boots, clothing for cold and wet weather, gear for routefinding and emergencies, rucksack to carry it all in, and best done in company of experienced companions or eased into gradually, conservatively.

Footsore describes short walks in and around Puget Sound City, outings suitable for a leisurely afternoon or even a spring-summer evening, as well as long walks that may keep a person hopping all day. For any walk, equipment demands no more than a passing thought; as for technique, the rule is just to pick 'em up and lay 'em down and look both ways before crossing the street.

Hikes are another matter and the novice must take care, when choosing a trip, to be aware of the difference and to make appropriate preparations. On every hike where a shout for help might not bring quick assistance to the lost or injured or ill, each person should carry the Ten Essentials:

1. Extra clothing—enough so that if a sunny-warm morning yields to rainy-windy afternoon, or if accident keeps the party out overnight, hypothermia ("exposure" or "freezing to death") will not be a threat
2. Extra food—enough so something is left over at the planned end of the trip, in case the actual end is the next day
3. Sunglasses—if travel on snow for more than a few minutes may be involved
4. Knife—for first aid and emergency firebuilding (making kindling)
5. Firestarter—a candle or chemical fuel for starting a fire with wet wood
6. First aid kit
7. Matches—in a waterproof container
8. Flashlight—with extra bulb and batteries
9. Map. Travel directions herein assume the reader has the proper highway maps for driving to the trip vicinity, from where the text and sketch maps zero in on the trailhead. For the walks no other maps are necessary. However, for many of the hikes a person is risking not achieving the destination—and not returning to civilization until carried there by a search party—if he lacks the appropriate U.S. Geological Survey maps, available at map shops and some backpacking shops.
10. Compass—with knowledge of use

Hiking isn't so complicated that a person needs a lot of instruction, but the same can be said of dying. To learn how to select and use the Essentials a novice lacking tutelage by a family member or friend may enroll in a course offered by an outing club, youth group, church, park department or professional wilderness guide. Alternatively, one can buy a book; the surveyor is partial to **Backpacking: One Step At A Time** but other mountain bums have to make a living too, and hundreds of them also have written manuals.

Some words about the information summary given for each trip:

The "round trip xx miles" and "elevation gain xxxx feet" tell a person if the trip fits his energy and ambition. Some hikers do 20 miles a day and gain 5000 feet without a deep breath, others gasp and grunt at 5 miles and 1500 feet. The novice will quickly learn his capacity. Note: the "elevation gain" is gross, not net; an upsy-downsy trail can gain hundreds of feet while going along "on the flat."

The "allow x hours" must be used with a personal conversion factor. The figures here are based on doing 1½ miles an hour on the flat (walking at a rate of 2 miles an hour but walking only 45 minutes in the hour) and an elevation gain of about 700 feet an hour, with added time for slow tracks—muddy, brushy, loggy. From these figures a hiker accustomed to doing 1 mile an hour or 3, or gaining 200 feet an hour or 2000, can calculate his own approximate travel time.

"High point xxxx feet" tells the knowing much about the vegetation and views to expect, as well as the probable amount of snow in any given month. The bottom line, the "all year" or "February-December" or whatever, attempts to spell this out. It does not suggest the "best time," which is a subjective judgment based on whether one likes spring flowers or fall mushrooms or what. The intent is to tell when, in an average normal year (whatever that is) a trail is probably sufficiently snowfree for pleasure walking, meaning less than a foot of snow or only occasional deeper patches. Several factors are involved. One is elevation. Another is distance from Puget Sound, whose large volume of above-freezing water warms winter air masses. In any locality, higher is generally snowier. But also,for identical elevations the farther from saltwater is generally snowier. And mountain valleys, acting like giant iceboxes, generally are snowier than nearby lowlands outside the mountain front. Finally, though south and west slopes get as much snow as north and east, they also get more sun (and also more sun than valley flats) and thus melt out faster.

These factors are taken into account, and eked out with guesswork, in coding the trips. To explain the code:

"All year" means the trail is always open—except during intervals when the snowline drops to sea level or near it.

"February-December" doesn't imply any prejudice against January, which may be no colder than adjacent months, but means an ordinary winter has maybe 4-8 weeks, from late December to late February, when the trail may be under more than a foot of snow. But it can be snowfree in a mid-January thaw or throughout a mild winter. And in a tough winter can be up to the knees from November to March.

"March-November" means a typical snowpack of several feet or so that begins piling up in November, early or late, and melts mostly out in March, early or late. Again, the path may be walkable in dead of winter. Or up to the crotch from October to May.

Foster Island trail in the University of Washington Arboretum

"April-November" means quite a deep snowpack that may begin accumulating in October (or December) and may melt in March (or June).

And so on. In short, the aim is to tell approximately how things usually have been, not predict what they will be.

ACKNOWLEDGMENTS 1-2

The primary debt owed by this and every other hiking guide to the Puget Sound region is to the tens of thousands of Mountaineers who have prowled the countryside for 75 years. Anyone setting out to survey the pedestrian pleasures of the territory starts, wittingly or not, from their group wisdom.

The debt to Janice Krenmayr and her famous **Footloose Around Puget Sound** is obvious. After a decade and three revisions she had enough, what with other projects demanding attention, and I—her old editor on that happy enterprise—became her pedestrian replacement.

Even before I met him I owed much to Stan Unger, who as a planner for King County played a key role in shaping the 1971 Urban Trails Plan. Reading that exhilarating document's schemes for paths interlacing throughout the county and tying to networks of adjoining counties inspired many explorations described herein. Very early in my surveying I was fortunate to be introduced to Stan by Tom Eksten of King County Parks, a fellow fanatic. At a first meeting Stan and Tom told me all manner of good places to walk. Stan himself had been mulling a guidebook; finding me already at work he graciously yielded the field and volunteered free access to his knowledge. In subsequent months he not only suggested trips but led me on several, demonstrating enviable form in crossing barbed-wire fences and heroic devotion to packing out litter, including beer cans, empty or not. Finally, Stan and Tom read and criticized the entire manuscript that became **Footsore 1** and 2.

If my expression of gratitude to others who helped on 1 and 2 is briefer it's solely because space considerations forbid proper thanks:

Don Campbell, Mt. Baker-Snoqualmie National Forest; Jack Mosby, Bureau of Outdoor Recreation; Dan Fryberger, Doug Bailey, and W. C. Alguard, U. S. Army Corps of Engineers; William A. Bush, Larry Kay, Bob Genoe, Don Malloy, Carl Nelson, Steve McBee, Bob Togstad, Jim Collins, Joe Cowan, and Monty Fields, Washington State Parks; Terry Patton and Joe Potter and Cassie Phillips, Washington Department of Natural Resources; W. M. Foster and Richard P. Wilson, Washington Department of Highways; Robert H. Barnard, Washington Department of Game; Gregory W. Lovelady, State Trails Coordinator in the Interagency Committee for Outdoor Recreation; Marjean Deach, Metro Transit; Bruce Finke, Seattle Office of Policy Planning; Larry E. Jones, Seattle Parks; Siegfried Semrau, Bellevue Parks; people in Mercer Island and Kent parks whose names I didn't catch; Pat Cummins, Green River Community College; Max Eckenburg, Camp Sheppard, and Dan Minzel, Camp Brinkley, of the Scouts; and in the Weyerhaeuser Company, James W. Crotts, Dave Mumper, and Howard Millan—the latter of whom was Senior Patrol Leader of Troop 324 when I was a Tenderfoot, **Footsore** thus providing a reunion on the trail with my Leader.

H.M. 1977

Fifteenmile Creek on Tiger Mountain

For the second editions of **F-1** and **F-2** I started with Tom Eksten of King County Parks and Larry Kay of Washington State Parks, always miles ahead of me. Bob Genoe of State Parks again was a gold mine of information, this time about Wallace Falls and the entire Skykomish. Robert Kinzebach's Pic-Tours Guide Maps were my guides to unsuspected wonders of the May Creek region. The Barber family brought me up to date on Anderson Cirque, more terrifying year by year. Contributions by comrades of the Issaquah Alps Trails Club defy listing—hundreds have shared In creating and popularizing the trail system. Most of what I know about Squak, and much about Tiger, I learned at the knee of our Chief Ranger, Bill Longwell. The O'Brians rediscovered the West Tiger Caves. Dave Kappler found Surprise Wall and pioneered the route to De Leo Wall, among others. Ralph and Peggy Owen hacked and stamped many new trails on Cougar Mountain. Irving Petite and Fred Rounds filled us with lore about bears, cougars, gypo loggers, coal miners, and other wild creatures. Beyond the Alps, Susan Bell and Gordon Fallicle introduced me to the wonderful world of wetlands on the East Sammamish Plateau, and Ed Alvorson to the Wild Sultan and other obscure marvels, and Sharon Steiner to Blue Heron Marsh, and Dick Burkhart to Youngs Lake. Linda Olson, Betty Nelson, and Edmunde Lewin straightened out some trips. Dick Brooks swung the machete that got us through the Beacon Greenbelt hellberry jungle. Florence Culp told me the history of Renton. Ira Spring occasionally had something to say that I didn't sneer at. I kept up with **Sunset Magazine** and **Signpost** and the newspapers. Aside from that there were the anonymous notes wrapped around rocks and hurled through my window. That's all right, a surveyor learns to live without love.

H.M. 1981

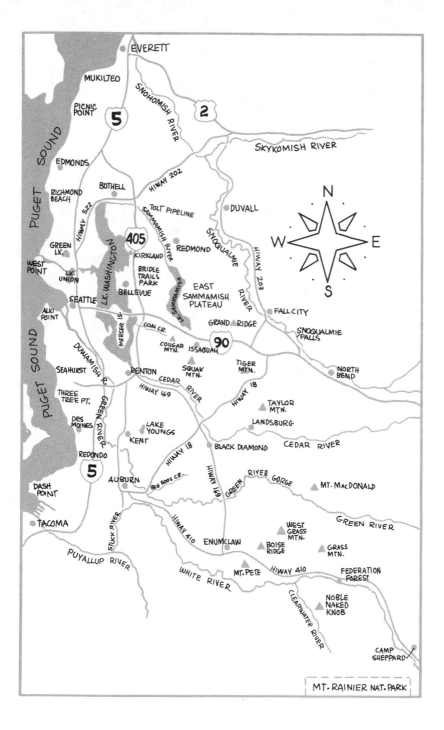

EVERETT

MUKILTEO

PICNIC POINT

PUGET SOUND

5

2

SNOHOMISH RIVER

SKYKOMISH RIVER

EDMONDS

RICHMOND BEACH

BOTHELL

HIWAY 202

HIWAY S-22

DUVALL

TOLT PIPELINE

SAMMAMISH RIVER

N

W E

S

GREEN LK.

405

KIRKLAND

REDMOND

SNOQUALMIE RIVER

HIWAY 203

WEST POINT

LK. UNION

BRIDLE TRAILS PARK

LK. WASHINGTON

EAST SAMMAMISH PLATEAU

SEATTLE

BELLEVUE

LK. SAMMAMISH

FALL CITY

ALKI POINT

MERCER IS.

COAL CR.

GRAND RIDGE

SNOQUALMIE FALLS

PUGET SOUND

DUWAMISH R.

COUGAR MTN.

ISSAQUAH

90

SEAHURST

RENTON

SQUAK MTN.

TIGER MTN.

NORTH BEND

GREEN RIVER

CEDAR RIVER

HIWAY 169

HIWAY 18

THREE TREE PT.

TAYLOR MTN.

DES MOINES

LAKE YOUNGS

KENT

LANDSBURG

CEDAR RIVER

REDONDO

BLACK DIAMOND

5

HIWAY 18

HIWAY 169

DASH POINT

AUBURN

BIG SOOS CR.

GREEN RIVER GORGE

MT. MacDONALD

GREEN RIVER

TACOMA

STUCK RIVER

HIWAY 410

WEST GRASS MTN.

ENUMCLAW

BOISE RIDGE

GRASS MTN.

PUYALLUP RIVER

WHITE RIVER

MT. PETE

HIWAY 410

FEDERATION FOREST

CLEARWATER RIVER

NOBLE NAKED KNOB

CAMP SHEPPARD

MT. RAINIER NAT. PARK

CONTENTS 1

Tolt Pipeline Trail

Seward Park

Green Lake

SEATTLE

Until the 1880s Seattle needed more trails like it needed more clams. After a decade of rampaging growth, however, citizens found their traditional quick and easy getaways so far dwindled they bought Woodland Park, way out north beyond the city limits, and laid rails there so folks could picnic on a Sunday in the "wilderness at the end of the streetcar line."

The growth continued at such pace the adolescent city, worried about losing its soul, engaged the Olmsteds (of Central Park) to plan a system of parks and boulevards, green ganglia for a flesh of residential and commercial wood and brick. The result, described herein as the "Olmsted Trail," remains to this day Seattle's best long walk.

Much more of the sort readily could have been done, then. But streetcar greenery paled in the brilliant morning of the automobile. Sunday picnics shifted to Lake Wilderness and Lake Serene, Flaming Geyser and Green River Gorge, Maloney's Grove and Snoqualmie Falls, and—incredibly to those of us who in less than a decade lived from Model T to Model A to V-8—Paradise Valley.

A glorious party it was, it was, a stupendous half-century binge. Then Seattle awoke. With a terrible hangover. The jug of cheap gas was empty. The nearby countryside had been filled overnight by new cities. The farther countryside was receding behind freeways clogged by mobs of cars. For quick and easy getaways Seattle of 1970 had to stay home—in a park system admirably suited to 1910.

Fortune smiled. When the military was forced to stop preparing for lovely old wars to invest in Armageddon, and the railroads junked the transportation business to pursue the big bucks of land development, civic opportunists alertly snapped up two new large parks and a second magnificent long trail. Yet even then the city famed for a Green Soul had the least close-to-home wildland— protected in parks or other preserves—of any metropolis of the West Coast. Vancouver was far ahead with Stanley Park, University Endowment Lands, and Grouse Mountain. So was Portland, with Forest Park. Also San Francisco with the Golden Gate Recreation Area and Oakland with the East Bay Regional Park System. The shocker was that so, too, with the San Gabriel Mountains, was the disaster area ill-famed as the Bellevue of the Southland—Los Angeles!

So it was, in the late 1970s, that Seattle humbly raised up its eyes eastward unto the hills, the Old Mountains that were its hope, the Issaquah Alps, the "wilderness on the Metro 210."

The Alps, upon whose foothills Seattle is built, are important because closer always is better. But by the same rule, closest is ever the best. The feet know that; very likely more miles are annually walked on paths described in this and the two following chapters than on all the National Scenic Trails combined. A half-dozen Burke-Gilmans scarcely would fill the demand. Indeed, just as freeways generate automobiles, trails breed pedestrians.

In the lack of a half-dozen Burke-Gilmans, not to be overlooked are the sort of routes that the new cities, if they have any, brag up as "trails" but old cities modestly call "sidewalks." Seattle has hundreds of miles of peaceful strolling under trees, beside gardens, in views, in quiet, in history. For a rich sampling consult Janice Krenmayr's two booklets, **Footloose in Seattle.**

USGS maps: Edmonds East, Seattle North, Kirkland, Shilshole Bay, Seattle South, Mercer Island

Seattle Greenbelts (Beacon Hill Greenbelt Trail) (Map-page 16)

In 1977 Seattle adopted an Urban Greenbelt Plan that proposed 14 areas for preservation either by purchase or regulatory measures (most greenbelts are bluffs of unstable glacial drift or wetlands that shouldn't be built on). Acquisition of the Southwest Queen Anne Greenbelt began in 1980. Some others on the list are Duwamish Head, East Duwamish, East Duwamish-South (Beacon Hill), Northeast Queen Anne, St. Mark's, and West Duwamish (Highland Park).

A greenbelt doesn't have to "do" anything. It serves by simply lying there making no noise (but soaking up a lot), polluting no air or water (but always cleaning), being looked at (to quote Rae Tufts, as "part of the urban fabric"), and being lived in (not by thee and me but by squirrels, rabbits, weasels, muskrats, raccoons, and beaver, and by red-tailed hawks, great blue herons, gulls, nighthawks, horned owls, screech owls, geese, jaegers, ducks, and grebes, and by moles, voles, mice, and rats, and by pigeons, wrens, and warblers, and by those sly old coyotes that everybody in the neighborhoods assumes are just plain dogs).

Some greenbelts invite a person to view the green from inside, to walk in wildland and philosophize, and—who knows?—maybe meet Old Coyote.

The surveyor did not inventory all Seattle greenbelts. He glanced at some, quailed at others, walked just one. What a walk. As his companion (the one with the machete) commented, "It's a different sort of city experience than rollerskating around Green Lake." What a mouthful.

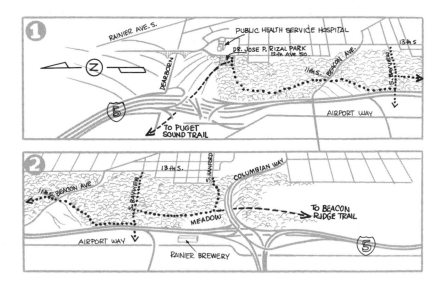

Seattle from Dr. Jose P. Rizal Park

Beacon Hill Greenbelt Trail

The larger significance of this trail is that it begins ½ mile from King Street Station (a link ought not be hard to arrange) and ends ¾ mile from the Beacon Ridge Trail (naught to bar the way but freeway fences which readily could be realigned to permit walking in forest and meadow beside and beneath a maze of skyways). Thus, a pedestrian route could connect the Puget Sound Trail to Beacon Ridge and (via another new link) to Renton and the Cedar River Trail.

The intrinsic importance is the green wildness of 1¼ miles of forested bluff. At times, trees mellowing the din of traffic, trillium 'and solomon's seal and fringecup in bloom, the walker is transported in spirit to true, distant wilderness. At other times one enjoys panoramas of the city's industrial guts, which ought not be scorned lest they wither and we starve.

Park at or near Dr. Jose P. Rizal Park, South Judkins and 12 Avenue South, on the slope just west of the former Public Health Service (Marine) Hospital on the north nose of Beacon Hill-Ridge. Elevation, 275 feet.

Linger long in the first of the great views of the on-going Industrial Revolution. Look from downtown towers, Smith's (Ivar's) humbly quaint against huge black boxes, to King Street and Union Stations, nostalgic next to Kingdome and freeways, and over Duwamish flats (once tideflats), crowded with factories and warehouses, to Elliott Bay and ferries and moored ships, Bainbridge Island and the Olympics.

Descend steps from the children's play area and find a rude trail down to an old street, the pavement invaded by ivy and hellberry. Turn left through a Highway Department plantation of native maples and exotic conifers. When the ancient roadway is chopped off by new freeway, climb left along an old road

Powerline trail along Beacon Ridge

grade. Evidences of a human past lie all along the route: traces of vanished houses; their kitchen middens; their garden escapes—weeping willow, teasel, ivy, blue sailors, and the omnipresent, ineffable hellberry; apple trees—the entire slope once was a row of orchards and local folks crop them still.

The path leads to several woods-hidden houses at the end of a single-lane gravel road that is, surprisingly, a public street, 11 Avenue South, that emerges on Beacon Avenue South. To here the survey took 40 minutes, leisurely, easy, no suffering.

Cross Beacon to a driveway and pause for a second stupendous industrial view. Then descend an alpine-like "talus" of andesite blocks strewn by the Highway Department to stabilize the slope. Hellberries force the route to the very edge of I-5. Reflect upon the scene. Doppelganger-like, see yourself there in the torrent of juggernauts—and then here, free of wheels and cares. Members of a party will have to muse separately because conversation is impossible. For a surreal experience walk under I-5, through the forest of pillars, and discover one of Seattle's least-known and least-objectionable motorcycle speedways. Discover, too, a path by which Beacon residents walk to work at plants in the Cudahy Bar S vicinity. The survey reached this point in 25 minutes from Beacon, most of the time spent gazing and musing.

Ascend the path (which leads via a stairway on the line of South Bayview to 13 Avenue South) and turn right on a trench hacked through hellberries by locals who enjoy pies, jelly, wine. The path ends on a meadow bench, recently a homesite, with apple trees that also yield many pies uncontaminated by agribusiness poisons. When the formal trail is dedicated this will become renowned as a charming nook to picnic among the apple blossoms.

Only machete and masochism made the next stretch possible. For 60 minutes there was chopping of hellberries, slithering up and slipping down steep mud. But—ah—the reward. The aroma that had been puzzling noses in the wildwood was revealed—upon emerging in a meadow above I-5—to be emanations from the mash cookers of Rainier Brewery. The surveyors paused for a long lunch, drinking in emanations, marveling at the myriad busy-nesses on Duwamish flats below, gazing from Ivar's Tower to Green and Gold Mountains.

During a final and easy ½ hour the intrepids reeled into a forest of great old cottonwoods, maples, and alders. The special feature is the festooning by long, tough vines that have the look of Hollywood fakes but are real, if exotic, and easily could be used by Tarzan and Cheetah to swing through the jungle in pursuit of Jane and Boy. The route turns uphill through an old clay mine that fed a brick factory and filled much bottomland around the brewery. It comes out through a heap of neighborhood hedge-trimmings and lawn-mowings at the deadend of South Hanford on 13 Avenue South, elevation 250 feet. For vines and brewery, start the hike here.

The endpoint has historic interest. The valley now used by Columbian Way to climb Beacon Ridge was dug not by Nature but Man—his first futile try at connecting Elliott Bay to Lake Washington.

Round trip 2½ miles, allow 4 hours
High point 275 feet, elevation gain 500 feet
All year
Bus: Metro 1, 60

Beacon Ridge (Map-page 21)

A 200-foot-wide green lawn rolling up hill and down dale for miles, in broad views west to saltwater and Olympics, east to Lake Washington and Cascades. And if you don't bother them the Seattle City Light power lines won't bother you. The hike can begin and end at any number of places; the full tour, starting at the north end, will be described here.

Park at or near Maple Wood Playground Park, Corson Avenue S and South Snoqualmie, in itself a nice little broad-view stroll around the greensward. Elevation, 200 feet.

Walk a long block north to the powerline lawn; here is a panorama over I-5 and the Duwamish industrial plain to Elliott Bay and downtown Seattle and Queen Anne Hill and Magnolia Bluff and Olympics.

Ascend the lawn 1 mile to the crossing of busy Beacon Avenue (good parking), just south of the Veterans Administration Hospital and Jefferson Park Golf Course. Here the lawn bends right to follow on or near the crest of Beacon Ridge. Streets (mostly quiet) are crossed and backyards merge into public lawn, but the walk-anywhere no-trail-needed strip is so spacious and calm (no motorcycles permitted) that despite the all-aroundness of Puget Sound City a person feels the green peace.

Ascending grassy knolls, dipping to hollows, the way offers looks south over Lake Washington to Renton and Rainier, up to jets sliding down to land, and east over Mercer Island to the Issaquah Alps. Beyond Empire Way the ridge assumes a rural air, often wildwooded on either side, pleasantly invaded by garden plots and orchards and horses pasturing and roosters crowing. And dogs barking. After crossing 51 Avenue S, the green lane drops a bit to fruit trees in a vale and rises to a hilltop weather station, 5 miles from the start and the recommended lunch spot and turnaround. The view extends back the full length of the route to the Veterans Hospital and beyond to downtown towers and Capitol Hill, as well as over the Duwamish Valley and Boeing Field to West Seattle and the Olympics.

Round trip 10 miles, allow 7 hours
High point 350 feet, elevation gain 800 feet
All year
Bus: Metro 3 and 31 and 48 to Beacon Avenue, 42 to Empire Way

The route goes on and has marvelous potential for connecting Seattle to Renton. But in dropping from Weather Station Knoll the powerline leaves the wide lawn and the city and enters a grubby motorcycle hell which continues to Skyway, relieved only by the oasis of Skyway County Park.

Olmsted Trail (Map-page 23)

In 1903, during the decade when Seattle established the bulk of what was to be its park system for the next 60-odd years, J.C. Olmsted designed for the city a magnificent park-and-boulevard network. A portion of the plan was implemented in those years before the automobile began to call the tune of urban development. To emphasize the unity and pre-freeway character, it might well be officially named "Olmsted Trail," linking the city's three major lakes, traversing kempt-lawn parks, an arboretum containing thousands of native and exotic plants, and a virgin-forest wildland, passing beaches, bird-busy marshes, sailboats on blue waters, and broad mountain views.

To experience the oneness, on the survey trip the entire trail was hiked in a day: the car was parked at East Green Lake; three Metro buses were taken to Seward Park, the total trip time 1½ hours; the trail was hiked back to the car, with the sustaining knowledge that if ambition failed or rain crushed the umbrella, always ready to rescue was Metro Transit. The hike is described here in the sequence of the survey; most people, of course, will prefer doing only short segments of the trail on any single excursion.

Mile 0-2½: Seward Park

Park at the entrance, just off Lake Washington Boulevard South at Juneau Street.

The Olmsted Trail properly begins by looping around Bailey Peninsula. Walk the shore in either direction, by fish hatchery and fishing piers, bathing beaches (on a hot day, break the hike for a dip) and views across Lake Washington to Mercer Island, south to Rainier.

Some Lake Washington facts: 210 feet is the deepest point; water level is now 20.0-21.85 feet above sealevel, having been lowered 10 feet in 1916; main tributaries are the Sammamish River and Cedar River, the latter diverted

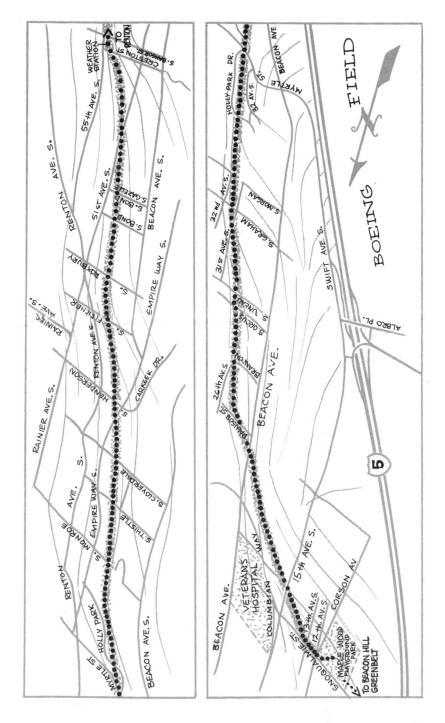

early in the century from the Green-Duwamish to the lake; former outlet was the Black River to the Green-Duwamish, present outlet is the Lake Washington Ship Canal.

The shore is not the sole attraction of 278-acre Seward Park. The peninsula spine features Seattle's largest virgin forest, close to 1 mile long and averaging ¼ mile wide. The old-growth Douglas firs are dazzlers, the maples are huge, and the supporting cast of native trees and shrubs forms a fine wild tangle. The forest trail system has entries around the peninsula; paths range from broad-flat to narrow-primitive. No map required. Just plunge in and explore. If lucky, get lost, thus making the wildland seem all the larger.

A basic introduction to Seward Park requires a 2½-mile shore loop plus a tour up and down the 1-mile-long peninsula; 4½ miles, 3 hours. For hikers intending to reach far points by day's end the short introduction is up either shore to the peninsula tip and back down the spine, a 2½-mile opening segment in the Olmsted Trail.

Mile 2½-9: Lake Washington Boulevard

Parking is plentiful (not summer Sundays) the whole route.

Officially known as Lake Washington Park and Parkway, the entire length is along streets, but most of the walking path is a decent distance from car lanes, traversing this or that pocket park; machines are easy to ignore if eyes are pointed over the water to the mountains.

Seward Park trail

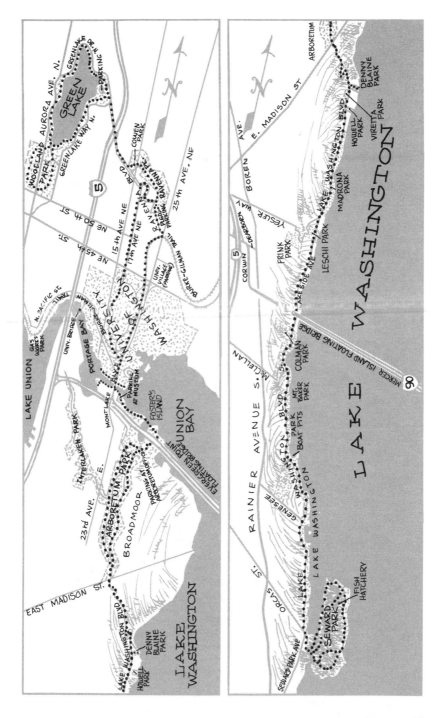

The first 3½ walking miles are trees and lawns and wall-to-wall ducks and coots and, in the reeds, redwing blackbirds. Some attractions, in order: pretty little Andrews Bay, enclosed by Bailey Peninsula; Japanese cherry trees; yacht moorage at Ohler's Island; dismal pits of Sayres Memorial Park; bathing beach at Mt. Baker Park, adjoined on the north by Colman Park; mountain views from Baker to Pilchuck to Index to Si to Issaquah Alps to Rainier.

For the next 1 mile the street changes name to Lakeside Avenue and is lined by private homes. But under Mercer Island Floating Bridge is public access to the water. For perhaps the best mountain views of the whole trip, walk up to the plaza and out on the bridge. See Glacier Peak.

At Leschi business district and yacht harbor the boulevard resumes; on the hillside are lawns and trees of Frink Park, on the water is Leschi Park. A little old ferry, now some sort of private enterprise, catches the sentimental eye, reminding of the pre-bridge era when this was the landing for the Mercer Island ferries. For a scant 1 mile the path is on the shore, passing the bathing beach of Madrona Park. (Ready for that swim yet?) Then private homes again preempt the water.

The final 1 mile leaves the lake and climbs the hill in a forest of private trees, plus the public trees of boulevard-side Howell and Viretta Parks. Not yet lost is the lake. Just down a deadend street is tiny Denny-Blaine Park. Note the handsome granite-block bulkhead, wonder why it is so high above the water—and realize that when built that's where the waves lapped. Above here the boulevard switchbacks through little Lakeview Park; dodge off the street in a secluded grassy hollow and climb a greensward knoll with a tree-screened look over the lake. Thence it's not far to East Madison Street and the Arboretum.

Mile 9-10: University of Washington Arboretum

Parking at Madison Playground at the south end, in several lots along the boulevard and Upper Road, and at the north Broadmoor entrance at the north end.

The full official name is University of Washington Arboretum in Washington Park. In the 200 acres of city park managed by the University as a scientific arboretum are thousands of shrubs and trees and other plants, native and from all over the world, arranged in logical groupings, placed in artful landscapings to exploit the natural terrain of ridges and valleys, marshes and ponds and creeks. A half-century of loving care and artistry are represented.

Attempting to summarize the Arboretum in this short space would be insulting. It needs to be visited plant by plant from one end to the other. When the tour is complete it's another season and the whole job has to be done over. The most cursory introduction requires four walk-throughs: along the valley of Lake Washington Boulevard (the main road), sidetripping in the Japanese Garden; along Arboretum Drive (Upper Road) on the ridge east of the valley; along the broad green valley-bottom lawn of Azalea Way; and along the hillside trails between Azalea Way and Arboretum Drive, passing the Lookout, a shelter (refuge in the rain) with views down Azalea Way and out the valley north to the University District. Before starting, visit the Arboretum offices at the northeast corner, by the north Broadmoor entrance, for a brochure describing the flowering seasons and the plant groupings. Total cursory introduction 4 miles, 4 hours.

A lifetime is too short. The only justification for treating the Arboretum as a mere 1 mile on the Olmsted Trail is to stress its connection to other good things.

Mile 10-11½: Foster's Island-Waterfront Trail-Montlake Bridge

One of which is coming right up.

Parking on the south at the north Broadmoor entrance, on the north at the Museum of History and Industry.

The concrete-and-thunder Evergreen Point Floating Bridge ripped off a fifth of the former acreage of the Arboretum, brutalizing Foster's Island and Union Bay marshes. But even the remnant is a wonderland. The damage could have been worse, and would have been, had not the "Save the Arboretum" campaign of the early 1960s halted the Thompson Expressway planned to blast down the middle of the Arboretum and across (or under) Union Bay; in Seattle, this battle was the start of something new.

From the parking lot at north Broadmoor entrance the path crosses a slough to Foster's Island. Lakeshore. Groves of water-loving trees. A passage under

Water trail in the University of Washington Arboretum

the concrete span of the bridge approach. Views of University stadium and campus, sailboats on Union Bay, Laurelhurst homes on the far shore, and mountains.

Here begins the Waterfront Trail built in 1968 through reeds, among a profusion of birds (and critters unseen), in cattails and bulrushes. The floating walkway has spurs to observation piers. (Incidentally, this marsh is not

Lake Washington Ship Canal from Montlake Bridge

"primeval" but "new"—the area was all open lake until the water level was lowered to that of Lake Union in 1916.) Competing for attention with marsh texture is freeway geometry.

The Waterfront Trail ends at the Museum of History and Industry parking lot. However, the Lake Washington Ship Canal Waterside Trail, a project of the U.S. Army Corps of Engineers and Seattle Garden Club, carries on without a break, rounding the corner to Montlake Cut connecting Portage Bay of Lake Union and Union Bay of Lake Washington. Ships pass through, and yachts, and racing-shell crews practice. The trail goes under quaint old Montlake Bridge, built in 1925.

Before climbing steps to the bridge, sidetrip ¼ mile west to the end of the cut and the public park by the Seattle Yacht Club. Fine view of Portage Bay. Some Lake Union facts: maximum depth 50 feet; due to filling and building, present size is about half the original.

Mile 11½-13½: University of Washington

Parking, for a reasonable fee, on campus.

Montlake Bridge has grand views west and east over the lakes, down to water traffic. On the north side is another waterside walkway.

There are three routes from here to Ravenna Park. For one, cross Montlake Boulevard to campus, hit the Burke-Gilman Trail (which see), follow it north 1½ miles to the vicinity of 25 Avenue, and there cut left to the park. For a second, at an unknown future date there will be a Union Bay Trail on the University campus, an extension of the Waterfront Trail leading near but not into wildlife sanctuaries, through a new arboretum, by water and marsh.

The third is through the campus, whose 600 acres offer miles and hours of strolling. Architecture from French Chateau to College Gothic to Concrete Brutal. Thousands of trees and shrubs, a veritable "other arboretum" used as such by botany and forestry classes. Windows out to Olympics, Lake Washington and Cascades, and Rainier.

For purposes of the Olmsted Trail the shortest line may be taken: up Rainier Vista (so named for the view of The Mountain which provides the campus its central axis) to Frosh Pond and resident ducks and onward to the vast brickery of Red Square, then up Memorial Way past the Astronomy Observatory and Washington State Museum, exiting from campus at NE 45 Street.

Turn right to reach the Burke-Gilman Trail. Alternatively, proceed north through Greek Row to Ravenna Boulevard and eastward to the lower end of Ravenna Park.

Mile 13½-15½: Ravenna and Cowen Parks

Street parking all around and at the lower end in Ravenna Playground.

A person can drive over (on bridges) the deep gulch of these parks and scarcely know they exist. But down in the dark hole, by the creek in big maples and firs, the city almost is silenced. Some ravine facts: before Seattle grew up this was the drainage of Green Lake to Lake Washington; the drainage continues but mainly underground in sewers and basements.

The ravine can be traversed along the bottom, on either sidehill, or by combinations; several trails interlace. Quiet semi-wild areas of native plants. Exotics, including a hellberry tangle only beloved by little, old winemakers and critters seeking a refuge from pussycats.

For 1 (walking) mile the ravine ascends from the level of Lake Washington to

Ravenna Park

that of Brooklyn Avenue. At Brooklyn take tree-lined Ravenna Boulevard under
I-5, by Boehm's Candy Kitchen, 1 mile to Green Lake, reached near the East
Green Lake business district.

Mile 15½-18½: Green Lake

Parking on streets and lots all around.

You can't get your ticket punched as having done the Olmsted Trail without
one 3-mile lap around Green Lake. Lawns and trees, views of surrounding
ridges and Rainier, resident mobs of waterfowl, who have their sanctuary,
Swan (Duck) Island. Beware of buzzing swarms of bicycles and thundering
herds of joggers; you could get knocked on the grass by endomorphins addicts
in oblivious ecstasy. Despite the popularity, many hours of many days the loop
is peaceful.

Bicyclists and rollerskaters are asked to travel in the lane farthest from the
lake, single-file, and in one direction only, counterclockwise. Walkers and
joggers should travel clockwise, in the lane closest to the lake, no more than
two abreast. A study shows that virtually all users approve of the rules but half
the walkers go the wrong way. You meet a lot of interesting people that way...

Some Green Lake facts: maximum depth 29 feet; lowered 7 feet in 1911 to
enlarge Green Lake Park; due to eutrophication (the "dying" which all lowland
lakes are doing) was once guaranteed to give any swimmer daring the waters
in summer a case of the "Green Lake Crud"; various attempts to clean up the
lake by dredging and poisoning having failed, eventually science was
consulted and Seattle City Water began diverting surplus water from the
mountains, and this flushing keeps Green Lake cleaner than some. Some of
the time.

By no means ignore the adjoining uplands of Woodland Park, one of
Seattle's oldest (1890) and still among its largest. Though entirely kempt, with
picnic grounds and rose gardens and zoo, it offers miles of serene green at
certain times of year and week. For a basic introduction do a 2-mile perimeter
loop, no guidebook or map required.

One-way trip 18½ miles, allow 12 hours
High point 250 feet, elevation gain 1000 feet
All year
Bus: Metro 39, Seward Park; 10, Colman Park; 27, Mercer Island Floating
    Bridge and Leschi Park; 2, Madrona Park; 11, 48, 4, Arboretum; 4, 7, 8,
    25, 30, 48, 76, 77, University; 7, 8, Ravenna-Cowen Parks; 16, 26, 48,
    East Green Lake; 6, West Green Lake

Burke-Gilman Trail (Map-page 31)

Any list of the nation's great urban trails would have to include the Burke-Gilman, whose 20 (ultimate) miles traverse scenes industrial, marine, commercial, academic, residential, and natural. There are views to ships and boats, over Salmon Bay and Lake Union to Seattle, Lake Washington to the Cascades, and Sammamish River to fields and forests. Sidetrips abound to parks and historic sites.

When Judge Thomas Burke and Daniel Gilman and fellow townboomers set out in 1885 to build the Seattle, Lake Shore and Eastern Railroad, their intent was to outwit Eastern financiers who controlled the American transcontinental railway lines by making an end run to the East via the Canadian transcontinental line. After appropriate chicanery these locals and the Easterners struck a deal and everybody got rich except the people. In the 1970s, however, the business of operating railroads became too much of a bother for the "railroad companies" that were energetically logging, mining, farming, and subdividing ill-gotten grant lands; the Burlington-Northern, mergerized product of a century of bamboozles, abandoned the Burke-Gilman line—which shortly was busier than ever with feet walking, jogging, and running, and bicycles. (No horses or motorized vehicles permitted.)

The official trail as of 1981 starts at Gasworks Park and ends at Kenmore Logboom Park, a distance of about 12½ miles, the cooperative effort of the City of Seattle, King County Parks, and the University of Washington. Eventually it will be extended to Chittenden Locks and Bothell Landing and thus these sections are described here.

Paved the entire 12½ miles, the trail is an easy day's up-and-back by bike. Hikers usually do as much as feels good and double back to the start. However, good bus service over the entire 20 miles permits any number of ingenuities. On the original survey, for example, the car was parked on Northlake and the walk ended in Bothell, 16 miles; a Metro bus (with one transfer) whisked the surveyor back to square one.

Chittenden Locks to Gasworks Park, 3¾ miles

Think of the railroad tracks (along this stretch, still in place) merely as the link between sidetrips. The rails run through grimy industrial backyards but at countless spots are close-by vista points that make this the most exciting working-waterfront walk in Seattle. (The Alaskan Way waterfront has more shops than ships and the Duwamish Waterway is hard to get intimate with.)

The first 1¼ miles from Chittenden Locks (see Puget Sound Trail) and the Ballard Bridge offer many short trips to docks and shipyards and every sort of craft from funky houseboats to fishing boats to medium-size freighters that serve the North—ships with such evocative names as **Pribiloff, Silver Clipper, Polar Merchant**. On the other side of the tracks lies Old Ballard, restored and revived and full of historic fun. Finish off this stretch by climbing the pedestrian stairway to Ballard Bridge for views west out Salmon Bay to the locks and east to the Fremont Cut.

The next 1¾ miles to Fremont Bridge start with more ships (**Trident, North Sea, Orion**) and views over the bay to Queen Anne Hill. After a dull mile inland, the tracks return to the water at Canal Street, just off Leary Way on 2nd SW, and pass Fremont Canal Park. Here where a creek used to flow from Lake Union to Salmon Bay now is the Fremont Cut, poplar-lined on both banks, ships and boats and canoes and ducks passing to and fro. Industry preempts the shore the final bit to Fremont Bridge. Climb from the tracks to visit the old Fremont District, platted 1875, now featuring Fat City Tavern, Deluxe Junk, Fremont Recycling Center, art shops, and the annual and far-famed Fremont Street Fair. At the northeast entry to the Fremont Bridge (built in 1917, 15 years before the higher Aurora Bridge) is the Rich Beyer sculpture, "Waiting for the Interurban," whose figures are so lifelike that fans often add embellishments — sweaters in cold weather, flowers in the hair in spring, bowl of dogfood for the dog.

The final ¾ mile to Gasworks Park is near Lake Union, passing a succession of marinas, rows of sailboats, stinkpots, fishing boats.

Gasworks Park to north end of University of Washington campus (NE 45th), 2¾ miles

Gasworks Park demands a tour. Inspect machinery of the plant which for decades generated gas from coal, walk the ¼ mile of frontage path on Lake Union. See tugboats, sailboats, police boats, climb the knoll for a view of downtown Seattle towering at the other end of the lake. Gulls, ducks, coots, crows, pigeons.

The official 1981 route begins here, following the Northlake Bikeway, a bluff-foot path separated from automobiles, to Latona Avenue NE, and turning up the bluff a block to NE Pacific Street and "Start" of Burke-Gilman Trail, ¾ mile from Gasworks Park.

On abandoned railroad grade the Burke-Gilman crosses under the Freeway Bridge and University Bridge over the ship canal and passes through the new West Campus to the old Central Campus beginning at 15 Avenue NE. Metro bus stops make this a good place for hikers-busriders to start.

The campus is among the best parts of the whole route. Views to Lake Union and Portage Bay, up Rainier Vista to the campus center and out to The Mountain, and over Union Bay to Lake Washington and the Cascades. Plentiful parking east of Montlake Boulevard. An intersection with the Olmsted Trail (which see) offers tempting sidetrips to campus and Arboretum. Eventually the University plans a nature trail through reconstituted natural areas on and around Union Bay, where for decades Seattle dumped its garbage.

At NE 45 Street the trail passes the tiny "Bob Pyle Wilderness" on the sidehill, crosses under the viaduct, and leaves campus. The traffic of students, professors, joggers, runners, strollers, bicyclers lessens.

North end of University campus to Sand Point (NE 65th), 3 miles

From campus the way passes close to University Village (parking, Metro buses, food, restrooms), swinging inland from the present lakeshore to curve around the former bay. Mostly residential, partly commercial, the way blooms in season with park plantings and private gardens. Urban birds sing.

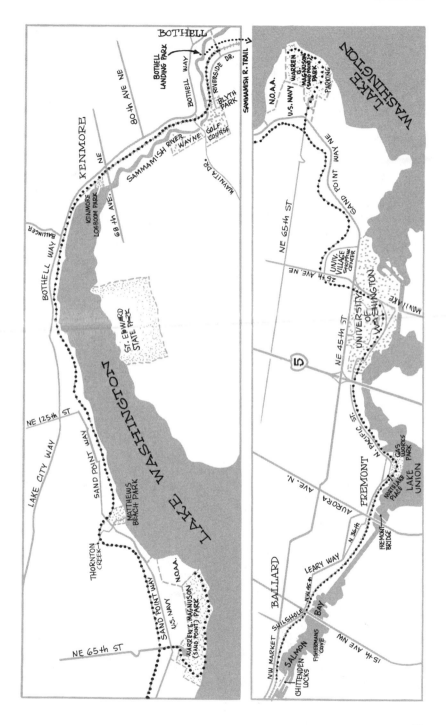

The trail returns to lake views at Sand Point. (For a sidetrip on NE 65 Street to Lake Washington beaches, see Warren G. Magnuson Park.)

At Princeton Bridge, just off Sand Point Way, a hillside gazebo is a neat spot to get out of the rain.

Sand Point to Seattle city limits (NE 145th), 4½ miles

Past Sand Point views are good over Lake Washington. At Thornton Creek are a Metro pumping station and a valley wildland of Himalaya berries penetrated by a path climbing the hill to a lake panorama.

A bit beyond is Matthews Beach Park. A sidetrip is mandatory out on the forested grassy knoll and down lawns to the shore to look over the waters to sailboats and mountains and fend off ducks and coots and gulls and crows that want your lunch.

A final 3 miles through residential neighborhoods on the water conclude at Seattle city limits.

City limits to Kenmore Logboom Park, 2½ miles

With no change except in style of signs and that the city's foot-saving lane of crushed rock beside the hard blacktop ceases, the trail enters King County jurisdiction, proceeding by more lakeside homes (Sheridan Beach, Lake Forest Park) to Kenmore Logboom Park, 1981 end of the Burke-Gilman. Access to the park is via 61 Avenue NE off Bothell Way.

The park's groves of cottonwood, willow, maple, and alder are an isle of cool peace on a hot day. The shore, mostly marshy-natural, provides refuge for myriad birds. The resident colony of ducks includes mallards, domestic whites, and weird exotics from China, gone wild (tame-wild). The park's chief glory is the long concrete pier, located where railroad cars once dumped logs in a "booming ground" where rafts were organized for towing to the mills. The pier provides splendid views down Lake Washington and across a stinkpot harbor to the mouth of Sammamish River.

Kenmore Logboom Park to Bothell Landing, 3½ miles

The bicycle route turns up onto Bothell Way. The foot route follows the railroad tracks, which here resume. The only feature of interest in a dreary industrial scene is the Kenmore Air Harbor.

However, the tracks soon leave the grime and diverge from the highway and enter the pastoral valley of the Sammamish River. Greenery of Wayne Golf Course pleases the eye. A sidetrip to a bridge gives vistas up and down the duck freeway. At 2½ miles from Logboom Park the railroad crosses the river on a solid, safe, and non-airy bridge and in a few steps from the far side comes to the entrance of Blyth Park, terminus of the Tolt Pipeline Trail (which see).

A ½-mile trail ultimately will connect Blyth Park to Bothell Landing Park. As of 1981 a detour is necessary along the railroad to 102 Avenue NE, then left to a trail intersection just before the river. To the right is the beginning of Sammamish River Trail (which see). To the left a scant ¼ mile (a scant 1 mile from Blyth Park) a handsome wooden footbridge arches over the river to The Park at Bothell Landing.

When Bothell turned its back on its beginnings it became just another backroad village. When it once again turned its face to the river it got Soul. The shops on the mall of Bothell Landing offer ice cream cones, books, and T-shirts—and they rent bicycles for the ride to Marymoor Park. The Park is a dandy spot to watch ducks and canoes, picnic, swim. Of special interest are the historic buildings: the 1885 Beckstrom Log House; 1896 Lytle House, now the

Senior Citizens Center; and the 1893 William Hannan Home, containing the Bothell Historical Museum (Sundays, 1-4 p.m.).

One-way distance from Chittenden Locks to Bothell Landing 20 miles
High point 150 feet, minor elevation gain
All year
Bus: Metro 17 and 43 at Chittenden Locks; 15, 17, 18, and 43 in Ballard; 26
and 28 at Fremont; a dozen lines in the University District; 30 in
Laurelhurst; 8 and 41 on Sand Point Way; 25 on 37th Ave. NE; 307 on
Bothell Way; many lines in Bothell

Sand Point (Warren G. Magnuson) Park (Map-page 31)

By the time the people of Seattle realized the local supply of waterfront was finite, somebody was sitting on just about every inch. How could the public obtain more room for children to go wading? Since only God and the military have the power to create a shore, and She finished Her engineering eons ago, it was left to the U.S. Navy to save the scene—by going away. The 196-acre park presently recalls all too vividly its past as an invasion of marsh and lake, as a desert of pavement reeking of aviation fuel. Future generations will stroll across the plain in cool shadows of stately trees (now being planted), along a shore restored to nature, and honor this as a jewel of the city. It's not too bad now.

From Sand Point Way turn east on NE 65 Street and follow signs to the parking area at the south end of the park. Elevation, 25 feet.

There's no shore trail and probably never should be. The walking is on old roads closed to motorized vehicles and on paths mowed or foot-beaten through tall grass. Countless sidepaths wend off through scotchbroom, hellberry, or willow thicket to nooks on the shore for looking out to sailboats, the north and south of Lake Washington, the Issaquah Alps, and the Cascades. The only developed areas are the boatlaunch (bring your canoe or sailing

Burke-Gilman Trail near Kenmore

Ocean-going tugboat in Hiram M. Chittenden Locks

surfboard) and the swimming beach. At 1 long mile from the south fence is the NOAA fence, guarding the base of the Great White Fleet of the scientific Rover Boys.

Until the New Forest grows tall the inland paths through the fields mainly will interest joggers. However, the birder will find a different bunch than along the shore. (On his initial tour the surveyor watched a vicious redwing blackbird chase a heron clear to the far side of the lake, then harass a hawk out of the country, after which the surveyor himself was sent packing.)

Round trip 2 miles, allow 1½ hours
High point 25 feet, no elevation gain
All year
Bus: Metro 8 and 41

Sound-To-Mountains Trail

For many years hikers have discussed how splendid and fitting a trail would be from saltwater beaches to the Cascade Crest. Routes have been proposed along the Nisqually River and Stillaguamish and Skagit.

The King County Urban Trails Plan published in 1971 proposed a route that would start in Seattle on Lakeside Avenue, cross the Mercer Island Floating Bridge, proceed to Bellefields Nature Park, Houghton, Bridle Trails State Park, and Marymoor Park, 15 miles to that point; thence via Evans and Patterson Creeks to the Snoqualmie River and parallel to Redmond-Fall City Road to Snoqualmie Falls, 20 miles; follow railroad tracks and river dikes to the Middle Fork Snoqualmie and thence on National Forest roads and trails to Dutch Miller Gap.

In 1972 a plan was published for the Lake Washington-to-Cascade Crest Ecology Trail, prepared by John Warth, who more than a decade before had drawn up the first boundary proposals for an Alpine Lakes Wilderness (at last achieved in 1976). Selected after 2 years of scouting trips, the Warth route traverses a great variety of ecosystems, thus being useful as (among other things) a laboratory for school instructional programs. His trail would go from Lake Washington up Coal Creek over the top of Cougar Mountain, cross Tibbetts Creek, Squak Mountain, Issaquah Creek, Tiger Mountain, East Fork Issaquah Creek, and Grand Ridge to the Snoqualmie River. It would then ascend Griffin Creek, go over the highland to the Tolt River at the forks, over another divide to Youngs Creek, climb Big Haystack Mountain, drop to the Proctor Trough, round the sides of Persis and Index, go through headwaters of the North and South Forks Tolt to Lennox in headwaters of the North Fork Snoqualmie, and proceed through the mountains to Lake Dorothy, down to the Middle Fork Snoqualmie, and up to Dutch Miller Gap. Wow.

Civilian hikers who long had applauded the dreams were startled in 1975 when the King County Division of Land Use Management suddenly brought forth a plan that was no distant vision but very near a reality. If it's not quite that, on August 20-24, 1975, Stan Unger hiked the whole 93 miles from West Point in Seattle to Snoqualmie Pass.

Pedestrians less determined than Mr. Unger are advised to wait for certain linkage problems to be solved and the trail officially opened. But most of the length is described in this book and can be walked now.

The 1975 version of the Sound-to Mountains Trail commences at West Point in Discovery Park and goes northeast to Chittenden Locks (see Puget Sound Trail—Seattle to Everett), east and then north on the Burke Gilman Trail (which see) to Blyth Park in Bothell. The way from there is the Tolt Pipeline Trail (which see) to the Snoqualmie River Trail (which see), this being followed to Snoqualmie Falls. The route then lies on abandoned railroad to Tanner, east of North Bend, and along the Middle Fork Snoqualmie road to the logging road up Granite Creek. Up on the ridge above Granite Lakes the Trail hits trail in National Forest and proceeds along slopes of Defiance and across Pratt River headwaters to Denny Creek, from there following the old wagon road to Snoqualmie Pass.

Mr. Unger's journal says he celebrated the inaugural tramp with "a nice tall beer." When asked whether it solaced dry mouth or sore feet, he answered, "Both."

Not content, at last word he was surveying the Unger Alternate and had got from Lake Washington over Cougar, Squak, Tiger, and Rattlesnake Mountains to the Cascade front, attained Mt. Washington, and was staring intently at the ridge east to McClellan's Butte. By now he very likely has again attained the Crest and has his feet in two buckets of beer.

As the Holy Grail became central to the "Matter of Britain," the Sound-to-Mountains more and more, year by year, is accepted as the organizing thread of the "Matter of Puget Sound Hiking." All major trails and trail systems are envisioned as hooking up: the Duwamish-Green Trail via Big Soos Creek and Cedar River; the Cedar River Trail via the Issaquah Alps; the Issaquah Alps via the Issaquah-Snoqualmie Falls Trail, not to forget the Unger Alternate; the East Sammamish Plateau Trail via the Issaquah Alps and the Tolt Pipeline Trail; etcetera.

This doesn't mean the trails mentioned have value only insofar as they attain the Crest; if memory serves, not very many knights actually achieved the Grail, but look at all the adventures they had, questing. The surveyor isn't sure he personally wants the Crest, yet is very happy that Mr. Unger keeps on questing.

Lighthouse on Alki Point

PUGET SOUND TRAIL—SEATTLE TO TACOMA

Having gotten devout pedestrians hysterical by proclaiming an unsuspected wonder, one must hasten to declare, "There is no Puget Sound Trail." Or rather, there's been one for eons, because for eons few of The People ever spent much time beyond the smell of saltwater. When European man arrived a century and odd decades ago he also leaned toward water-side living, and still does. If, between Seattle and Tacoma, a strip of shore is lacking houses it's primarily due to the steepness and instability of the wave-cut bluffs of morainal materials deposited by the Puget Glacier.

Only secondarily is it due to public parks. There are a number of these, mostly in ravines of creeks whose slipping-sliding slopes frustrated builders until government awoke to the need. Government took its time. Upon attainment of statehood in 1889 all saltwater beaches in Washington were public property. But the selling commenced immediately and continued until the scandalously late date of 1969, when 60 percent of the beach length had been sold, including perhaps 99 percent of what anybody might want for residential purposes.

Is it, then, possible to wall off the public from Puget Sound? If the law says so, then "the law, sir, is a ass." As well attempt to wall off the sky. And indeed, many scholars feel the eons of continuous uoo have firmly established a public highway beside the water and there is no such thing on tidal beaches as completely private property.

But who wants to go hiking with his lawyer? It therefore is the first commandment of this book that "Thou shalt not bug the people who live by the beach." If you want to argue philosophical and legal points about land ownership, go to court. Don't do it on the beach.

The most any legal expert claims for the (European-Asian) public is the right of passage, of walking through "private" property. Everyone agrees that except for The People there is no right to dig clams or pick oysters, gather pebbles or driftwood, or to camp or build a fire or have a picnic lunch or even to sit down. Certainly there is no right to leave garbage or anything else.

Legal theory aside, no rational walker wants to get into a squabble. Thus the second commandment of this book is "Thou shalt instantly depart when somebody tells you to get off his property." With an apology. (To finish off the commandments, a third: "Thou shalt not trespass with thy dog, which shalt be left at home.")

No brief is made here that the Declaration of Independence and Bill of Rights endorse trespassing. However, during the surveys in many seasons over many years many local residents were interviewed. Most are nature-sensitive folk; that's why they live on the beach. Most sympathize with other nature-sensitives and are apologetic about "owning" the beach. Even amid thickets of "No Trespassing" signs most say, "Oh, nobody minds if you walk their beach, as long as you don't make a nuisance." Whatever the property rights of beach residents they have human rights—the right to live in peace, not subjected to dumping of garbage in yards, to noisy picnics and wild night-time beach orgies; the right to sunbathe in privacy, not subjected to the stares of a thousand foreigners marching by.

Some of the signs say "Trespassing by Permission Only." And this is the

Anchor recovered from bay, Alki Beach

key to the Puget Sound Trail: the beach traditionally has been walked by tacit permission. Interviews with local residents revealed some rules as to the times and places when such permission is least likely to be revoked, your presence least likely to be challenged.

Good days are bad. On weekends the year around and on fine evenings of spring and summer, stay away. At such times if you must go to the beach visit the public parks described here or (for reasons discussed in that chapter) walk the Puget Sound Trail north of Seattle.

Crowded beaches are the worst. If you see a mob of people walking past and ignoring "No Trespassing" signs, do not suppose there is safety in numbers. The numbers will just be infuriating residents, who will be calling the police.

Walking off the ends of public park beaches onto private beaches is the most inviting to the ignorant—and to residents the most irritating.

The "wild" beaches, those with bluffs that keep houses at a distance from the water, are the most open to tolerated trespassing.

Low tide, when the "trail" lies at the water's edge far out from houses, is better than high.

When trespassing, be clean and quiet. No garbage. Carry a litterbag and use it. No shouting. No dogs. Don't come in gangs but alone or in small groups. Keep moving. Don't stare at the houses, fascinated though you may be by littoral architecture; burglars also stare when casing jobs.

If challenged, politely apologize and retreat and go someplace else.

If you avoid built-up stretches (who wants to walk in a succession of front yards anyway?) in favor of wilder areas, and pick the off-seasons and off-days (a stormy Wednesday morning in December) you can walk from Seattle to Tacoma with no greeting from the locals but a friendly hello.

Advanced pedestrians can walk the entire trail. Probably not on a single day. Aside from the miles there are the tides. Unlike the trail north of Seattle there is no all-tides route provided by the railway. The surveyor was constantly running out of beach, waves lapping tanglewood cliffy bluffs or residential bulkheads, and forced to return another day. And he constantly had to keep in mind the possibility of having his retreat cut off. The long-distance walker must coordinate map and tide table.

The attractions of beach-walking probably need no praise here. But the importance of the Puget Sound Trail should be stressed. First, it is close to the homes of just about everybody—within a half-hour of 90 percent of Puget Sounders. Second, it's an all-year route, never blocked by snow except during the infrequent Ice Ages. Third, due to a partial rainshadow from the Olympics, the weather is better than farther east in—say—the Issaquah Alps. Frequently when storms are chasing each others' tails over the Northwest and the mountains and foothills never free themselves of one storm's murk before the next descends, "Blue Holes" open along the beach. These interludes are superb for walking—clouds boiling around the Olympics, whitecaps gleaming in the sun, surf rattling the gravel, wind nipping the nose.

Of course, when the inland weather is sunny-blue, fogs may linger long on the water. But that's not a bad time for walking either, foghorns sounding, ghost ships sliding through mists, seagulls wailing at the mystery of it all.

USGS maps: Seattle South, Duwamish Head, Vashon, Des Moines, Poverty Bay, Tacoma North

Mile 0-5½: Pioneer Square-Duwamish River-Duwamish Head-Hamilton Viewpoint Park (Map-page 41)

Fanatics committed to doing every inch of the Trail must hoof it from Pioneer Square to the waterfront, south to Spokane Street, west over the Duwamish Waterways to West Seattle, and north to the start of open beach. This is comparable to walking a highway shoulder across the Mojave Desert to "do" Canada-Mexico. There are much better places to study commerce and industry, humanity and nature. But folks continue to haul packs across the Mojave, so there it is...

Hamilton Viewpoint Park on Duwamish Head is the best spot anywhere to watch marine traffic: Bainbridge Island ferries passing close, ships and barges and tugs to and from Duwamish Waterways, sailboats and motorboats to and from marinas. Views too of downtown Seattle, Queen Anne Hill, Magnolia Bluff, Winslow and Eagle Harbor on Bainbridge Island, the Olympics.

Mile 5½-8: Alki Beach Park-Alki Point Lighthouse (Map-page 41)

This may be the most popular beach walk in Seattle. A favorite time is winter storms, when ocean-size breakers smash over the seawall. The sidewalk is open at any tide; at low tide one can stroll the beach and there, below the wall, the busy street and the houses are out of sight and mind.

The entire strip beyond Duwamish Head is called Alki Beach Park. At the south end is the sandy bathing beach, where there is beach at even the highest tide, and the usual gangs of gulls and crows and pigeons and ducks and blackbirds and sandpipers whose presence the rest of the route will not be further mentioned.

A stretch of private beach intervenes between bathing beach and the historic Alki Point Lighthouse. (Visiting hours on weekends and holidays, 1-4 p.m.)

Schmitz Park (Map-page 41)

An inland sidetrip from Alki Avenue the short way up SW Stevens Street or 59 Avenue S to Alki Recreation Center, which abuts the lower end of Schmitz Park. (Alternatively, drive up SW Admiral Way and at Stevens go down the park entrance road to the small parking area.)

Started from one of three gifts of land by Ferdinand and Emma Schmitz, this 50-acre park contains one of Seattle's few bits of genuine virgin forest— Douglas firs up to 5 feet in diameter and cedars even thicker, nurselogs supporting rows of hemlocks, and thickets of salmonberry, walls of swordfern.

The "birthplace of Seattle" monument close by (on Alki Point at 63 Avenue SW) causes one to reflect that when the schooner **Exact** landed the first settlers a century and a third ago this forested ravine was just about exactly as it is now. And this was what the country looked like all the way from the Sound to the mountains.

From Alki Recreation Center walk a blockaded old street, now a path, up the ravine, complete with a creek that here is not, as are most city streams, in a storm sewer. At the parking lot old street yields to old trail continuing up the ravine, definitely not city-park-kempt but natural-wild. The trail divides and redivides in a maze of paths down to and along the creek, up tributaries, along sidehills, by sandbanks, onto knolls. To fully sample the park ascend the ravine along one side to where it's about to enter residences, swing to the far side, and loop back down. Though small, the park contains nearly 2 miles of paths.

Sample round trip from beach 2 miles, allow 1½ hours
High point 250 feet

Mile 8-12: Me-Kwa-Mooks Park-Lowman Beach Park-Williams Point-Lincoln Park (Map-page 41)

South of Alki Point the bluff, which temporarily has receded inland, returns to the beach. Also here is one of the few outcrops of non-glacial rock, sandstone ledges atop which rest glacial debris.

Immediately south of the point are homes on the beach. Then the beachfront drive prevents construction and permits public access for a bit. Walking is halted by pilings of Harbor West, a condominium perilously built on a dock. Cheek-by-jowl homes extend 2 miles south; even though in spitting distance of the water one can't see it.

Right in the middle, however, is a small opening. At Oregon Street is a 32-acre park, half a wooded upland on the base of the bluff, half shorelands.

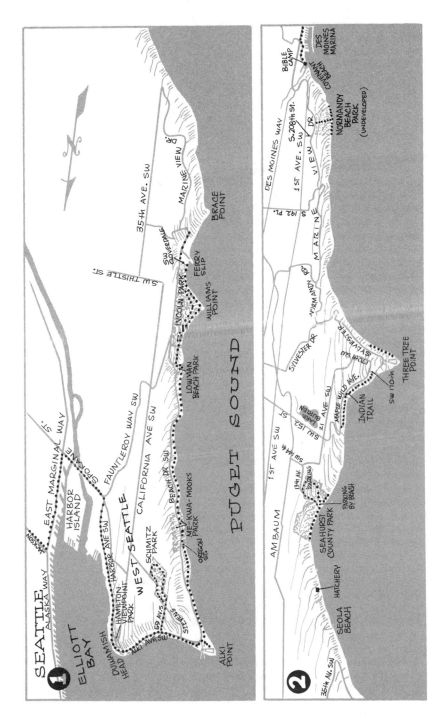

Another Schmitz gift, to avoid confusion it has been renamed from Emma Schmitz Memorial Viewpoint to Me-Kwa-Mooks ("entire Alki area"). The opening permits a walker to see the view has changed. Bainbridge Island is being replaced by Blake Island and the Kitsap Peninsula. Now prominent to the south is the green-and-white ferry shuttling from Fauntleroy Cove to Vashon Island.

Private beach ends at Lowman Beach Park. A public alley-street leads behind homes to the beach at Lincoln Park. The next 1 mile through the park requires separate treatment.

Lincoln Park (Map-page 41)

The best beach park in Seattle? Only Discovery Park can contest the claim. The 107 acres, served by buses and many parking lots, have been a favorite for generations.

For a basic introductory loop start from the parking area off Fauntleroy Avenue SW at Cloverdale Street. Head for the water, following steps or ramp down to the bulkhead walkway, which destroys the naturalness of beach but does permit high-tide walking. (At low tide one can walk natural beach.) The bluff, partly green jungle, partly gray sand cliff, rises 175 very vertical feet, topped by magnificent madrona groves. Smackdab on climactic Williams Point is Colman Pool, a good thing in the wrong place, reminding us that a sewage plant was built on West Point—and an aquarium was not built on Meadow Point, Seattle by then having learned to leave points alone.

Having walked 1 splendid mile north to homes, retreat to the first of three good (safe) paths that climb the bluff to the top. Walk the rim path, lawns and groves left, wild bluff right. Views over the water to Vashon ferry, Bainbridge ferry, Olympics.

Basic loop trip 2 miles, allow 1½ hours
High point 175 feet

Mile 12-16½: Fauntleroy Cove-Vashon Ferry Slip-Brace Point-Seahurst (Ed Munro) Park (Map-page 41)

Just south of Lincoln Park in Fauntleroy Cove is the Vashon ferry slip. Always worthwhile to a ferry fan is pausing to watch the docking. An excellent rest stop on a long-distance walk is a trip over to the island and back.

In the 3 miles south from the slip there is no formal and darn little informal access to the beach. Breaks in the bluff, such as on the flats of Brace Point and in the creek valleys of Arroyo Beach and Seola Beach, permit homes to be built by the water. But three strips of beach, each ¼ mile long, are kept wild by tall bluffs, the northernmost rising 300 steep feet from beach to top, a stunningly prominent feature of the shoreline.

The fourth and best wild stretch is in Seahurst Park, and this nearly 1-mile haven from **No Trespassing** signs must be treated separately.

Seahurst (Ed Munro) Park (Map-page 41)

Seahurst (King County) Park, 185 acres of woods and nearly 1 mile of beach, is reached from Ambaum Boulevard in Burien via SW 144 Street. Like most

Puget Sound and Olympic Mountains from Lincoln Park

beach parks this consists of a creek valley that couldn't easily be built in and so remained wild until acquired in the 1960s.

The parking area by the creek mouth gives access to a unique combination of an upper concrete seawall protecting a picnic-area path usable at highest tides, a lower gabian wall atop which is beach walkable at middle tides, and the outside natural beach open at low tides. All this eventually ends, and in ½ mile north so does the park, at a row of homes. All the way is a fine high bluff. Park beach also extends a scant ½ mile south from the creek; wild beach continues south.

To beach the park adds wildwoods. On the south side of the creek, by the bridge, an unmarked path climbs the bluff, then contours steep slopes, crossing above the large inland parking lot and diverging up a roadless tributary valley. The gulch is wild, the firs big, the bushes a green snarl. The way swings around the valley, crossing creeks, sidepaths branch this way and that, permitting quite a long trip. In the park are about 3 miles of trail, ranging from primitive to downright mean. For the introduction, loop down to the entry road and return on it to the beach.

Basic woods-walk loop trip 2 miles, allow 1½ hours
High point 300 feet

House built on steep hillside along the Indian Trail near Three Tree Point

Mile 16½-23½: Three Tree Point-Indian Trail-Normandy Beach Park (Map-page 41)

The ¼ mile south from Seahurst Park is below a tall wild sliding bluff, houses unseen atop, slumping trees hanging boughs over the sand. Homes begin and continue 2 miles to Three Tree Point (Point Pully).

Maplewild Avenue SW leads to the beach just south of Three Tree Point and the light—which is on private property and can't be visited. Parking here for a half-dozen cars and access to a short piece of public beach.

The Indian Trail. Said to be part of an old Indian route, this 4-foot-wide public walkway extends about 1 mile north from the point. To find it (unmarked) turn off Maplewild at SW 170 Street, just by Three Tree Point Store. A street-end (which goes to the beach, providing public access) has parking for two or three cars. Off it, north, stairs lead up a path. The only signing is to forbid public use between sunset and sunrise. (Orgies were ruining the neighborhood.) The path goes north in backyards along the steep bluff, giving intimate glimpses of bluff-suited architecture and views through firs and madronas to the water and the Olympics. The trail ends at Maplewild—no parking at this end. A short bit south of the north end a public path drops to the beach, permitting a waterside return for a 2-mile loop. Don't do the Indian Trail on weekends or summer evenings; come on a winter morning. Don't park stupidly; park by the beach at the public spot or on a shoulder somewhere in the neighborhood in such a manner as not to block a street or driveway; if you can't find a good parking place, go away and return some other day.

From the above-mentioned public access just south of Three Tree Point, a landmark visible for many miles, new vistas open south, including Rainier. The next 1 mile the road is close by the beach, house-lined most of the way.

A wild bluff then rears up, marking the start of the Normandy Park area. For very long stretches nobody lives on the beach or even close, up there atop the bluff. Moreover, near the south end of this stretch is a park, a palpable park, discussed below.

For about 1 mile from the wild bluff, in a broad valley, habitations are by the beach but not many. The bluff rears up to protect wildness of the next ¾ mile. A little valley has a few houses, then comes ¼ mile of high wild lovely bluff, 200 nearly vertical feet from the shore, and no houses atop. For ¼ mile a marshy valley borders the beach; a house is situated inland and an unused road leads to the beach. A bluff then has several houses and after that is 1 mile with only a couple inhabited spots. This excellent stretch (which includes 1000 feet of waterfront in the veritable park) ends at a row of houses built on pilings at the foot of a cliff, the houses having only trail access at high tide, car access via the beach at low. This access is from the gulch occupied by Covenant Beach Bible Camp; a road leads to the entrance and the beach.

The last ½ mile of this segment is the huge pier (and public parking area) of Des Moines Marina, close by the town, where the highway nears the water after a long absence. The marina is a good place for boatwatching. And waterlooking.

Normandy Beach Park (Map-page 41)

After lo how many years the City of Normandy Park obtained, via Forward Thrust, a genuine public park, and the citizenry is still in a state of shock. As of 1981, however, they have not found themselves overwhelmed by the feared invasion of unwashed outlanders. The park is unmarked and the only trail down the precipice is mainly used by 10-year-old boys who don't want to become 11. Ah, but what wild delights await the doughty mountaineer-beachwalker!

From 1 Avenue South turn west on South 208 Street, then south on Marine View Drive. In the one and only short stretch without houses spot a woods road that in several hundred feet ends on the brink of the bluff, elevation 225 feet.

Don't expect to necessarily get to the beach in one unbroken piece. And getting back up the bluff in any condition whatsoever may prove impossible. Engineering a safe and easy trail down the glacial drift will take a bit of money, which the City may not ever wish to spend.

The obvious old woods road that sets out amiably over the brink soon ends. The main trail down from there has three stretches that can abrade and contuse and a final drop to the beach that could kill. An alternate path off the end of the woods road tours splendid madrona groves and magnificent old-growth Douglas fir snagtops, snags, and stumps, mortally wounded by a fire of a century-odd ago but some likely to survive another century or more, alive or dead, as eagle perches.

Don't take the children on this walk—not until and unless the City builds a genuine trail in its only genuine park.

Round trip to big fir snagtops ½ mile, allow 1 hour
High point 225 feet

Mile 23½-25½: Saltwater State Park (Map-page 47)

Due to solid barriers of private yacht club and then homes it is not practical to get off the Des Moines Marina onto the beach at the south end. Don't sweat; just 1½ miles south is Saltwater State Park.

From the marina the first ¾ mile is beach houses, there being virtually no bluff in the broad Des Moines valley. But the next 1 mile is something else—the bluff abruptly leaps up 150 feet and though homes are on top and some paths come down, the beach is quite wild because the bluff is exceptionally vertical, formed here of hard sandstones-shales and, atop a discontinuity, 90-degree gravels. This fine long stretch of naked cliff is striking from miles away. Imbedded in forest river gravels are large granite erratics dropped from icebergs. Layers of black, partly-carbonized wood are an early step toward coal. Tree clumps from the top of the bluff have slid to the bottom, there growing on the sand—until the next big storm makes driftwood of them.

The final ¼ mile of this segment is in Saltwater State Park, whose north end has a great big fence signed against trespassing.

Saltwater State Park (Map-page 47)

Because of the disproportion between public beaches and public here-abouts, Saltwater State Park gets some 1,000,000 visitations a year. Quite a lot for 88 acres with just 1445 feet of public beach.

Reach the park from Marine View Drive SW, Highway 509, the route having many twists and turns but guided by signs leading to the park.

In addition to beach there is forest in the valley of Smith Creek. For the basic introductory loop, park near the beach. By the restroom on the south side of the parking lot, find the unmarked trail switchbacking up the bluff, then contouring the sidehill in big firs and hemlocks and maples, crossing little creeks. Pass under the highway bridge and climb to the plateau top, with views down to the creek. Amid a rather confusing maze of paths choose a route that turns up a tributary ravine nearly to private homes, contours past privies and campsites of the Youth Camp, then drops to the campground area, where two valleys join.

To do the loop, cross the two bridges over the two creeks just above their union, switchback to the plateau, hike through a fine conifer grove, descend to the valley, find a path ascending a tributary, pass under the highway bridge, on the opposite side of the valley from before, and hit the entrance road.

For a sidetrip, cross the road and walk out to a superb bluff-top viewpoint. Then return to the entry road and walk it down to the car.

Basic introductory loop trip 1½ miles, allow 1 hour
High point 125 feet

Mile 25½-27: Poverty Bay-Redondo Beach (Map-page 47)

A handful of homes abut Saltwater State Park to the south and signs sternly forbid trespassing. But in a very short distance begins a long stretch of mostly empty beach. For ½ mile a 125-foot cliff keeps houses respectfully at a vertical distance. Then there is a short strip of homes reached via a piling-protected road along the water from Woodmont Beach on the south. At Woodmont a public road comes to the beach but PRIVATE signs bar parking and access.

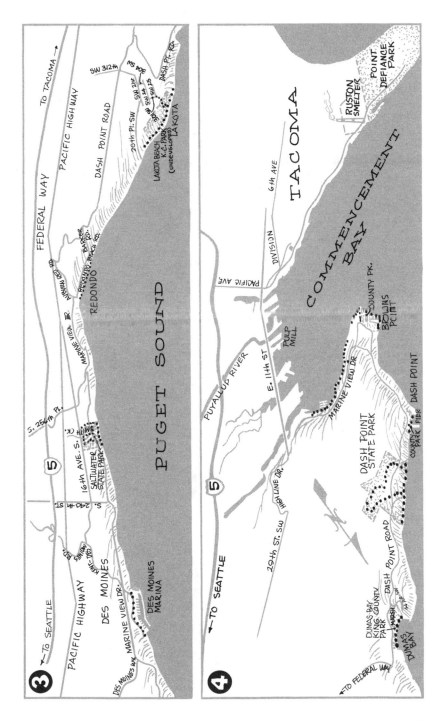

The bluff is low, scarcely more than a bank, and houses are solid and water-close the final scant 1 mile to Redondo Beach. Here, north of the marina, is public parking and a moderately long public beach. (From Highway 509 just off Highway 99 in Federal Way, take Redondo Way down the ravine to Redondo Beach Drive and the marina.)

The views now are over the water to Maury Island, close across the here-narrow Sound; southward appears Point Defiance and the tall stack of the ASARCO Smelter; when south winds are blowing, sniff for it, but learn to distinguish between smelter stink and pulpmill stink, both of which are in the air.

Mile 27-31½: Lakota Beach Park-Dumas Bay Park-Dash Point State Park

Three parks. And many wild bits, many delights of bluff and beach, creeks and marshes.

For 1 mile south from Redondo Beach houses are at waterside, and half that distance the road is there too before veering uphill and away. After ½ mile of high bluff and wild beach, the ¼ mile of Adelaide valley is inhabited. A street-end gives public access to the (private) beach; from 21 Avenue SW (see Lakota beach, below) turn right on 20 Place SW to very limited parking at the driftwood.

There is then ½ mile of wild bluff, partly occupied by undeveloped Lakota Beach or Poverty Bay (King County) Park, discussed below.

The wild bluff ends in a low bank and valley of densely-dwelt-in Lakota Beach, extending ½ mile to a point featuring huge granite boulders, houses on bulkheads, and the north boundary point of Dumas Bay.

Dumas Bay, about 1 long mile by shoreline from point to point, is very unlike any other part of the Trail. At low tide the bay empties and the wide flat permits a shortcut across the mouth, far from shore. Three creeks enter, one through a deep green ravine where two red houses catch the eye. There aren't many more houses than that, partly because the highway is at the bluff-lip part of the way; the cliff here is not a practical access to the beach.

But the main show is Dumas Bay (King County) Park, discussed below.

Dumas Bay ends in a bluff at the west point. Houses are atop at first but soon yield to wildwoods. In the next 1 mile are notably large granite erratics on the beach, the hulk of a beached barge, the **Biltgood,** and non-public paths to the top of the bluff. Humanity then intrudes in the form of a dozen houses at the bluff base, accessible solely by trails hacked in the 150-foot cliff.

At the end of this intriguing neighborhood is Dash Point State Park and its long ½ mile of beach.

Lakota Beach (Poverty Bay) Park (Map-page 47)

A halfmile long by a quarter-mile wide and 300 feet from bottom to top, this undeveloped King County park has naught to offer funseekers but a maze of trails through wildland forest, a cathedral choir of birds and squirrels, and a halfmile strip of lonesome beach in broad view of the Gravel Coast of Maury Island.

The turnoff from SW Dash Point Road is at a confusing intersection. Where SW 312th intersects Dash Point Road at a stoplight just south of a shopping center, turn west on 21 Place SW, unsigned at the intersection. It bends north as 21 Avenue SW. In a scant ¾ mile turn left on unsigned SW 304 Street, which bends right as 24 Avenue. Turn left on 301 Street, which at a jog becomes 25

Saltwater State Park

Black brant, a small goose, near Alki Point

Avenue. The "25 Avenue" sign points across the street into the woods. Room at the deadend stub for a couple cars to park. Step over the pile of neighborhood lawn-clippings and hedge-trimmings and find a very decent trail descending a scant ½ mile to the beach. Other trails meander about the bluff in excellent mixed forest.

**Round trip to beach 1 mile, allow 1 hour
High point 275 feet**

Dumas Bay Park (Map-page 47)

Yes, it's a public access to the beach, and that's appreciated. But the glory of this King County park—undeveloped as of 1981 and planned never to have any development except a better parking area and perhaps a few tiger traps for motorcycles—is the birding. Most of the park is a vast lagoon marsh cut off from the saltwater eons ago by a baymouth bar. From the edge of the driftwood an impenetrable wilderness of cattails and reeds extends inland a quarter-mile to the foot of the bluff; in season there's such a racket of redwinged blackbirds and frogs and other marsh racketeers one can hardly hear the crows and the gulls. As for the shallow little bay, its seaweeds and mucks (and two creeks) nourish such a rich assortment of tasty bites that at times one can hardly see the water. A fine April afternoon the surveyor found fleets of black brant, terns, mallard, and goldeneyes, the motley mob dominated by a solitary white-fronted goose. Mergansers and surf scoters patrolled offshore, cormorants posed on rocks, the sands were alive with killdeer and peep, and kingfishers scolded.—Not to mention the great blue herons standing in the water pretending to be driftwood: the park contains a large heronry (nesting area) whose existence in an urban area testifies to the natural defenses of the wetland.

From Dash Point Drive turn north on 44 Avenue SW for ¼ mile. At the only gap in houses, at SW 310 Street, spot a side-by-side pair of undrivable woods roads, elevation 80 feet. Walk either of the roads (they join) ¼ mile down through alder forest, beside the creek that feeds the marsh, to a little meadow by the driftwood.

Round trip ½ mile, allow hours
High point 80 feet

Dash Point State Park (Map-page 47)

The 297-acre park has 3500 feet of sandy beach beneath a 225-foot bluff of vertical clay and sand topped by forests. It also has, de rigeur, a ravine.

From Federal Way drive via SW 320 Street, then right on 47th and finally left on Dash Point Road, south to the park entrance. Descend the ravine to the parking lot upstream a bit from the beach.

One trail leads through a tunnel under the entry road to the beach. There, on the east side of the valley, look for a broad path ascending the bluff to a viewpoint and a second picnic area.

For the main trail, the boundary loop, find the path at the upstream end of the parking lot, going up the gorgeous valley in ferns and alders. Passing under the highway bridge and by a massive cedar stump, the way crosses the creek in a wide maple-alder flat, at ¼ mile from the parking lot reaching a Y.

Take the right fork, switchbacking to the plateau and park boundary. The trail proceeds across the upland in fir forest and alder-maple, marshes, delightful ravines, no sights or sounds of residences in the wildland. Ignoring minor sidepaths, at a major intersection with a road trail turn left, soon joining the paved campground road. Turn left down the campground loop road to the bottom end of the camp and a sign, "Trail to Beach." Drop to the valley-floor Y, completing the loop, and return to the parking lot.

Boundary trail loop 2½ miles, allow 1½ hours
High point 250 feet

Mile 31½-40: Dash Point County Park-Browns Point County Park-Commencement Bay (Map-page 47)

Some ¾ mile along the beach from the state park is Dash Point proper. The absolute tip is a private home but short of it is Dash Point (Pierce County) Park, with parking, a public beach, and a long fishing pier the hiker should walk out on for northward views nearly to Three Tree Point (Point Robinson on Maury Island blocks it out), but mainly across the mouth of Commencement Bay (not yet quite seen) to Point Defiance—and the tall stack of the smelter. Also look across East Passage to points on Vashon-Maury Islands and into Dalco Passage, leading to the west side.

Beachside homes continue past the point ¼ mile; then a 175-foot cliff leaps up from the water, atop it being Marine View Drive, protecting wildness of the

Browns Point Light

beach for ½ mile. At the outward bulge of Browns Point the bluff retreats inland, allowing solid houses the next 1½ miles around the point.

The road off the boulevard down to the lighthouse on Browns Point leads to the adjacent Browns Bay Improvement Club and Library, with public parking. Enclosing the lighthouse (beach access via the lawns) is Browns Point (Pierce County) Park. Picturesque lighthouse. Nice views, variations on those from Dash Point.

As the shore swings around Browns Point to turn easterly into Commencement Bay, a very short stretch of wild bluff 100 feet high provides a grand viewpoint. Just by the boulevard is a small, unmarked parking area. Paths lead down to the beach and also out on the madrona-decorated promontory. For the first time on the Trail, here is a look directly into Commencement Bay, to the industrial waterway and across open waters to downtown Tacoma.

Now comes a long ¼ mile of homes on beach and bluff. But just as one expects increased urbanization, wildness rules. (The beach, not the view.) For nearly 1 mile the beach is guarded by a tall bluff atop which is Marine View Drive with many splendid viewpoints but apparently no paths down. For a bit the bluff is an amazingly vertical 160-foot gravel wall atop which is perched a restaurant. Other entertainments are an old beached barge, newer barges moored offshore, driftwood and dune lines and even a tiny lagoon marsh, and views to ships, and directly across to Ruston and its smelter stack and, farther out, Point Defiance.

The beach becomes industrial-filthy and ends in a marina. The unsigned road down from Marine View Drive to the marina parking lot gives access to this beach, which offers the unusual combination of lonesome beachwalking in full view of the metropolis.

Past the marina the beachwalking is difficult but Marine View Drive is beside the water, with many turnouts, and the next 1 mile of shore cottages and shacks, derelict (or nearly) houseboats, is picturesque, as are log rafts, and gray and rusting Navy escort vessels.

The bluff continues on up the Puyallup River, indeed growing higher; right in the city is a wildland bluff strip more than 3 miles long and up to ½ mile wide, rising abruptly from sealevel to over 400 feet.

The Trail leaves the bluffs for a final 3 miles on 11 Street East across waterways of the Puyallup River flat. In a nature-oriented book the scenes will be simply noted: crudely industrial, workaday-grimy, where the world makes its money so it can afford time off for beachwalking; rows of ships berthed along waterways; lumber yards and factories; a pulpmill belching clouds of steam. One is likely to feel, after closely studying this terminus of the Puyallup-Carbon-White Rivers, three of the major streams flowing from Rainier glaciers, that no similar use should be made of the outlet of another Rainier river, the Nisqually.

At long last the Puget Sound Trail enters Tacoma. To end? By no means. Tacoma has some of the best parts. But those and the way south are for **Footsore 4**.

Bus: Duwamish Head-Alki Point, 37 and 15; Lincoln Park, 18 and 34; Seahurst Park, 136 to Ambaum and SW 144, walk a few blocks to park; Three Tree Point, 136 to Marine View Drive at SW 170, walk to point; Des Moines, 130 and 132; Saltwater State Park, 130 to Marine View Drive at S 248, walk ¼ mile to park

Cormorant in Commencement Bay

PUGET SOUND TRAIL—SEATTLE TO EVERETT

Most of the way north from Seattle the Puget Sound Trail has two lanes: the low-tide path on the beach; the high-tide path atop the handsome seawall of granite blocks. While lamenting the miles-long violation of natural beach one must score this point—the all-tides easy walking—for the railroad. And immediately score a second point for the way it has kept homes at a distance from the water, thus providing a quasi-public access lacking the NO TRESPASSING problems so common on the Trail south from Seattle.

As characteristic of the Puget Sound Trail North as the railroad is the bluff, lifting an abrupt 200 to 400 feet above the shore—and constantly slumping down to the shore. Composed partly of concrete-like glacial till, partly of bedded sand and gravel and varved blue clay, it ranges from quite to extremely unstable. Homes are built on top by people gambling the bluff edge will not, in their lifetimes, retreat to the point occupied by their houses. Sometimes homes even are built on terraces formed by chunks of the bluff slumping off the top, the hope then being the slump terrace will descend at a rate no faster than inches a year. Sometimes homes are built below the bluffs, the residents sleeping restlessly on wet winter nights. But mainly the bluff is given up as a lost cause, permitted to remain houseless. Extending nearly the full length of the Trail is thus a strip wilderness, houses pretty much out of sight at the top, the steep, wooded, vine-tangled slope harboring a thriving population of birds and small beasts, the water-side walker for hours at a time "away from it all" while right in the middle of it all, strolling along in the heart of Puget Sound City.

And deeply sliced into the bluffs are numerous creeks, some in slot canyons, others in wide-bottomed, steep-walled valleys. From the shore wildland these short-to-long fingers of wildland poke into urbs and suburbs. Many (more than have been noted in the following route description) have trails inland; due to private property or lack of parking, they generally are not good accesses to the beach except for local residents, but for a hiker on the beach they provide a change of beauties, walking up a trail into a cool canyon of tangled greenery and splashing waterfalls.

So much for the land side of the Trail. What about the water side? Well, it's just your standard, routine, Puget Sound mix: waves on the beach, shorebirds on the sands and waterfowl swimming and gulls and crows above, the changing panorama across the waters to islands, Kitsap Peninsula, and Olympics, the parade of tugs and lografts and barges and freighters and ferries and fishing boats and sailboats, and memories of the water traffic that was, the old pilings, remnants of docks last used half-a-century ago, ghosts of the vanished mosquito fleet.

Special hot tip for carfree walkers: A **Footsore** reader who gets to all her trailheads by bus reports a really gaudy way to do the Trail North, in 2 days. One morning take Metro 306 from Seattle to Everett, hit the tracks south, and in afternoon, at Edmonds, catch the 316 or 376 back to Seattle. Another morning ride 305 to Richmond Beach and walk south to West Point and the gaggle of Metro lines that serve Discovery Park.

USGS maps: Seattle South, Seattle North, Shilshole Bay, Edmonds West, Edmonds East, Mukilteo, Everett

---

Edmonds-Kingston ferry and the Olympic Mountains   55

Mile 0-1½: Union and King Street Stations-Klondike Gold Rush National Historic Park-Skidroad-Alaskan Way-Waterfront Park (Map-page 59)

The only wildlife here is when the Domed Stadium erupts 50,000 football fans into the hundred-odd places of refreshment. The only solitude is in the late hours of a dark and stormy night when the panhandlers all have crawled into garbage cans for shelter. However, the complete pedestrian goes a-walking not always for birds and flowers but sometimes for people. And history. This opening segment of Puget Sound Trail North may just be the best lowdown, downtown, waterfront walk in the West. Or East.

Begin inside the Union Station and the King Street Station on South Jackson Street. Within the echoing vaults listen for conspiratorial whispers of ghosts plotting how to bribe the Congresses of Heaven and Hell into giving them land grants (alternate sections in a 40-mile strip either side of the tracks) for the Great Heaven Railroad, the Northern Hell, and the Union Eternal. From Jackson turn right on 2nd Avenue South to South Main and turn left to Pioneer Square, Klondike Gold Rush National Historic Park, benches, bricks, trees and bistros of Occidental and Pioneer Place Parks, and guided tours of Underground Seattle. Via Main or Yesler or whatever, cross under the highway viaduct to Alaskan Way, nee Railroad Avenue.

Start the waterfront at Washington Street Public Boat Landing, where during Fleet Week in the 1920s-30s the liberty parties from the battlewagons used to debark, later to be embarked, the worse for wear, by the Shore Patrol. On your way north you, too, may choose to embark on over-the-water extensions of the Puget Sound Trail: The blue-and-white Alaska ferries will take you up the Inland Passage. The green-and-white Washington ferries will take you to Bremerton to visit the **U.S.S. Missouri,** to Winslow to walk Bainbridge Island beaches. The **Sightseer** offers harbor tours. So does the **Good Times** fleet, which additionally voyages to Blake Island State Park for baked salmon at Tillicum Village and the best beach-and-forest hiking so near Seattle (see **Footsore 4**). The **Princess Marguerite** in a single day will whisk you to and from a foreign nation and the city named for Queen Victoria. Or perhaps you'll be content just to look at these vessels, along with the fireboats and fishing boats and grain ships.

A nice thing about the waterfront is you don't have to be neat or even clean—the scene is casual and the whole place reeks anyway. If all the fish and chips consumed here on a fine summer Sunday were laid end to end a person would need a very long stick to shake at them. If all the ivory carvings sold here in a season weren't, the Eskimos of Hong Kong would be destitute.

There's a Tsutakawa fountain at the ferry terminal. Waterfront Park with benches to lounge on while sipping clam nectar. Seattle Aquarium with tidal basin, fish ladder, underwater viewing room, and marine life indigenous to local waters. Plaques noting historic spots, such as the first **maru** to arrive from Japan and the landing used by sailors of the Great White Fleet. And much more, including stairways climbing the bluff to Pike Place Market, a whole other story.

Mile 1½-3: Myrtle Edwards Park-Elliott Bay Park (Map-page 59)

At Broad Street, Alaskan Way ends and Myrtle Edwards Park begins. A large metered area extending to Bay Street permits parking long enough for a leisurely walk north to Smith Cove and back. The 1200-foot length of Myrtle

Myrtle Edwards Park

Edwards Park (City of Seattle) is succeeded by 4000-foot-long Elliott Bay Park (Port of Seattle).

In the whole of its green-lawn 1¼ (walking distance) miles through the two parks the path is close by the seawall; at low tide the beach can be walked instead. New-planted trees in time will make the lane a shady stroll. Train-watching (adjacent tracks are fenced off) is superb, and ferry-watching and general ship-watching. Also available for watching are ducks, gulls, crows, joggers, bicyclers (most of the way on a separate path), Elliott Bay, and the Olympics. The 200 tons of granite and concrete arranged in a sculpture have caused considerable remark. So too, notably among residents of Queen Anne Hill, has the huge grain terminal at Pier 86, next to which a fishing (viewing, too) pier juts 100 feet out from shore.

The path ends at Pier 89 on Smith Cove. A large parking lot (free) on 16th West (¼ mile from Elliott Avenue and reached via West Galer Street) permits the walk to be done from this end.

Mile 3-3½: The Smith Cove Lacuna

When enough walkers express enough interest the Port of Seattle, whose directors are elected by the public, will devise a pedestrian-bicycle route across Smith Cove and past Piers 90 and 91, linking the waterfront to Magnolia Bluff.

Until that happy time a person bent on connecting Elliott Bay Park to Discovery Park must walk from West Galer on railroad tracks to the stairway up to Garfield Street Bridge, then follow Magnolia Boulevard (glorious blufftop views over Elliott Bay and Seattle) to 32 Avenue, which descends a gulch to a deadend at the beach. Or, if the tide is high and there is no beach, stay with

Magnolia Boulevard (more stupendous views) to Emerson Street and the South Gate of Discovery Park and use the Loop Trail (see below) to attain West Point.

Mile 3½-7: Smith Cove Park-Magnolia Bluff-West Point (Map-page 59)

Most of the Magnolia Bluff beach is private property; for comment on that, see Puget Sound Trail—Seattle to Tacoma. However, the route can be done in seasons of high toleration, at hours of low tide. (This was the first scheduled walk by The Mountaineers, weeks after founding of the club, and the connection with 1907 is among the special pleasures of following in their footsteps today.)

The Port of Seattle's Smith Cove Park (also called simply "Public Viewpoint") provides a put-in. From 15 Avenue West turn west on West Dravus, turn south on 20 Avenue West, which bends right to become Thorndyke. Pass a sign that leads left to "Pier 91, trucks only," and turn left on 21 Avenue West, marked "Pier 91—Port of Seattle—Public Viewpoint." Miles of Datsuns and Toyotas, the largest parking lot in the West, end at the little park at the mouth of Smith Cove. A stone's throw across a slip ships are docked at Pier 91, unloading Datsuns and Toyotas. Ferries shuttle through Elliott Bay. Views extend to Alki Point, Blake and Vashon Islands, Restoration Point on Bainbridge Island, the Green and Gold Mountains on the Kitsap Peninsula. It's a nice spot to sit and look. But also it lets the feet down the riprap onto the beach—the first natural beach of the Trail and the only natural shoreline on Elliott Bay.

Particularly in the first 2 miles from Smith Cove the major attraction is the "working bay"—the parade of ships and ferries and other boats to and from the downtown waterfront and the industrial Duwamish Waterways. Other views are to Four Mile Rock and across the mouth of Elliott Bay to Alki Point where it all began. Look up the vertical till bluff to the line of madronas (when that fellow gave the bluff the name he thought they were magnolias). Gamblers Row, where Perkins Lane follows slump terraces down the very face of the bluff and where residents so value the combination of nearness to city and distance of mood they are willing to risk losing homes in a slippery spell, intrigues the passerby who has no stake in the game. Old pilings at the bluff foot and litters of boards on the slope speak of gambles lost over the decades.

The way swings from westerly to northwesterly to northerly, Seattle and its towers lost around the corner, the view now over the water to Bainbridge Island and the Olympics. At low tide the beach is a broad tideflat, the walker at such distance from the bluff he is scarcely aware of houses tucked in the trees. A sign announces "End of Public Beach"; this is the entry to Discovery Park. Now the bluff is a great wilderness of trees and bushes, outcrops at the base of blue clay continuing to be carved by waves, and up high, the famous sand cliffs.

Then comes West Point, the finest spit on the entire Seattle-to-Everett route. On its tip stands the near-century-old West Point Lighthouse, destination of The Mountaineers in 1907, and on 80 acres that have the potential to be one of the best parts of Discovery Park is the Metro sewage-treatment plant. Many citizens feel Metro, though a very Worthy Cause, can and should locate its facilities elsewhere and that when the existing plant requires replacement, 30-40 years from now, a new site should be chosen and West Point returned to its pristine natural beauty.

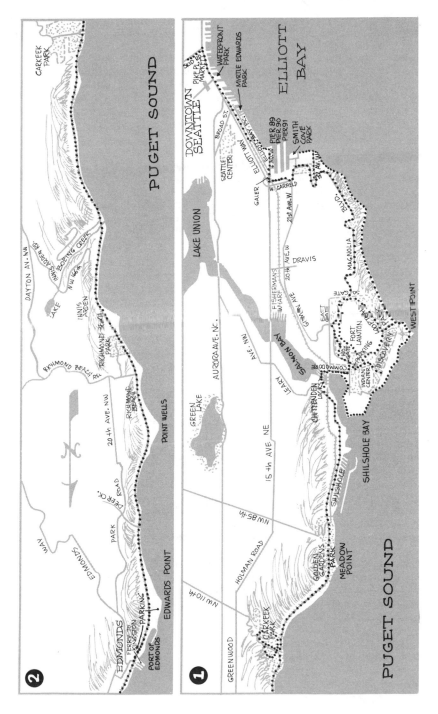

Mile 7-9½: West Point-Discovery Park-Commodore Park-Chittenden Locks (Map-page 59)

Metro and Seattle Parks have cooperated to ameliorate the disturbance on West Point. In 1981 the sewage lagoon built in 1966 was removed and the south beach was once again manhandled, but this time to eliminate effects of earlier manhandling, thus restoring (it is hoped) the look of naturehandling. A path was built past the treatment plant to give easy access to the north beach. That the work was planned by Wolf Bauer is all the assurance needed that it's an honest attempt to do right.

In a low enough tide the beach can be walked all the way around the shore of Shilshole Bay into Salmon Bay. But don't do it when homeowners are sunbathing on private sands and hollering at peasants and calling the police.

When the tide is high or toleration low, go inland. From West Point climb the service road-trail to the Loop Trail, which leads to the North Parking Area. From there exit through the North Gate onto 40 Avenue, turn right on Commodore to Commodore Park, where the beach route joins. This over-the-hill way is about 2 miles, about the same as the beach, but with more elevation gain.

Commodore Park is a jimdandy. Look out saltwater Salmon Bay past railroad bridge and jetties to Shilshole Bay and Puget Sound. On a sunny day admire the parade of vessels lined up to go through the Big Lock or the Little Lock into freshwater Salmon Bay.

Follow the promenade path through the park to the pedestrian walkway over Chittenden Locks.

Pause to examine the fish ladder which salmon and trout ascend on their way to spawning grounds in the Lake Washington basin. A below-ground viewing gallery gives the best close looks at big fish available outside a fish market. (After studying the fish you may wish to study fishing boats, another endangered species. For a sidetrip, walk east on Commodore 1 mile to the fleet based at Salmon Bay Terminal, "Fishermen's Wharf.")

Hiram M. Chittenden Locks ("Ballard Locks") are the key component of a navigation system dedicated in 1917. A channel was dredged from Puget Sound through Shilshole Bay to Salmon Bay, joining this body of water via the Fremont Cut to Lake Union, and that body via the Montlake Cut to Lake Washington. The latter was lowered from the natural elevation above sealevel of 29-33 feet to the level of Lake Union, 21 feet, and Salmon Bay was raised by the dam at the locks. Lake Washington, which formerly emptied via the Black River to the Duwamish River, thence to Elliott Bay, now drains through the Lake Washington Ship Canal to Shilshole Bay. The Black River virtually ceased to be. The Cedar River, which flowed into the Black and thus the Duwamish, was diverted into Lake Washington, which it thus furnishes a constant source of flushing water from the mountains, the uncelebrated other half of the clean-up-the-lake success story for which Metro is always given full credit. Awareness of all this fooling around with Mother Nature adds interest to watching ships and boats being lowered or raised through the locks. Footnote: the Ship Canal never made Lake Washington, as everyone imagined would happen, a great seaport.

Adjoining the locks are the 7 acres of the Carl English Botanical Gardens, displaying plants from lands all over the world.

Discovery Park (Map-page 59)

Though the English anthem requests the Deity to attack the nation's foes by confounding their politics, frustrating their knavish tricks, Seattle has cause to bless the Spanish or the British or whoever gave the Department of War (as we then called it) an excuse to build Fort Lawton. When the Department of Defense (as by then we'd renamed it) couldn't afford enough lawnmowers to maintain empires of useless landscapes, Seattle gained a splendid new park. Though a host of Worthy Causes immediately descended to claim hunks, most were beaten off and the bulk of the disgorged land saved for a dispersed-use, nature-oriented park. Nature. Since summer 1981, when one was caught there, the word has been, "Watch out for cougars." (And lions and tigers and bears—and LIONS and TIGERS and BEARS...)

The principal access to Discovery Park is the very large North Parking Area (and bus stop) located by the North Gate. A dependable way for strangers to get here is: from 15 Avenue NW turn west on Dravus, then north on 20th Avenue which becomes Gilman Avenue which becomes Government Way and leads to the East Gate. At the East Gate turn right and follow the winding road to the parking.

Wolf Tree Nature Trail

From the North Parking a ½-mile self-guided nature trail circles through forest and mucky bottom, along the sidehill and over Scheuerman Creek, named for the Christian who bought the land in 1807 and with his Native American wife, Rebecca, lived in a log cabin with their 10 children. We learn

Fish ladder at Hiram M. Chittenden Locks

this from the pamphlet available at the trailhead, and also much more, including explanations of "a dog hair stand," the "wolf tree," and "witches broom."

Round trip ½ mile, allow 1 hour

Loop Trail

The loop roughly circles the periphery, connects to all park entrances, and is accessible by many Metro buses. Though the generations of military maneuvering largely converted the vegetation to species from the East, Europe, Macedonia, and the domains of Cyrus the Great, volunteers are patiently working to reintroduce local plants and protect them from invasive foreigners. The trail—and the park—will get better and better, year by year.

Every park entry leads to the Loop Trail. From the North Parking ascend the hill on any of several paths ¼ mile to intersect the Loop. In the counterclockwise direction (those of you with digitals, ask an oldtimer what that means) it soon passes a sidepath to North Bluff, with views north out Puget Sound, and then the service road down to West Point (see below). South Bluff, atop the famous sand cliffs, has glorious Sound views; inland are old dunes dating from a drier climate of the past. Upsy-downsy, by old Army buildings where once upon a time a war with Spain was considered serious business, through woods, the Loop self-completes.

Loop trip 3 miles, allow 2 hours
High point 300 feet, elevation gain 500 feet

Discovery Park beach

The Beach

The Discovery Park beach has a number of claims to being the very best on the entire Puget Sound Trail: There is no railroad. The bluff offers not only the usual tills and gravels but some of the tallest walls of sand. There is the West Point Lighthouse, as pretty as they come. The parade of ships and boats and cockleshells makes it hard to get a nap, so much is always going on. Are birds your game? Clouds? Waves? Storms?

Moreover, you get here afoot, from bus stops. From the North Parking it's 1 mile via Loop Trail and service road to the beach. Another ¼ mile leads past the Metro plant to the lighthouse. Or, some 3½ miles lead south around Magnolia Bluff to Smith Cove. Or, some 2 miles lead north to Salmon Bay.

Total round-trip beach walk 11 miles, allow two tides

Mile 9½-13½: Chittenden Locks-Golden Gardens Park-Meadow Point-Carkeek Park (Map-page 59)

At Chittenden Locks begins a connection on streets to the Burke-Gilman Trail (which see). Onto it from the Puget Sound Trail turns the Sound-to-Mountains Trail (which see).

The Puget Sound Trail proceeds westward from the locks on the north shore of Salmon Bay. Staying close to the water on sidewalks and dirt paths, in 1 mile a walker leaves Salmon Bay for Shilshole Bay and its enormous jetty-protected moorage for hundreds (or is it thousands?) of pleasure boats. The Port of Seattle has decorated the way with Leif Ericson's statue, a monster 19th-century wrought-iron anchor, and other marine artifacts. Across the street is Gordo's, which makes the greatest peanut-butter milkshake available on any trip in this book.

The moorage at last yields to the 76 acres of Golden Gardens Park, with bathing beach and unobstructed Sound views. Meadow Point is the last point in Seattle retaining all elements of a complete beach: driftwood line, dune line, lagoon. It does not have a swimming pool (as does Colman) or a sewage plant (as does West). There was a plot to decorate it with an aquarium but saner heads squelched that dizzy idea.

The railroad tracks having joined the route at Chittenden Locks, from Meadow Point on north to Everett they constitute the high-tide lane.

The bank above the tracks is not high and is quite solidly built-up through the Blue Ridge area and what used to be called North Beach.

Then the bluff suddenly rears up 200 feet from the water, tall and steep and unstable. From now on a common feature of the route is the sensor wire at the base of the bluff; when chunks of bluff slide over the tracks, as they do every winter, all winter, a light blinks on in a control room and trains are signalled to watch out.

Carkeek Park (Map-page 59)

Carkeek Park is mostly a second-growth wilderness, one of the two largest on the Trail; few traces remain of long-ago logging or even a once-thriving brickyard. The park features an excellent beach and in its spacious 192 acres

Beach at Carkeek Park

an extensive network of trails being built by Seattle Parks and Scouts of the Viking District.

Drive from Greenwood Avenue, turning west on 110 Street to find the entrance roadway winding down Piper's Canyon. From the large water-view parking area a skybridge crosses the railroad tracks to the beach.

The major trail is that up Piper's Creek. Near the tracks by the creek find a path leading upstream to the Metro sewage-treatment plant (yes, this park also has a Worthy Cause), a small parking area off the entry road, and a sign, "Carkeek Trail." The way ascends the steepwalled canyon floor in lush mixed forest, passing a dozen basalt-boulder half-dams that reduce erosion. Crossing and recrossing the sandy creek, the trail climbs the narrowing canyon, at last leaving it to ascend steeply to a small parking area at the street-end of 6 Avenue NW, which leads to a bus stop on NW 100 Place close to Holman Road NW. This trail is 1¼ miles in length.

For a loop return, find one of the several paths climbing into wildwoods south of the canyon and wander along the hillside out to a bluff 175 precipitous feet above the tracks and beach, giving fine views over the water and south to Meadow Point.

For a separate walk on the north side of the canyon, from the beach parking area climb the bluff edge to the high flat and follow the path along the rim in woods ⅓ mile to the unmarked park edge. For a loop return, take a path inland and descend to the picnic and parking area on a path where red rubble shows this to be the site of the brickyard.

For the wildest walk of all, on the latter path watch for a slippery track dropping to a skimpy trail contouring the tanglewood bluff halfway between rim and beach. Take care not to become part of the slide terrain; the mucky slopes are tricky.

Total park sampler loop trips 5 miles, allow 3 hours
High point 275 feet

Mile 13½-18: Boeing Creek-Richmond Beach Park (Map-page 59)

From Carkeek Park northward the bluff wildland-and-wildlife-refuge is a near-constant presence. Beside the high-tide lane atop the seawall are alders and maples, flowers in season, frogs croaking in marshy ditches, creeks tumbling down little gorges. One scarcely believes houses are at blufftop, usually set back from the lip a goodly distance. And with winter wind blowing by the ears and winter surf pounding, one may not hear trains creeping up behind; to avoid being crushed or—nearly as bad—being impelled on a leap into outer space by a train horn blowing in your ear, keep looking over your shoulder. Unless of course, it's low tide and you're down on the beach, enjoying that other and parallel wildland and wildlife refuge.

North 1 mile from Carkeek Park is a canyon in clay and sand; generations of local kids have worked away at eroding the deposit while trying to break their necks climbing the vertical walls.

At 2 miles from the park (and all this way no houses by the beach, presence of a city seeming impossible) is Highlands Point and the wide valley of Boeing Creek, named for the logger-aircraft manufacturer who kept this section of forest as a private retreat; not until World War II was the magnificent virgin Douglas fir of the "Boeing Tract" logged. The newspapers enjoyed the picturesqueness of 19th-century-style logging so near the city so late in history; only a few people mourned the loss of the equivalent of a dozen Seward Parks.

On the south side of Boeing Creek a private road ascends the wild creek, in big trees that weren't worth logging (snagtops and the like) to The Highlands residential park. On the north side a road-trail with greenbelt easement but gated on the upper, inland side to keep out vehicles, ascends ½ mile to Innis Arden Way at NW 166 (very limited shoulder parking). A footpath goes around the gate, permitting beach access. In the valley bottom at NW 166 is a wide flat through which the creek meanders; until a flood took out the dam, this was Hidden Lake, Boeing's private fishing pond. King County owns half the lakesite and is considering a plan to rebuild the dam.

North from Boeing Creek is more wild bluff. Approaching Richmond Beach, keep a sharp eye for a path up a gulch to Innis Arden; this private trail makes an interesting sidetrip ½ mile up to a road.

At 4 miles from Carkeek Park is a sand hill that formerly was the site of shipwrecking; wooden ships were stripped of metal fittings and then set afire, the clouds of black smoke attracting throngs from all over the north Seattle area. Here is Richmond Beach (King County) Park. A skybridge crosses the railroad tracks to the parking area in a great amphitheater that until a quarter-century ago was a gravel mine and another favorite spot for local kids to get bruises and contusions and minor fractures. From the top of the park, elevation 200 feet, the view across the Sound is superb.

To reach Richmond Beach Park, on Aurora Avenue at 185 Street turn west on the Richmond Beach Road and follow it down the steps of wave-cut bluffs, each representing a different former level of the water. When nearing the water, only one more bluff to go, turn left at a sign directing to the park.

Mile 18-22: Point Wells-Edwards Point-Edmonds Ferry Slip-Sunset Beach Park (Map-pages 59, 69)

From the park the Trail goes through the old community of Richmond Beach to Point Wells, which in a pristine condition was perhaps second in beauty only to West Point (in a pristine condition) but ages ago was preempted by Standard Oil for an oil tanker terminal, oil storage tanks, and asphalt refinery. Wild bluff resumes at the complex, at whose north end, nearly 2 miles from the park, is a tiny strip of natural beach, trees growing to the driftwood line.

The ravine of Deer Creek has a tempting (unsurveyed) trail inland. At the palatial bluff-top estates of Woodway Park begins one of the most spectacular slide areas of the route, the naked muck slopes in motion from an elevation of 220 feet down to the tracks, which often are blocked by chunks of former palatial estate. But except for the kempt-looking bluff rim giving away the existence of lawns up there, one would never suspect homes, here or anywhere from Point Wells to Edmonds.

This metropolis is entered, 3 miles from the park, at Edwards Point, site of another tanker terminal (Union), storage tanks, and small refinery. But a considerable portion of the natural beach at the point is undisturbed.

At Edwards Point begins a 1-mile breach in the bluffs; in the cavity is a broad marshy valley, a pioneers' landing that became Edmonds.

The large parking lot at the point is accessible via shoreline streets from the ferry dock to the north. At the public beach begins the Port of Edmonds, the long breakwater-protected yacht basin offering a display of boats comparable to that at Shilshole Bay. A public observation pier and a public (city) beach enliven the walk. The aroma from a fish-and-chips restaurant is calculated to drive a long-distance hiker insane.

The best thing about Edmonds is the ferry. For a lunch stop and an incomparable viewpoint, take the voyage to Kingston on the Kitsap Peninsula and back. At least pause to watch the ferry ease in to the slip, unload, and load.

Adjoining the dock on the north is Edmonds Underwater Park, sunken ships providing homes for marine life that scuba divers can look at but mustn't touch. Connecting to the underwater park is the abovewater Sunset Beach Park, located at historic Brackett's Landing.

To reach the park follow signs from I-5 to the Edmonds-Kingston Ferry and cross the ferry lane into the park, where cars may be parked for 4 hours maximum, enough for short walks. If using this as a base for a longer trip, park south of the ferry dock in the vast free lots of the Port of Edmonds.

Another feature to note here is the only Amtrak station between Seattle and Everett.

Mile 22-26½: Browns Bay-Meadowdale Beach Park (Map-page 69)

For many years one of the favorite stretches of the Puget Sound Trail has been from Edmonds to Meadowdale (and onward to Picnic Point). The overwater views become distinctly and dramatically different. The north-of-Seattle shore and Bainbridge Island fade south in haze, the vista now being across to the Kitsap Peninsula. But one sees out northwest between the peninsula and the white cliffs of Whidbey Island to Admiralty Inlet, the route to the ocean. For the first time, and only briefly, there is a water horizon.

Richmond Beach Park

Immediately north of Edmonds there's no bluff and houses crowd the way. Then the wilderness wall rises again, cut by gulches and a sand canyon, offering a series of trails inland—doubtless to private property and thus not public accesses to the beach.

At about 3 miles the shore bends in to Browns Bay. In a lovely gulch is Lynnwood's sewage-treatment plant (the old story) and the first road access to the beach since Edmonds, via a sideroad off 76 Avenue W (see Meadowdale).

At 4 miles a structure juts out on the waterside of the tracks—Laebugten Fishing Wharf. On slumping hillsides above is the village of Meadowdale. To the north ½ mile is the fine broad sandy Meadowdale Beach at the mouth of Lunds Gulch.

Meadowdale Beach Park (Map-page 69)

The delta-point thrusting far out in the waves, views up and down the Sound virtually the full length of the Trail, the large creek gushing from wide Lunds Gulch and rippling over the beach, these are the features most famed in this undeveloped Snohomish County Park. But in addition, Lunds Gulch is one of the two largest chunks of wildland (Carkeek Park the other) on the shore between Seattle and Everett.

The village of Meadowdale is reached from Olympic View Drive (known from logging days of the 19th century as the Snake Trail, so sinuous is the route) via 76 Avenue W from an intersection signed "Laebugten Wharf." (Partway to the beach a sideroad drops left down a ravine to the Lynnwood sewage treatment plant—see above—and a public parking lot with beach access.)

Parking on Laebugten Wharf is strictly for customers. Parking elsewhere in

Meadowdale, entirely on road shoulders, is extremely limited. The public is an obvious pain to residents, who barely have room on their ever-sliding hillside for houses and streets much less visitors. This therefore is not a place to go on weekends and summer evenings.

Park with care wherever possible on a road shoulder, not blocking traffic or driveways. One route north the ½ mile to the gulch is the beach. Another is 75 Place W, barricaded at the edge of residences but as a foot trail continuing, the grade partly slid out, across the face of the bluff in woods, and descending to the valley bottom.

Meadowdale Country Club, it once was, a good long while ago. Nature is reclaiming foundations and charred timbers of the burned lodge, fields of what must have been a rather minute golf course, and valley roads.

To explore the wildland, walk upvalley on an old road that dwindles to trail. The creek flows over sandbars and little waterfalls. The valley walls, rising steeply to the plateau top at 450 feet, are massed alders, fern-hung maples, hemlocks growing from huge cedar stumps notched for the fallers' springboards, and appropriate other vegetation. At 1 mile from the beach the trail, still ½ mile from the head of the gulch, comes to a Y, the two branches scrambling up mossy-lush, black-mucky slopes on either side of the gulch to suburbia. Downvalley from the Y several other paths similarly climb the walls. A trail system built at various levels of the gulch on both sides could have a total length of up to 10 miles.

Sample gulch round trip 3 miles, allow 1½ hours
High point 450 feet

Mile 26½-28: Norma Beach-Picnic Point Park (Map-page 69)

Just around the corner, ½ mile north of Lunds Gulch, is another fishing wharf; this one at Norma Beach shows its half-century age, seeming about to sag to the sands. Public cars have little space to park, but the public feet easily can gain the beach via the railroad tracks.

A high sand cliff catches the eye, and a trail to the blufftop; there's another way there (see below). Then, on a slump terrace above the beach, appears a row of homes (see below).

Ghosts now crowd the beach—lines of old pilings, remnants of docks, visions of the vessels of the mosquito fleet that steamed up and down the water road until the 1920s. More ghosts—concrete foundations of beach cabins. Are those mandolins we hear in the summer twilight?

All this, 1 mile from Norma Beach, is none other than far-famed Picnic Point, a great sandy spit at the mouth of a superb valley, a lovely creek rushing across the beach.

Picnic Point Park (Map-page 69)

Candidate for honors as one of the best places on the whole Puget Sound Trail, Picnic Point does not have a sewage plant, swimming pool, or aquarium. But it almost had a refinery. When the oilers realized they'd better seek a more cooperative county to the north, they decided to turn a profit another way. Chevron Land Development Co. plans to build a city on the uplands and shore.

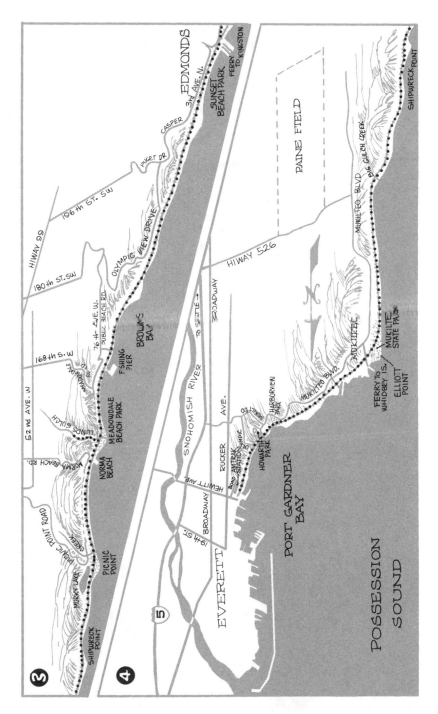

PUGET SOUND TRAIL-SEATTLE TO EVERETT

Meanwhile it has leased (not sold) an itty-bitty piece to Snohomish County for a park which essentially is just a parking lot and an access to the beach.

But what a beach!

Take the Paine Field exit from I-5. Drive west to Highway 99 and turn south to the Mukilteo Road, Highway 525. Turn northwest (right) to the Beverly Park-Edmonds Road. Turn southwest (left) a short way to a yellow blinker. Turn northwest (right) on the Picnic Point Road and descend a forested, undeveloped, beautiful, wild, parkless gulch (passing the Alderwood Manor wastewater treatment plant, that the valley should not be a total loss) to the beach parking area.

There's no park to put a trail system in but there is a nice bluff walk from here. Maps still show Puget Sound Boulevard contouring the bluff face south to Norma Beach. But it doesn't make it all the way and hasn't since about 1960. Don't drive south of Picnic Point on what road remains; the residents on the slump terrace need every bit of single-lane pavement. From the parking area walk ¾ mile along the row of houses (that are, seen from the geologist's vantage, riding the sliding hill down to the waves), to the road-end (no parking). Trail continues on the remnant grade (haunted by ghosts of Model Ts) across the bluff. The sand cliff admired from the beach (see above) is what finally discouraged the highway department; not a scrap of grade lingers here.

Here on the vanished section a hiker can sit in the woods, high above the beach, far below the blufftop, protected on every side from the 20th century. Gazing over the broad waters, one feels as remote from civilization as anywhere on the Puget Sound Trail.

It's not a large sanctuary—in ⅓ mile from drivable road is the edge of inhabited Norma Beach. But as one sits in the wild spot it grows in the direction of infinity.

Round trip 2½ miles, allow 1½ hours
High point 100 feet

Great blue heron hunting at low tide near Picnic Point

Partly salvaged hulk at Shipwrecking Point

Mile 28-33: Shipwrecking Point-Big Gulch-Mukilteo State Park-Elliot Point-Mukilteo Ferry Slip (Map-page 69)

The hiker who started the journey in Seattle now is aware of having come very far north. Indeed the route here leaves Puget Sound for Possession Sound, across whose relatively narrow width is Whidbey Island. Still in view are the Olympics but now very close to the north, above Camano Island, is the white volcano of Baker. At hike's start the Bainbridge Island ferry shuttled back and forth from Seattle to Winslow. Then came the shuttling of the Edmonds-Kingston ferry, which now retreats southward in the distance as to the north becomes more prominent the green-and-white vessels ceaselessly voyaging between Mukilteo and Columbia Beach on Whidbey.

Just north of Picnic Point the way passes a murky lake dammed by the railroad fill; homes line the inland shore, leaders of flycasters festoon the telephone wires.

At 1 mile is "Shipwrecking Point," a sandspit once used for stripping and burning wooden ships; a carcass and some ribcages remain to be seen but not explored—on the privately-owned point is an inhabited house. A footpath of steps cut in clay ascends the bluff to a waterfall (in hard rock, a rare exposure of non-glacial materials) and, atop the plateau, a path along the creek in wildwoods to Marine View Drive at 116 Street SW.

In ¼ mile more is a substantial ravine up which goes a trail. Homes of so-called Chenault Beach (which has no beach) then are seen atop the bluff.

In 1 mile more (2¼ miles from Picnic Point) is a point with a very wide beach at low tide, the mouth of the wild valley of Big Gulch. Not a park. In fact, it once was degraded to an open ditch down which ran raw sewage from Paine Field Air Force Base. Cleaned up and looking nice, it now harbors a Worthy Cause—

71

the Olympus Terrace Sewage Treatment Plant. No public access. Thus lonesome country. The solitary plant operator frequently sights deer and bear and weasels and seals, eagles perched in favorite snags, fleets of thousands upon thousands of waterfowl swimming by.

North ½ mile is the first close house in a long while, in a creek valley on a flat beside the tracks; the road access is private. Shortly a public road descends a slump terrace to within 50 feet of the tracks, but is not recommended as a public beach access, having very little parking. An interesting portion of this community is built outside the railroad tracks on a bulkheaded invasion of the beach; the dozen cottages have walk-in trail access only; the residents tend not to buy new refrigerators very often.

After this ½ mile of scattered dwellings, in the final 1¾ miles mankind retreats from the beach, up to the top of the tall, wild bluff. The way features a tangled-green slot of a gorge, a great vertical cliff of white glacial till, another creek tumbling out of a gulch.

Rounding Elliot Point the railway swings inland and is fenced off through Mukilteo. The Trail thus follows the beach to small Mukilteo State Park. On the tip is Elliot Point Lighthouse, the first since West Point, a dandy. Adjacent is the ferry dock, suggesting a sidetrip over the water to Columbia Beach, a nice rest stop after the 5 miles from Picnic Point, before starting back.

Mukilteo is reached from I-5 via Highway 526-525.

Mile 33-38: Powder Mill Gulch-Merrill and Ring Creek-Harborview Park-Howarth Park-Pigeon Creeks No. 2 and 1—Weyerhaeuser Mill-Port Gardner Bay-Everett Amtrak Station (Map-page 69)

Gazing from Mukilteo to the industrial sprawl of Port Gardner Bay, the hiker may ask, "Who needs it?" But the wild bluff continues to guard the beach and the assemblage of wild ravines is arguably the best on the entire Puget Sound Trail.

The shore, previously trending north, bends sharply eastward at Elliot Point. The view thus is across Possession Sound past little Gedney (Hat) Island to Saratoga Passage between Whidbey and Camano Islands and to Port Susan between the latter island and the mainland. No longer is there a parade of ships to and from the ocean and various ports of Puget Sound, but there is considerable traffic along Possession Sound to Everett.

Easterly for a scant 1 mile from the Mukilteo ferry dock the beach is blocked by another oil terminal and a series of storage tanks. A public road extends along the fence to a public parking area and beach at the far end, a good start for walking to Everett.

Passing a ravine and a trail-staircase up the bluff to a viewpoint, then the prettiest exposure of varved blue clay on the route, in 1 scant mile of continuous vertical cliff is the first of the exceptional wildland valleys, Powder Mill Gulch, with a large creek, a broad delta-point, and a path up the gulch an unsurveyed distance inland.

In ½ mile is a nameless but noble creek and in ¼ mile more is larger and superb Merrill and Ring Creek whose prominent delta pushes far out in the waves and supports a driftwood line and dunes.

The bluff lowers and houses creep near the next ¼ mile to a small creek and little Harborview (Everett) Park, located on Mukilteo Boulevard at Dover Street. An excellent view of the harbor. At the north edge, a deep green ravine.

In a scant ½ mile (3 miles from Mukilteo ferry dock) is Howarth Park, for

Beach access at Howarth Park

which be praised and congratulated the Everett Park Department. The park is reached from Mukilteo Boulevard at Seahurst Avenue; parking is provided at the upper, blufftop level and, via Olympic Boulevard which descends to the floor of Pigeon Creek No. 2, at the beach level by the railroad tracks. Extending from Pigeon 2 south to a nameless ravine, the park has enough paths—on blufftop and in gulch depths and on sidehills, on wide-view lawns and in wildwoods—to permit 2 miles of walking with scarcely any repetition. Access to the beach is via a skybridge over the tracks. On the beach side a stairway winds around and down a wooden tower resembling a donjon keep but actually serving utilitarian needs for stairs and restrooms.

The final 2 miles of the Trail have a different appeal. Or to some tastes, perhaps none. Port Gardner Bay is entered and Everett Junction reached. Here is Pigeon Creek No. 1, which in another location surely would have been a park but here is a mucked-up truck road to the Port of Everett. From the Junction the tracks lie between surprisingly wild bluff and the onetime site of a mammoth Weyerhaeuser pulpmill complex. Then comes Port of Everett Pier 1 and the Amtrak Rail Passenger Station, at Bond Street off Hewitt Avenue. Plentiful parking.

Bus: Seattle waterfront, in walking distance of a bushel of routes; Magnolia Park, Metro 19, 24, and 33; Discovery Park, 19 to South Gate, 24 to East Gate, 33 to North Gate; Chittenden Locks, 17 and 30; Golden Gardens Park, 17, 30, and 48; Carkeek Park, 28 (to trail at upper end of Piper's Canyon); Richmond Beach, 305; Edmonds, Metro 316 and 376; Everett, Metro 306.

OVERLAKE: MERCER ISLAND
TO EAST SAMMAMISH PLATEAU

Urban and suburban and rural and wild, that's the 1980s mix in the overlake section of Puget Sound City. Close to home and largely bus-accessible, elevations topping out around 600 feet and thus open the year around, ranging from lakeshores to pastures to forests, it's an important walking province and a rich one. But less rich actually than potentially.

The survey for this book found few hikes of regional (as distinguished from local) significance on Mercer Island and the glacierized flats and bumps and bogs of the upland between Lakes Washington and Sammamish, and these mainly have been provided not by the municipalities but by King County and the State of Washington. The New Cities here pretty well blew their chances for spacious parks in the 1950s and '60s, when the land-planning was being done by speculators and their servants in government, taxpayers were concentrating on building schools and roads, and the suburban ideal in recreation was to buy $50,000 worth of toys and burn a barrel of gas a weekend dragging the portable kindergarten around the freeways. By the time the New Cities emerged from childhood into adolescence the land prices had rocketed out of sight. Their only chance now for large close-to-home parks is in the Issaquah Alps.

Quite another story is the second major segment of this overlake province, the Sammamish Valley. Not for future massive bond issues but right-now walking are the grand trail along the river and the magnificent county park at the north end of Lake Sammamish and the splendid state park at the south.

Still a third story is the broad highland between the Sammamish and Snoqualmie valleys, the area called Pine Lake-Beaver Lake Plateau in the south and Bear Creek Plateau in the north and East Sammamish Plateau in sum. Presently mostly wildland forest and gracious pastures generously wetted by myriad lakes and ponds and bogs and swamps and creeks, the area is proposed to have a dozen Bellevues, with a score of Issaquahs thrown in for good measure. The swarm of developers—from California, Canada, Las Vegas, and Kuwait—are engaged in civil war to see who will get the most rich the most fast, but form a united front to oppose the imposition of a public plan on their separate schemes. Follow the real-estate pages of your newspaper to learn why the plateau is the "hottest spot" in King County. Pedestrians and horsefolk despair of cooling it but do hope the New Bellevues have sidewalks.

USGS maps: Mercer Island, Bothell, Maltby, Kirkland, Redmond, Issaquah, Fall City

Mercer Island (Map-page 76)

Before War I the entirety of Mercer Island could have been purchased with the City of Seattle's petty cash and made into one of the world's great urban parks, a park for all of Puget Sound City for the ages. The acquisition was seriously proposed—and not by wild-eyed birdwatchers but pillars of the community. However, the petty cash was wanted for paper clips and pen nibs.

Mercer Island still is all forest ringed by bright waters. However, it has become some thousands of private parks, entry only by invitation. The City of Mercer Island, as it now is, must look east to the Issaquah Alps for walks longer

Beach trail in St. Edward State Park

than over-the-lawn and around-the-patio. Two remnants of the Old Island provide a little close-to-home exercise, and glimpses of what might have been.

PIONEER PARK

Logged so long ago the firs now are quite big and very tall, Pioneer Park consists of three pieces, each a quarter-mile square, separated by streets but each block large enough to preserve an inner peace.

Drive Island Crest Way to SE 68 Street, turn west, and park in the small shopping center.

For an introductory loop, cross SE 68 into the Northwest Block and weave through on any combination of the maze of unmarked paths. Loop back to SE 68, cross Island Crest Way, and similarly weave-loop through the Southeast Block. Finally cross SE 68 to the Northeast Block and there, on Island Crest Way, find either entrance to the Nature Trail. Follow it across the island-crest plateau, along the rim of a deep green ravine containing a year-round stream, and return to Island Crest Way and the start.

Sample loop trip 2 miles, allow 1½ hours
High point 332 feet, no elevation gain
All year
Bus: Metro 202

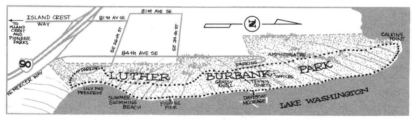

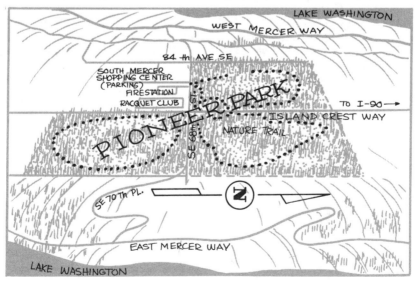

LUTHER BURBANK COUNTY PARK

Come out of deep woods into wide-view meadows beside the lake under the big sky. On the 77-acre grounds of a former school for delinquents are fields, marshes, trees, and 3000 feet of waterfront.

From the Mercer Island business district cross under I-90 onto 84 Avenue SE and from it at SE 24 Street enter the park.

To methodically "do" the park, walk a loop. From the parking lot by the headquarters building and tennis courts head north. Pass the amphitheater and a froggy cattail marsh to Calkins Point and views north over the water to Meydenbauer Bay and towers of the University District. Walk the meadow shore south, by clumps of willow and cottonwood, to views of the East Channel Bridge and the peaks of Cougar Mountain enclosing Coal Creek. Pass below the old school building, by the old brick power plant, walk out on docks where, in season, boats moor for picnicking. Follow the waterfront trail in willow-madrona-Indian plum woods to the fishing pier, lawns by the swimming beach, and the marsh at the park border. Loop back inland through meadows, including an ascent of the Grassy Knoll.

Loop trip 1½ miles, allow 1 hour
High point 50 feet, elevation gain 50 feet
Bus: Metro 202, 210, 226, and 235

Mercer Slough-Enetai Beach (Map-page 81)

The lowering of Lake Washington narrowed a bay to a slough through newly-exposed wetland, some of which was drained to grow the blueberries that once were Bellevue's chief claim to fame. When the village grew to a city, changing in hue from green to concrete-gray and subdivision-brown, a small but

Canoeing at the mouth of Mercer Slough

persistent voice in the community cried out, "Save **something**." Not enough was, and most of that in Mercer Slough, and most of that not by the city but Washington State Parks. Between 118 Avenue SE on the east and Bellevue Way on the west, Lake Washington on the south and Bellefields Nature Park on the north, an expanse of wetland more than a mile long and a halfmile wide has been purchased by the state. Tentative plans are to leave most of the area just as it is, with nature trails built where the wild vegetation won't suffer and the wild critters won't mind. Off Bellevue Way, where now a blueberry farm lingers on lease, will be parking, nature center, and entry to trails that will circle several ponds, cross and recross the slough, and wind through the natural area—something like 7 or 8 miles in total. Probably the park will be turned over to Bellevue as a magnificent enlargement of Bellefields Nature Park.

As of 1981 the bulk of the park is strictly for the birds (and muskrats), though in harvest time a person can visit the farm to buy delicious pick-'em-yourself blueberries. Aside from that there is a delicious little walk.

Surrealistic, that's what it is: the wide expanse of cattails and willow thickets a-rustle with flitting birds, the lakewater a-ripple with swimming birds, all manner of wary critters skulking in the bushes—and inches away from this wildland, the concrete jungle of I-90. Indeed, this walk is possible by courtesy of the State Highway Department.

On Bellevue Way just north of I-90, where 113th goes west, a road unmarked save for a bicycle symbol goes east down to undeveloped Sweyolocken Park, which presently consists solely of a boat-launching ramp (note ancient wood piling of an old, old bridge), a Metro pumping station, and a parking lot.

Walk the blacktop bicycle path on a graceful sky bridge over Mercer Slough, then a floating path through reeds beside and under I-90, in ½ mile reaching the far east side of the wide valley and 118 Avenue SE. Less than 1 mile south along this little old onetime-highway-become-backroad is Coal Creek (which see). And 1 mile north is Bellefields Nature Park (which see). Opportunities thus are excellent for creative combinations of walks.

Meanwhile, back on the west side of the valley, a footpath turns off the bike path and goes a short bit to the shore of Lake Washington and views over the water to the marina and homes of Newport Shores and to the west slopes of Cougar Mountain. The path leads to SE Lake Road, which in a scant ¼ mile reaches Enetai Bathing Beach Park, a dandy place to sit and watch ducks and sailboats and look over the East Channel to Mercer Island and Coal Creek.

Complete round trip 2 miles, allow 1 hour
High point 25 feet, no elevation gain
All year
Bus: Metro 226 and 235

Bellefields Nature Park (Map-page 81)

Something there is about a marsh that makes man want to fill it or drain it and turn it into "useful" land—a farm, freeway, or subdivision. Or maybe a golf course or baseball field. Siegfried K. Semrau, former Bellevue Park Director, was among the earliest folk hereabouts to appreciate the intrinsic value of marshes. Thanks to his leadership, here is a beautifully useless soggy tanglewood.

Leave Highway 405 on Richards Road exit, drive west to 118 Avenue SE, and turn south 1 mile to the park sign and a small parking area. Spot the sign, "To the Trails," and go.

Artfully arranged to make the 48 acres seem a dozen times larger, the 3 miles of trails weave through forest, over little creeks, beside Mercer Slough and its (often) hundreds of ducks and coots. Most of the trails are literally floating on a deep peat deposit. Brush from trail-clearing was placed as a base, over which was spread a layer of sandy loam from the hillside, then a layer of wood chips, also from the trail-clearing. The result is a unique springy surface. Names of the paths, signed at intersections, are evocative and entertaining as well as descriptive: Mud Lake Boulevard, Nightshade Avenue, Willow Grove, Skunk Cabbage Lane, Cottonwood Avenue, Cattail Way, Fireweed Lane, Gooseberry Avenue, Bee Trail, and so forth.

No map or guide is needed to savor this "living museum of natural history." Start on any trail, take any turns, keep going until it's time to go home. A good introduction is a perimeter loop, taking lefts at all junctions and thus circling the edge of the park. Then, on a second go-around, take all the right turns. Finally criss-cross to make sure you haven't missed anything.

Perimeter loop and embellishments 2 miles, allow 1½ hours
High point 50 feet, elevation gain 30 feet

Mud Lake, Bellefields Nature Park

Bellefields Office Park (Map-page 81)

In Bellevue's youth the common joke (in other cities) was that the citizens were too busy keeping their Cadillacs from being repossessed to worry about such frills as sidewalks, storm drains, and parks. So, at a time when a minor bond issue could vastly have enlarged Bellefields Nature Park, the voters shrugged; after all, most expected to be transferred soon to Houston. Developers therefore proceeded to convert 200 acres of wetland-wildland into an Office Park. Though the "park" consists almost entirely of buildings, blacktop roads, and blacktop parking lots (office occupants apparently drive two cars apiece, like rollerskates) the development was done with some sensitivity, recognizing that natural amenities so ameliorate the humdrum of workaday that rents can be higher. The developers dredged a second slough parallel to Mercer Slough, creating a 160-acre island. They set the buildings back from the sloughs and surrounded them with lawns and trees. Along the sloughs are paths with spots to fish, launch canoes, picnic, and watch ducks, coots, gulls, crows, banties, and weird hybrids.

Enter the Office Park either from 112 Avenue SE at SE 15 Street, or SE 8 Street. Park in any non-reserved space in any of the lots. Circle the island shore on cinder paths and lawns, eked out with connections across roads and lots. This is couth and kempt slough compared to that of the Nature Park but not bad, not bad at all. There also are paths in the strip along 112 Avenue.

Island loop 2 miles, allow 1½ hours
High point 50 feet, no elevation gain
Bus: Metro 226 to Bellevue Way, walk ¼ mile to island entrance

Kelsey Creek Park (Map-page 81)

That the agricultural past of the Bellevue area be not utterly forgotten, and that children may know animals other than dogs and cats, this former farm has been revived, complete with barns and pastures, cows, pigs, horses, burros, goats and sheep. Other attractions of the 80-acre park are the Fraser House, a cabin of squared-off logs built nearby in 1888 and moved here to be preserved, and an Oriental Garden to commemorate Bellevue's sister city, Yao, in Japan. There also are undeveloped natural areas, both valley marshes and hillside forests.

Leave Highway 405 on the Lake Hills Connector, turn north on SE 7 Place, then take 128 Place SE and finally SE 4 Place into the park. Some of these turns are signed only "Kelsey Creek Park."

The maximissimo walk is the Kelsey Figure-Eight: the Farm Loop plus the Hillside Loop. Start in the entrance parking lot and spend much time in the Oriental Garden. Then turn right to the path along the west edge of the lawns, with views to barns atop the central ridge. Bend left over West Fork Kelsey Creek to the Fraser House and cross the Barn parking lot to the trail along fenced-off preserves of cows and sheep and horses. Keep bending left, now upstream along East Fork Kelsey Creek, pastures on the left, wild wetlands on the right.

At about 1 mile from the start the Hillside Loop takes off from the Farm Loop.

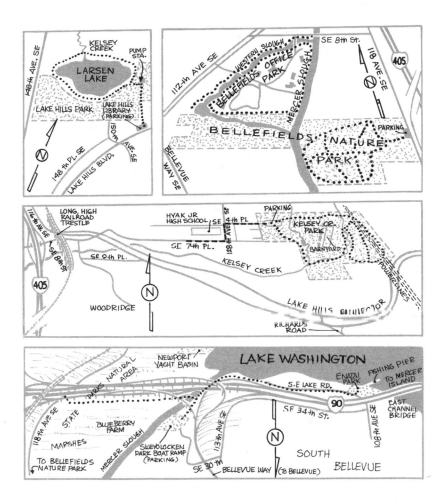

Turn right over East Fork into forest, to a T. For the recommended clockwise direction, take the left. On trail that invariably has solid boardwalks over ook and creeks and staircases up mucky slopes, ascend in a glory of mostly deciduous forest. The way turns right and sidehills; several sidetrails climb left a short way to the powerline and neighborhoods. After crossing several nice gullies from which Kelsey draws watery substance, the way drops back to the bottom and recrosses the tributaries to the T, closing the loop in about 1 long mile.

Finish the Farm Loop by climbing over the ridge of Douglas fir and dropping back to the north parking lot.

Kelsey Figure-Eight Loops 2½ miles, allow 2 hours
High point 160 feet, elevation gain 300 feet
All year

Larsen Lake (Map-page 81)

Want to search for the roots of old Bellevue, to insulate from freeways and shopping centers, to immerse in sheer bogginess? Where the blackbirds in nesting season are as tyrannical as motorcycles?

Drive Lake Hills Boulevard to halfway between 148 and 156 Avenues NE and park behind the Lake Hills Library, elevation 275 feet.

At the east end of the parking lot find a path into the grass and follow it ¼ mile north, backyards and barking dogs on the right, thickets of hardhack and willow on the left. Just before a pumphouse that sucks water from a drainage ditch so the neighbors won't drown, turn left into tall grass on a well-beaten path. In a few steps is a Y, the two ends of the lake loop.

If you choose the right fork in high summer, progress soon will be slowed by big, sweet, blueberries on bushes of an abandoned farm. Time also must be spent on sorties to the lakeshore to make the frogs splash, ducks paddle, fish swim, and to see the pond lilies, in bloom or pad. Do not disdain a "ditch" crossed on a plank—that is Kelsey Creek! Issuing from its headwaters. You must now cease eating the blueberries because from this point on a farmer wants to sell them. Pass a grove of fir and cedar that harbor different birds, then willow thickets preferred by still another crowd. In ½ mile return to the Y, and so home.

Loop trip 1½ miles, allow 1 hour
High point 275 feet, no elevation gain
All year
Bus: Metro 252

Robinswood Park (Map-page 83)

A calendar-pretty, Christmas-card-idealized farm, centered on a small lake in a pasture vale ringed by forest, a most pleasing scene as viewed from a grassy slope, the neater for not being messed by animals. The Bellevue park retains and uses the farm buildings; for examples, the Main House is a community-center meeting place, the barn is a teen center.

Drive 148 Avenue SE to the park entrance at SE 24 Street.

For an introductory loop that saves the centerpiece lake for last, walk south from the parking lot on a path near 148th. Enter a fir forest and hit an old, narrow blacktop road now closed to cars. Turn left (east) on it to houses at the park's east boundary.

From this junction find a path left into park forest. Emerge from firs on the greensward beside the air-supported tennis domes above the lake. Admire the prospect from this eminence, then descend the meadow to weeping willows and cattails and circle the shore. A couple times. Complete the loop up to the parking lot.

Loop trip 1½ miles, allow 1 hour
High point 425 feet, elevation gain 200 feet
All year
Bus: Metro 252

Weowna Park (Map-page 84)

A 1-mile-long, ¼-mile-wide strip of virgin forest here, of all places, in Bellevue? Yes! Astounding. A hiker accustomed to second-growth of the

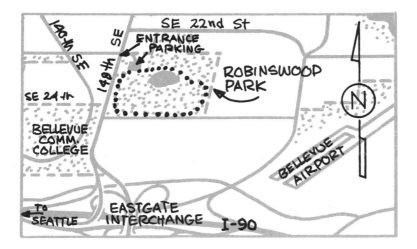

vicinity cannot but be staggered by the Douglas firs, up to 6 feet in diameter, and the equally fine cedars and hemlocks, and that special quality of dark green lushness that aside from tree size characterizes old-growth.

Douglas fir in Weowna Park

83

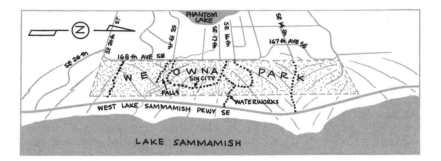

And the ravines! The creeks! Located on the brink of the Lake Hills Highland and the steep slope to Lake Sammamish, the park is deeply incised by streams. The outstanding one is Phantom Creek, the outlet of Phantom Lake just ¼ mile away. The creek enters the park in a 5-foot-deep trench hand-dug in glacial till decades ago to lower the lake and make more pasture. Shortly the creek plunges over a till cliff in a superb waterfall, flows in an impressive canyon, then waterfalls over another cliff, this of blue glacial clay.

That the virgin forest has been preserved seems due to the difficulty of logging the precipice in early days, then perhaps the nostalgia for deep woods felt by the owner, a logger himself, and then a subdivision scheme (don't try to figure out an Indian source for the name—it's "We own a park"—catch?), and finally a Forward Thrust purchase. There is no development, not even a sign announcing the park name, just signs saying "No Dumping. Cut No Trees. King County Parks." Things never will change much; plans are to keep it a wilderness park, little done except to systematize the trails.

The trails are accessible from the bottom, West Lake Sammamish Parkway SE, elevation 100 feet, but parking is a problem—the west shoulder is bikeway-walkway and the east shoulder is very skinny. Bottom accesses will be noted but the wise plan is to hike from the top.

Drive to 168 Avenue SE, which runs most of the park length on the upper side. Park carefully on shoulders to not block traffic. Elevation, 275 feet.

Local folks have beaten out many paths over the years but not with any system. For a full survey one must either fight brush to hook up trails or return frequently to 168th. The most important paths are here described in sequence from the south.

North 350 feet from the paper-deliverers' shelter where 168th curves down to the park an obvious trail enters the woods and descends easily and pleasantly. Note evergreen huckleberry, unusual hereabouts, and a fruity reason for visiting Weowna in fall. At a T go left and continue down to Sammamish Parkway; the trail widens to a blacktop stub and is chained; a highway sign just here says "Speed Zone Ahead."

The park's chief spectacularity is Phantom Creek, its pretty falls located among some of the largest of the Douglas firs. By SE 19th spot a pair of white concrete posts marking the culvert and take the path on the right (south) side. Hang onto the children! The way skirts the perilous brinks of "Till Falls," frothing to a cirque-like basin, and then "Clay Grotto Falls," where the creek goes underground and plunges into a clay-walled cave. Sidepaths permit safe explorations of the bottoms of both falls. The main trail ends but a root ladder drops into the gorge jungle; a doughty soul could slither on down to Sammamish Parkway and likely find secret nooks that would excite Tarzan, and even Boy.

North of SE 17th at a "Bus 225" sign a good path, not obvious at the start, winds across a splendid flat of mixed forest to a Y. The right fork sidehills through Sinners' City (not a Boy Scout camp, according to evidence of beer bottles and pinup girls scattered around shacks and treehouses) and connects to the falls area of Phantom Creek. The left fork samples superb groves of big alders and maples, big firs, big madronas, and eventually comes out on 168th at SE 16th, obscured by neighborhood lawn-clippings and hedge-trimmings. Loveliest of all, the Trillium Trail takes off—very obscurely—from this fork and descends a luscious big-tree ravine, passes a fenced watershed and covered reservoir, an old waterworks, and hits Sammamish Parkway 500 feet south of the gated road noted below.

For the final path, turn right from 168th onto SE 14th, right onto 167th, and right on SE 12th to the deadend. Skid down to a trail-road in the gully and descend by a series of concrete retaining dams and stormwater drains to Sammamish Parkway, where the trail-road is prominently gated. The feature of this walk is a 7-foot Douglas fir snag.

Total of all round trips about 4 miles, allow 3 hours
High point 275 feet, elevation gain 800 feet
All year
Bus: Metro 252 to SE 16th and 148th, walk 1 mile to park

Bridle Trails State Park (Map-page 86)

Smackdab in the midst of suburbia-urbia are 481.5 acres of second-growth Douglas fir and some big old-growth specimens too firescarred to interest the loggers, plus hemlock and cedar and the usual array of understory and groundcover. And honeycombing the forest are 28 miles of trails—28 miles! As the ranger warns newcomers, "You can get lost in there." But not dangerously. Just long enough for the fun of escaping the maze.

In south Kirkland or north Bellevue exit from Highway 405 onto the close-by and paralleling 116 Avenue NE. Between NE 40 and NE 60 Streets turn into the main park entrance and parking lot, elevation 400 feet.

Hikers should keep in mind that on all trails where horses are permitted, not just in this park, the animals have the right of way. The hiker should step off the path, act nonchalant, talk to the beast so it'll recognize the stranger as a human, and avoid sudden motions. Because of the park name, one may suppose hikers are not welcome and/or might be trampled by the cavalry. Neither is true. Despite the popularity with horsefolk the park is too large to get crowded; on an ordinary day a hiker won't meet many horses, particularly if he stays off the main trails that in winter are anyway churned to muck. Moreover, improvements of the early 1980s drained and turnpiked mudholes, easing the way for both hooves and feet.

To describe the complete 28 miles would require many pages—and be superfluous. There is little in the way of views out and the plateau has minor topographical variety; one place is much like another, one trail like another—wild and great. Getting confused is a distinct possibility but to stay lost long

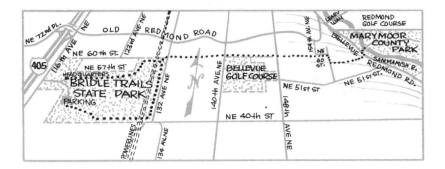

would require dedication; listening for the roar of Highway 405 gives a western baseline; the powerline swath down the center of the park provides north-south orientation. But since there are no signs at junctions, and myriad feeder trails enter from horse ranches, riding academies, and stables all around, even describing a basic introduction could get out of hand. One can only try.

For an introductory perimeter loop, start on the prominent wide trail taking off to the left from near the parking area entrance. At major trails take right turns, avoiding minor paths, and shortly reach the south boundary. Proceed easterly (shunning paths that enter the park), cross the powerline, reenter woods, and reach the east boundary, 132 Avenue NE. Turn left to the north boundary, NE 60, and turn left, west, jogging left to pass a large indentation of ranches. Return by the headquarter corrals to the parking lot.

That's the basic introduction — but not the best hike. To escape the churned major trails, to lose the sights and nearly the sounds of civilization, leave the perimeter, dive into the interior on the smaller paths. Get lost.

Perimeter loop 4 miles, allow 2½ hours
High point 566 feet, minor elevation gain
All year
Bus: Metro 251 to NE 70 and 116th, walk ¾ mile to park

Kirkland: Juanita Bay, Moss Bay, Yarrow Bay (Map-page 88)

Many an American city started with little of God's bounty and quickly gave it all away; the traveler stepping from his motel in morning may have to consult a calendar to see if he's in Iowa or California or Oregon. Consider Bellevue, which might have become the City Between the Lakes — except that when Beaux Arts, Medina, Hunts Point, and Yarrow Point seceded to escape the subdividers they took Lake Washington with them — and fenced it off. In Bellevue, if you want to see the lake, you have to go to Seattle.

Or Kirkland. Through historical circumstance (luck) and civic vision, this is the Lake City, reminding of the English Bay section of Vancouver, the natural and the human combined. A place worth living. And worth walking, too. The city hopes ultimately to provide a formal shore (or near) trail the entire length of the route described here. But don't wait. Your feet are votes in support of the plan.

To do the entire walk starting from the north, leave the car or get off the bus at Juanita Beach (King County) Park, located on NE Juanita Drive, elevation 20 feet.

Begin in the park, walking the ¼-mile promenade that encloses the swimming beach. Views past Juanita and Nelson Points across the lake to Sand Point and the tip of the Space Needle, down the lake to Hunts Point and the Evergreen Point Bridge. Beware of the ducks and geese and crows— they'll grab your lunch.

Leave the park and walk Juanita Drive a short bit to the next delight, a ½-mile stretch of abandoned highway now dedicated to bicycles and feet. On the shore side is a marsh-swamp tangle of cattails and bulrushes, willow and hardhack; birds nest undisturbed, muskrats ramble, and salmon spawn in Forbes Creek. On the lake side a line of old dock pilings topped with little gardens points out through acres of lily pads, gorgeous in season with large white flowers.

Near the south end of the abandoned highway (what a happy sight, green grass growing from cracks in sterile concrete!) a dirt lane winds through sprawling fields and groves of weeping willow in abandoned Juanita Golf Course. The city wants a park here but the issue remains in doubt.

Round trip 3 miles, allow 2 hours
High point 50 feet, minor elevation gain
All year
Bus: Metro 241

So few automobiles disturb the quiet residential streets one may walk down the middle without attracting attention, except from the dogs, who make sure you stay in the middle. Two small shore parks and a wide-view boulevard reward the stroller.

From the southwest edge of the golf course climb a path to public streets. Walk 10 Street W; at a Y, follow it left, uphill, then right. When it bends left find a path down the bluff to Kiwanis Park, with huge cottonwoods on a smidgeon of wild shore. Return to the street, go left on 8th, right on 16th, right on 7th, left on 14th, right on 6th, and finally right on Waverly Way, reached at its northern deadend. Descend through forest to the beach of Waverly ("Skinnydipper") Park and walk out on the fishing pier for views south to Moss Bay. Return to Waverly and proceed south. The bluff side is free of houses, opening long views north past Champaign Point and across to Sand Point and the tips of Seattle towers. At Market Street turn right, downhill, to the shore. (Kirkland plans a new Waverly Way Strip Park along the bluff to connect Waverly and Marina Parks.)

Round trip 4 miles, allow 2½ hours
High point 175 feet, elevation gain 400 feet
Bus: Metro 241

So much for the wild bit and the neighborhood bit. Now comes the downtown bit, the shops and the boats, the condos and the restaurants—a downtown that is not graveyard-empty at night because people live there.

Market Street used to run out onto a ferry dock; until the end of War II a

person could walk on the boat, debark 4 miles later at Madison Park, and catch the bus to downtown Seattle—gracious living of a style that can live again if we all keep the faith. Marina Park preserves the memory. Benches permit relaxed watching of sailors and scullers. The dock of a public moorage lets a person examine boats close-up.

Return via Kirkland Avenue to Lake Street South and walk past shops and bistros to the Port of Moss Bay Marina, present home of Northwest Seaport. Admire the ships being preserved and restored by the Seaport (contributions deductible): the **Relief,** Lightship No. 83, dating from 1904; the **Arthur Foss,** a handsome big tugboat from 1889.

The sidewalk southward wouldn't be worth walking had not pains been taken. But they were and it is. Three small beach parks (nameless, Marsh, and Houghton Beach) provide openings in the line of medium-rise apartment houses; several of these provide public walkways that are in effect additional parklets.

Beyond the last park is the site of the Lake Washington Shipyard, which built ferries, War I wooden freighters, postwar steel freighters, and in War II, destroyer escorts and seaplane tenders. Now wasteland, the area is in process of development; the city hopes to obtain a trail corridor.

Neighboring to the south is a large green lawn which a billboard calls "Home of the Seahawks," whatever they are. Conclude with a sidetrip down to Yarrow Bay Marina to check the pricetags.

Round trip 4 miles, allow 2½ hours
Minor elevation gain
Bus: Metro 235, 251, 254

Complete round trip 11 miles, allow 7 hours
(Ride the bus one way and cut the walking in half)

O.O. Denny Park-Big Finn Hill Park (Map-page 90)

Stroll a sandy beach in views across Lake Washington. Leave the sun for cool shadows of Big Finn Canyon. And suddenly yelp in surprise, ambushed by a genuine, flabbergasting, holy-cow and oh-my-golly of a Douglas fir claimed to be the largest in (urban?) King County.

From Juanita Drive NE turn off on Holmes Point Drive to O.O. Denny (Seattle City) Park, located on Holmes Point, elevation 20 feet.

The park is well-known for its ¼ mile of beach, Cougar Mountain rising on the horizon to the south and Sand Point jutting from the west. Fewer folks are familiar with the two trail systems, one on either side of Big Finn Creek.

Find the start of one just south of the culvert under the highway. A broad path ascends beside the gorge through impressive forest of cedar and fir and hemlock, yew and hazelnut and huckleberry, coolwort and fairy bells. Skidpaths plummet to the creek jungle. The path ends at a gravel road, 175 feet, that drops to the creek and someday may be an access to Big Finn Hill (King County) Park.

The gorge section of Big Finn Park presently has no trails worth recommending, just 80 acres of creek and wildwood walls, a critter preserve. Getting the land set aside from the usual process of maximizing the tax base took local activists 10 years of crusading. Ultimately 1-mile trails might be built along both sides of the gorge, if the critters don't mount a crusade against it. (Also, 120 acres on the plateau east of Juanita Drive may be added; this woodland already has meandering paths beaten out by local feet.)

The major trail system of the gorge area begins at a sign, "No Motor Vehicles," at the overflow parking lot northeast of the creek. The path soon forks, and each fork forks again, and each eventually ends in somebody's back yard. However, along the way...

At the first split, a short bit from the parking lot, the left ascends a tributary ravine in mixed forest of big old conifers and hardwoods, splendid but not

"King County's largest" Douglas fir in O.O. Denny Park

unusual. Then the eye is caught by large Douglas firs—and larger—the bark blackened by charcoal. The walker suddenly sees the history of the park area: burned a century-odd ago by a forest fire that killed all but the thick-barked old-growth firs; the second-growth attaining size rivalling the old-growth; the Denny family acquiring the property as a summer retreat, then giving it to the city of Seattle. The path repeatedly divides, each piece worth wandering up ravine walls through spacious green chambers of the forest. One climbs to the top of a 300-foot ridge, where a final split leads (left) to a skywide vista over the gorge and (right) to a madrona grove where kids long have camped out. These endpoints are about ¾ mile from the parking lot.

Now, back to that first split: Take the right fork up the main valley, near the creek, through plants lushly growing from black ook. A sidepath climbs left; follow it a few yards and gasp and wow-ee—these are the biggest old firs yet, and the young cedars aren't much smaller. Return from the sidetrip, take a few more steps. For maximum effect keep your eyes on the ground. There, spot the plaque:

"King County's Largest Douglas Fir
Height 255 feet
Circumference 26.3 feet
Bark thickness 12 inches
Age 575 years
Shatanka Campfire Girls, Kirkland, 1978"

Now lift your eyes.

The trail continues, dwindling, a bit farther, and at a long ⅓ mile from the parking lot peters out at a derelict house. Don't bother. End the trip at the Big Tree, on your knees.

Round trip all trails 4 miles, allow 3 hours
High point 300 feet, elevation gain all trails 1000 feet
All year
Bus: Metro 240 to NE 122 Place and Juanita Drive NE, walk 1 long mile to
O.O. Denny Park

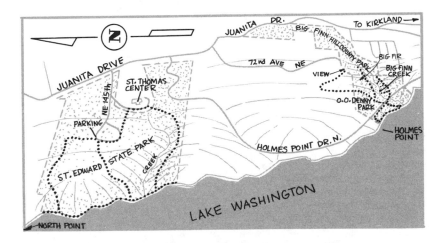

St. Edward State Park (Map-page 90)

Thanks to a property owner (the Archdiocese of Seattle) with soul, and a partnership of alert state and federal legislators and officials, in 1977 the people obtained—half a century after any realist would have said the last chances were gone—a large wildland park on the shore of Lake Washington. Unlike Sand Point Park obtained the same year, this is ready to go as is, no remodeling necessary, the forests already installed. Development will be concentrated on the plateau bench, in and around the former seminary buildings; most of the 316 acres—all the steep bluff and the several superb ravines and the 3000 feet of waterfront—will remain green and quiet.

Drive Juanita Drive NE north from Kirkland or south from Kenmore to the park entrance at NE 145th. Turn west, avoiding the road left to St. Thomas Center, following signs to the parking area behind the main St. Edward building, elevation 350 feet.

Where to walk? Where seminary students did for years and the deer and coyote still do, beating out a trail system of a dozen-odd miles. For openers, to sample just about all the good things, do a figure-8 loop. (Ultimately there may be a perimeter trail of 3-4 miles plus a network of interior connectors.)

At the front of the seminary building take the Beach Trail ⅔ mile, losing 338 feet, to the lake. Always at an easy grade, this onetime woods road winds down the bluff, in and out of valleys, through a forest of maple, alder, dogwood, hazelnut, and cedar but especially notable for the combination of two dominant species, Douglas fir and madrona. Views into shadowed vales give the feeling

Trail in St. Edward State Park

Footbridge across Issaquah Creek, Lake Sammamish State Park

of touring the great halls of a forest mansion. Sidetrails invite left and right; mentally note them for later.

At the lakeshore picnic lawn watch mallard hens lead flotillas of ducklings, gaze over log rafts to boats on the water, look up the lake to Kenmore, down to Sand Point.

For the first loop of the figure 8, follow the shore trail down the waterside terrace (underwater until the lake was lowered), through alders and cottonwoods leaning far out from the bank, ¼ mile to the south boundary. Now, having satisfied your curiosity about **that,** retreat all the way back to the trickle-creek just south of the picnic lawn, and just south of this ooze take the prominent path up the bluff. The way ascends slopes of a ravine and tops out on the narrow crest of a ridge crowned with a cathedral of a fir forest. At ⅔ mile from the shore the way leaves trees for grass at the St. Thomas water tower; follow roads and lawns north ½ mile to the start.

For the second loop, again descend the Beach Trail—or one of those mentally-noted sidepaths. Turn north on the shore through a succession of monster cottonwoods, two with caves that invite kids to crawl in. In ½ mile the park ends. Retreat a few hundred steps to the only major up-trail. (There are several lesser up-paths.) The way climbs steeply through glorious fir forest, then sidehills a jungle gorge where devils club grows tall as trees. At a Y the left fork drops to the creek and climbs to suburbia; take the right a final bit up to the plateau and at ⅔ mile from the lake return to the parking lot.

Figure-8 loop trip 4½ miles, allow 3 hours
High point 350 feet, elevation gain 700 feet
All year
Bus: Metro 240 to NE 153rd, walk to entrance

Lake Sammamish State Park (Map-page 93)

Not for a hot summer Sunday, when this is the most Coney Island-crowded of state parks, but for any quieter day, and a particular joy in lonesome winter, is the shoreline walk starting on lawns crowded with ducks and coots, proceeding into marsh. Frequently sailplanes are soaring, parachutists floating from the adjoining Issaquah Sky Sports Center, located in historic Pickering Farm. All along are views up the lake and to the Issaquah Alps — Grand, Cougar, Squak, and Tiger — dramatically huge above the Great Green Plain. The topper is an unsuspected trail in a wildwood gorge to a secret waterfall.

Leave I-90 on Exit 15, drive a short bit north to SE 56 Street, and turn left to the park entrance. To maximize the walk, park at the first opportunity. Elevation, 25 feet.

Cross lawns through groves of cottonwood and weeping willow to the lake and follow the sandy shore east to the mouth of Issaquah Creek. Turn right

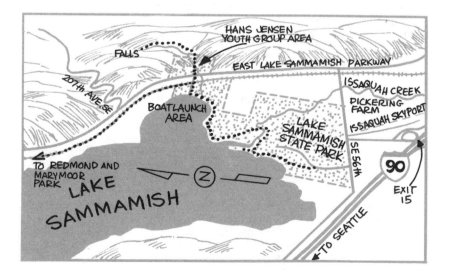

upstream to the handsome footbridge and return downstream nearly to the mouth. Manicured park yields to reeds and tall grass and willow tangles and masses of lilypads, and to soggy footing of a meager mucky path that may require getting the ankles wet. The cause is worthy. Soon the path improves and pavement is reached at the boat-launch area, some 1¾ miles by this devious route from the start. For a 3½-mile round trip, turn back.

For the second main feature, go on. Cross railroad tracks and East Lake Sammamish Parkway, jog right, and enter the least-known section of the park, the Hans Jensen Youth Group Area. Proceed through the campground field up the valley of Laughing Jacob's Creek to the edge of the woods. There, in a cool-shadowed cedar grove by babbling water, the trail splits.

For one tour, cross the little bridge and ascend a steep ¼ mile up the gorge wall on a rude path. On the rim are big firs and views some 200 vertical feet down to the fine frenzy of greenery along the creek.

For the other, don't cross the bridge, continue on the trail up the gorge into a pocket wilderness. In about ⅓ mile, ¾ mile from the highway, gentlefolk may wish to conclude the tour. Walkers willing to brave the tangle can continue some ¼ mile and be bewitched. There it is, the water splashing down moss-black sandstone slabs in a jackstraw of moss-green logs, Laughing Jacob's Falls.

Complete-tour round trip 6 miles, allow 4 hours
High point 350 feet, elevation gain 400 feet
All year
Bus: Metro 210 to Exit 15 (Highway 900), walk ½ mile to park

Marymoor Park (Map-page 95)

Largest of King County Parks, Marymoor occupies 485 acres of the flats at the north end of Lake Sammamish and along its outlet, the Sammamish River. In this spacious plain are soccer and baseball fields, children's play area, archery butts, model airplane airport, tennis courts, bicycle track, picnic tables, Pea Patch. In an open-air shelter is an exhibit of the archeological dig that established the fact of human residence on this spot 7000 years ago. An historical museum occupies the 28-room Clise (Marymoor) Mansion, headquarters of what began in 1904 as the Clise family hunting preserve, called Willowmoor, then was a dairy farm until purchased for a park in 1963. And there are lines of majestic poplars up to 4 feet in diameter, and groves of Douglas fir. A Dutch-like windmill. A river. A lake.

Just south of the center of Redmond, cross the bridge from West Lake Sammamish Parkway over the river to the park, elevation 36 feet.

What's to be done in the way of walking? By no means disdain simply striking off in the grass and roaming the fields. This book spends most of its time in forests. It's bracing to wander wide-open spaces under the big sky of pastures and lake.

The basic walk, of course, is downstream along the machine-free riverbank, first in fields and by the Pea Patch, then in willow thickets, finally in people-free marshes, a great big critter refuge. Mingle with ducks and coots, blackbirds and hawks. In pre-park days the walk would have ended in the frustration of impassable marshes; now, a wooden walkway leads through muck and reeds

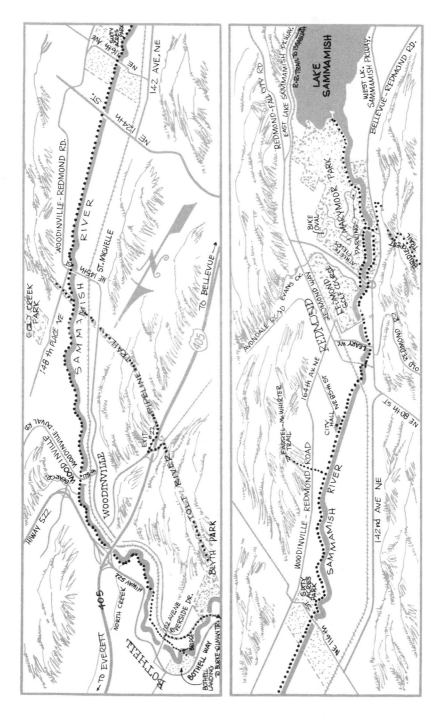

to a concrete viewing pier at the meeting of marsh and open lake, by the beginning of the Sammamish River, with views down the 9-mile-long lake to Tiger Mountain rising a tall 3000 feet above the south end.

Described separately, but best done as a walk from Marymoor Park, is the Bridlecrest Trail (which see).

Round trip to lake 2 miles, allow 1½ hours
High point 35 feet, no elevation gain
All year
Bus: Metro 251, 253, and 254 to West Lake Sammamish Parkway, walk ½ mile to park

Bridlecrest Trail (Map-page 95)

A gorgeous forest seemingly virgin, of huge firs, including a snagtop some 7 feet in diameter, and big hemlocks and maples. That's the best part of a trail that connects Marymoor Park to Bridle Trails State Park. Most of the route is rather undistinguished and primarily of interest to horseriders and local walkers, but no hiker visiting Marymoor should miss the first stretch.

From Marymoor Park (which see) walk out the entrance road. Cross the river bridge, walk the riverbank trail south, cross Lake Sammamish Parkway to a "Bridlecrest" sign and enter the forest.

Ascend the steep hill in the marvelous trees. Down in the mossy bottom of the creek to the right, spot an ancient bridge, an old concrete water tank, nurselogs. The trail climbs above the splendid ravine to a ridge between two gullies, through a fine alder-maple jungle, to lawns of a Redmond city park at 156 Avenue NE. This is as far as most hikers will care to go. But the way west has attractions, particularly to a fan of horses, an admirer of horse ranches. There also are cows and views to the Cascades.

From the neighborhood park the trail jogs north a block, then turns west on the line of NE 60 Street, which except for a couple blocks at the start is not cut through, so the trail is a lane between fences, removed from vehicles except for crossings of 148th and 140th Avenues. Passing pastures, a posh apartment complex, greensward of a golf course, at 132nd Avenue the trail reaches the northeast corner of Bridle Trails State Park.

Round trip 4 miles, allow 2½ hours
High point 500 feet, elevation gain 450 feet
All year
Bus: Metro 251 to NE 70 and 116th, walk ¾ mile to Bridle Trails Park, thence to the trail; Metro 251, 253, and 254 to West Lake Sammamish Parkway, walk ¾ mile to trail

Sammamish River Trail (Map-page 95)

Pastures and cornfields and "instant lawn" farms sprawling table-flat east and west to forested valley walls. The murky river floating ducks and coots for 15 meandering miles. Tweety birds flitting in reeds, clouds of gulls circling, hawks on patrol above. The path along the bank, far out in the quiet plain, distant from noisy roads. To a hiker accustomed to skulking in dank woods, an airy, wide-sky, liberated trail sure to have sun if there's any to be had.

Sammamish River Trail

On first survey in 1977, before the trail formally existed, the solitary walker met only bored cows and friendly horses. On a fine Saturday in the summer of 1981 the entire 9.4 miles between the Park at Bothell Landing and Marymoor Park were one big smile: bicyclists by the family (bike rentals in Bothell and Redmond), rollerskaters by the platoon (rentals on fine weekends at the Leary Way crossing in Redmond), horses (with riders), runners, joggers, walkers, not to forget paddlers in canoes and rubber rafts. There were tiny children carried on mothers' backs, in kiddyseats on bikes, in strollers being pushed by fathers on rollerskates. There were seniors enjoying the scenery from a flat, paved, no-problem path. Where were all these folks before the trail was created through the efforts of Save the Sammamish Valley Trail Association, King County Parks, Forward Thrust, and IAC? Wherever, they weren't having this much fun. Anybody who supposes motorized recreation is the future, quiet travel is the past, should spend a day here—and then get active promoting more urban-area trails.

The walk can begin at either end or any number of convenient spots along the way. To emphasize the connection to the Burke-Gilman Trail, the following description is from the north end.

The Park at Bothell Landing, elevation 20 feet, lies just off Bothell Way. At 0.2 mile from its graceful wooden bridge over the Sammamish River is 102 Avenue NE, where paved trail begins, fields and woods on the right, river on the left. At 0.7 mile the trail crosses the river to another popular parking-starting place just off Highway 522. For a short bit the way is a sidewalk along the old

Beginning of the Sammamish River Trail at Bothell Landing

Bothell-Woodinville Road, which now deadends at the river. A bridge over North Creek leads to a forest of concrete pillars whose foliage is concrete ramps—the interchanges of Highways 405 and 522 and whatnot.

At 2.2 miles, crossing Bear Creek on a bridge and then going under NE 175 Street in Woodinville (parking), the scene changes. To this point there have been river and greenery but also trailer courts, apartment houses, assorted urbia, and concrete—pleasant walking but "busy." Now begins ruralia as the broad trail and companion river strike out into the center of the peaceful plain. At 3.8 miles is the junction with the Tolt Pipeline Trail (which see), and at 4.2 miles the underpass crossing of NE 145 Street (parking, and a sidetrip to Ste. Michelle Winery, ¼ mile away, to buy cheese and crackers and refreshments for lunch). Shortly beyond the underpass crossing of NE 124 Street (parking), at 6.7 miles is NE 116 Street and the county's Sixty Acres Park, mainly soccer fields. At 7½ miles is the junction with the Farrel-McWhirter Trail (which see).

At 8.1 miles the scene again changes at Redmond City Hall, located beside the river at the deadend of NE 85 Street (parking). Leaving farms, the trail follows the river through city greenery, passing under the Redmond-Issaquah Railroad Trail (which see) and lofty masses of concrete, and at 8.8 miles crossing Leary Way (parking) next to downtown (if any) Redmond. Across the river lies the picturesque golf course, then the mouth of Evans Creek. And voila, Marymoor Park (which see), the entrance reached at 9.4 miles, every step a smile.

One way from Bothell Landing to Marymoor Park 9.4 miles
Allow minutes or all day
High point 35 feet, minor elevation gain
All year
Bus: Metro 307 to Bothell; 251, 253, and 254 to Redmond

Farrel-McWhirter Park and Trail (Map-page 99)

In 1971, when Elise Farrel-McWhirter bequeathed Redmond the 68 acres of pasture and forest that had been her summer retreat since 1938, she gave the city what became in 1980 "the jewel of its park system." Candidly, it's much too tiny a system (barely 200 acres total!): during the years of emergence from country hamlet the civic energies were focused more on shopping centers than parks; for large expanses of close-to-home green and quiet the citizens must look to the Issaquah Alps. However, the 2 miles of in-park trails and the 3-mile trail to the Sammamish River provide excellent entertainment for horses and have some interest for walkers.

The recommended itinerary is to start at (near, that is) the Sammamish, saving the park for the luncheon climax. Drive Woodinville-Redmond Road 1½ miles north of NE Redmond Way (via 164th), 1½ miles south of NE 124 Street (via 140 Place NE) to the pushbutton traffic signal signed "Trail Crossing." Park on the shoulder, elevation 175 feet.

The "Puget Power City of Redmond Trail" descends the powerline swath west ¼ mile to the Sammamish River Trail at 25 feet. The park, however, lies east. Ascend alder forest to the powerline swath and plateau top, 275 feet, with a view back over the Sammamish valley. In the first 1 mile the swath zigs left, zags right, crosses two streets (bus stop at NE 110) and a private drive—very suburban. The next 1¼ miles to Avondale Road have long woodland vistas and a country feel. Houses are few, cows many, fields and woods line the way. Twice, to dodge a swamp bottom and a farm fence, the trail swings from powerline through woodland cool. Two well-beaten sidetrails lead right into nicer and wilder forest than anything on the main route. The swath drops from a high point of 300 feet to 82 feet at "Trail Crossing" (and bus stop) of Avondale Road. The final ½ mile to the park boundary crosses the fish avenue of Bear Creek and winds through birdy woods of willow, alder, ocean spray, and honeysuckle.

A perimeter (approximately) trail covers park highlights in a 1½-mile loop. From the Equestrian Show Ring veer left to the powerline and climb to the 175-foot top of Novelty Hill. Turn right along 196 Avenue NE to the park's horse-trailer entrance. Continue through middling Douglas fir shading a floor of

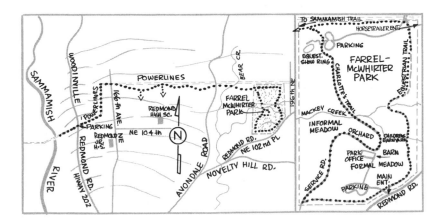

bracken and coolwort, dip to Mackey Creek, climb to the park's main entrance on Redmond Road, and proceed to a service road—the old farm road. Turn right beside picnic grounds of the Formal Meadow to the Orchard, the Red Barn (display of old farm implements) and Children's Barnyard (animals to pet), and Grain Silo (restrooms and observation deck). Skirt the Informal Meadow, recross Mackey Creek, and return to the Show Ring.

To drive to the park, take Avondale Road northeast from Redmond 1½ miles, turn right ½ mile on Novelty Hill Road, and turn left ½ mile on Redmond Road.

Round trip 7 miles, allow 4 hours
High point 300 feet, elevation gain 500 feet
All year
Bus: Metro 251 to trail crossing of Avondale Road; 254 to trail crossing of
NE 110

East Sammamish Plateau Trail (Map-page 101)

Between the valleys of Sammamish Lake and River and the Snoqualmie River is a great, sprawling up-and-downland, plateauland. Logged early in the century and homesteaded before that, later pioneered for stumpranches, dairy farms, horse ranches, and hideaway homes, it now is on the frontier of Urbia. If all the developers with all their plans had everything all their own way, there never would be enough people to fill up the planned houses without importing the total populations of several foreign nations. The area is a battleground of developers, each seeking governmental approval of its New City. But there is another voice, not of anti-development but of cool development—growth that retains the quality of Plateau life, space for cows to munch, trees to grow, horses to gallop and feet to plod. If a developer were to pave over Lake Washington the boaters would rise in revolt, claiming historic rights; Plateau folk who came here for the trails similarly resist being overwhelmed by Instant New Cities.

The Plateau is of more than local significance, it's a **regional** resource. Even more important than the vast woodlands interlaced with old logging-railroad grades ideal for riding horses, and more so than the views of downtown Seattle and the Olympics, the Issaquah Alps and Rainier, and the skyful of rushing clouds, are the **wetlands**: Lakes, some edged by houses, some wild. Creeks up which salmon struggle from the distant ocean. Marshes where blackbirds nest, frogs sing. Swamps. Bogs (including cranberry bogs). Bottoms drained for pasture—but with reedy potholes left for the ducks. This was what the land once was like all the way from Everett to Tacoma, but Puget Sound City put most of the water in ditches and underground pipes. The Plateau offers the region's last chance to preserve a generous near-City sample of the pristine post-glacial landscape—or waterscape.

The central axis sought by King County and environmentalists is a regional trail that would extend 18 miles from the Issaquah-Snoqualmie Falls Trail to the Tolt Pipeline Trail, both of which are routes of the Sound-To-Mountains Trail. The Plateau Trail would connect them. (A horse party already has ridden from Yellow Lake to Ellensburg!) It also would connect the many sidetrails into new communities under construction.

The approximate general route of the proposed trail is the wide swath of the

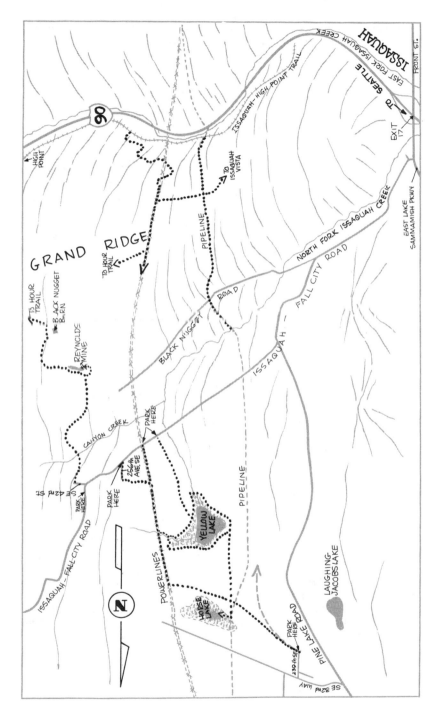

OVERLAKE: MERCER ISLAND TO EAST SAMMAMISH PLATEAU

Northwest Natural Gas Pipeline. Fences and other problems currently block the swath at this point and that. Following are sections easily open as of late 1981.

East Fork Issaquah Creek-Grand Ridge-North Fork Issaquah Creek

From the Issaquah-High Point Trail (which see) at 1½ miles west of High Point, ¾ mile east of the site of the old railroad trestle, turn steeply up the gas line swath, climbing from 325 feet to the gentling out of Grand Ridge at 500 feet. Gaze south to the Tradition Plateau, Tiger and Squak.

In ⅓ mile intersect the telephone cable (buried): the woods road left leads to Issaquah Vista; the right connects in a scant ½ mile to the Bonneville powerline swath, which runs south to the Issaquah-High Point Trail and north to SE Black Nugget Road—on the way passing a sidetrail to the Hour Trail (which see).

From the high point of 550 feet the gas line slopes gently, then plummets to the valley of North Fork Issaquah Creek, crossing the Black Nugget Road at 375 feet. (To drive to this point, go ¾ mile from Issaquah-Fall City Road.)

For the best part of this whole section, cross the road, climb a 100-foot ridge, and drop to the broad bottom of the North Fork. The gas line has dammed the vigorous creek of "mountain tea" into a dark-watered pond-marsh-swamp, a place of cattails and pond lilies, fish and frogs and blackbirds.

Round trip from Issaquah-High Point Trail 3 miles, allow 2 hours
High point 550 feet, elevation gain 400 feet

Yellow Lake-Reynolds Mine-Hour Trail

On Issaquah-Fall City Road spot SE 42 Street, a narrow gravel lane going off east; park just beyond on the wide shoulder, elevation 475 feet.

The neighborhood is friendly to horses and hikers, though not to motorcycles; relying on "tolerated trespassing," walk SE 42 past private drives. The way drops to the bottom of Canyon Creek, 350 feet, and an excellent large swamp-bog. On the far side the graveled road turns right into a pasture, ½ mile from the county road. Continue ahead, past a deadend spur left. Cross a creek to big cedars and start uphill in a magic forest of cedar groves, vine maple, bigleaf maple with licorice fern growing a hundred feet toward the sky, silvery-barked alder, fir, hemlock—and stumps with ladderways of three vertical steps notched for springboards. The way goes up and down in fine ravines and bogs, ¾ mile from the pasture to a T with a woods road.

Step right a couple feet on this road (which leads to the Black Nugget Road) and go left on a path that drops to a creek in a weird, unnatural-looking ravine—a trench dug to surface-mine coal—the Reynolds Mine, dating from a half-century ago. Turn left up the trench. Poke about in sandstone rubble for fossils. Come to another trench full of bilious water, shown on the map as a lake. See methane bubbles break the surface—on a calm day, do not light a match! To the left find a waterfall splashing down a cliff to a clear pool. A few feet beyond is the exposed seam of coal, black nuggets interlayered with brown peaty sub-sub-bituminous. Elevation, 500 feet.

Back at the woods road, walk left, past the clearing of a homestead-cabin, to a cottonwood bottom. The path turns uphill and at a long ½ mile from the mine junction nears the Black Nugget Barn. Turn left, uphill, beside a barbed-wire fence, then diverge left. In a few feet meet a downhill path signed "Trail." You now are at about 800 feet on the Hour Trail (which see) and can continue blithely on over Grand Ridge.

Round trip to Hour Trail 4 miles, allow 3 hours
High point 800 feet, elevation gain 800 feet

Yellow Lake-Horse Lake-North Fork Issaquah Creek

Chances seem good that King County, local environmentalists, and the owner proposing massive development of the 883-acre "Hestnes Property" will reach an agreement that will preserve one of the Plateau's richest wetland ecosystems, a place of cougar, bear, coyote, otter, muskrat, mountain beaver, and deer, and of eagle, osprey, red-tailed hawk, great blue heron, snow geese, Canada geese, and many species of duck, of sphagnum moss and Labrador tea, aspen and birch, and miles and miles of trails through second-growth wildland, so many miles the surveyor spent hours and hours happily semi-lost. Accesses from surrounding neighborhoods are as numerous as the trails. Following are several that are easy to find. Note: The trail system will differ after development, but the pledge has been made to keep both lakes and the North Fork "as natural as possible."

From East Lake Sammamish Parkway north of I-90's Exit 17, drive 1000 qual-Fall City Road (Before the Sunset Highway was built from Issaquah to the Raging River, this was the Snoqualmie Pass Highway.) At a Y in ¾ mile keep right on Issaquah-Fall City Road. (For another approach, noted below, keep left on Issaquah-Pine Lake Road.) In the next 1½ miles cross the gas pipeline (no access); North Fork Issaquah Creek (hardly noticeable); an old woods road to Yellow Lake (walkable—and sport-drivable, too, sorry to say); the Bonneville swath (walkable, and good parking); and come to 256 Avenue SE. This road is gated and posted to keep out hoodlums but quiet walkers and horseriders are tolerated to date. Park outside the gate in such way as not to block entry. Elevation, 470 feet. If tolerance ceases, go in from the Bonneville swath.

At a scant ⅛ mile on the narrow lane of 256th, where it is grownover and blocked by posts, turn left on a horse path that in ¼ mile of pleasant woods intersects the Bonneville swath. At ½ mile from the Issaquah-Fall City Road the swath descends to a wet vale, the inlet of Yellow Lake, and enters a huge old gravel mine become a motorcycle romper room. Stay alert. At the very bottom of the swale go off left on a path. A razzer track joins from the right, another goes off left, several squirrel off right into the pit, all in 2 minutes, culminating in a confusion of paths left and right, ahead right and ahead left. Take the last one, ahead left, several steps to a Y. The lesser path, downhill right, is the way to the north side of Yellow Lake. Take the larger path, left.

The route from the Bonneville swath to the gas pipeline is ¾ mile, easy to follow despite a maze of trails. So far as the lake is concerned, this is the climax. But don't expect to go swimming, or even picnicking on the shore. Yellow Lake is a marvel, a joy, but impenetrable thickets of hardhack bar human access. At only one spot, site of an old hunting camp, can a person stand next to water; the only view—screened—is from a knoll of Douglas firs, a tantalizing glimpse of cattails and lilypads, open water a-leaping with fish, a-swimming with ducks, a-slinking with critters. A formal trail system likely will provide a few viewing blinds; meanwhile one can take satisfaction in the continued existence of what may be—and may remain—the Plateau's greatest wildlife refuge.

The way rounds the lake, crosses a swampy low spot that is the head of North Fork Issaquah Creek, and emerges on the gas line. Turn right and in about 1 minute drop to a low spot near the lake. In about 2 more minutes look sharp to spot the north-shore trail, which loops back ⅔ mile to the Bonneville line, at no point letting you see the lake. But you can feel its presence.

For the best walk continue on the gas line ½ mile to the intersection of a crosstrail.

The left is another recommended entry. For this, at the Y where Issaquah-Fall City Road goes right, stay left on Issaquah-Pine Lake Road a scant 2 miles and turn right on SE 32 Way. In a scant ⅓ mile turn right on 239 Avenue SE ¼ mile to its end (1981), just past SE 35 Street. Park on the shoulder, elevation 375 feet. Walk east a short bit on what appears to be a private drive but isn't, to white posts marking the present end. Bear right on a large trail a few feet to a junction; the right is an old logging railroad grade, a lovely walk; however, for present purposes cross it, ascend a slope, and shortly cross another path. In a long ¼ mile from the streetend step out of woods onto gas line.

This crosstrail—the recommended return—continues a long ⅓ mile from the gas line to the Bonneville line, which in 1 mile returns to Issaquah-Fall City Road.

First, a mandatory sidetrip. Descend the gas line to the shore of Horse Lake, so called because in summer horses love to wade in to wet their bellies. Hikers would wet more than that if they tried to wade. However, the exploring is easier than at Yellow Lake because the swath breaks through the hardhack, providing access to spongey mats of sphagnum moss. Water squishes and gurgles underfoot and maybe over-ankle—the moss mats are floating. Step from mound to mound through acres of Labrador tea, marvelously aromatic (take home a few leaves to brew up in the samovar); in spring there are acres of bog flowers in bloom.

**Suggested introductory loop trip, with sidetrip, 4 miles, allow 3 hours
High point 475 feet, elevation gain 300 feet
All year**

Yellow Lake to Tolt Pipeline Trail

Though just about every segment of the proposed Plateau Trail currently is used by local residents, the linkages need perfecting. Following are accesses suggested as of late 1981:

SE 8 Street—From 228 Avenue SE turn east on SE 8 to the end in ⅔ mile. A woods road continues a short bit to the gas line, which is open to public feet a mile south and a mile north. The woods road continues to the Bonneville line. Dozens of miles of paths go off from the two lines, interconnecting and looping.

Union Hill Road—Drive the Union Hill Road between Redmond and the Snoqualmie valley to the gas line, open to walking in both directions, more than a mile south to Evans Creek, perhaps twice that north toward Novelty Hill Road.

Novelty Hill Road—Drive the Novelty Hill Road between the Sammamish and the Snoqualmie valleys. Walk the gas line south to Union Hill Road, north to Seidel Road (which is firmly fenced in both directions).

Tolt Pipeline Trail—From the Plateau east of Struve Creek walk nearly a mile south to the fenced Seidel Road.

Tolt Pipeline Trail (Map-page 107)

When the Seattle Water Department built the pipeline in 1963 from its new Tolt River Reservoir 30 miles to the city, it acquired for the purpose a strip of land some 100 feet wide. As an admirable demonstration of multiple use of such utility corridors (hundreds of miles of which traverse Puget Sound country), cooperation with King County Parks led to establishment of the first King County Forward Thrust trail. The route is 12 miles, up hill and down dale, from city's edge through suburbia to wildland, from Bothell to the Snoqualmie River valley.

January morning hike on the Tolt Pipeline Trail

OVERLAKE: MERCER ISLAND TO EAST SAMMAMISH PLATEAU

The trail may be hiked straight through if return transportation can be arranged. Most hikers, of course, start at one end or somewhere in the middle and walk this way or that as far as inclination leads. Parking availability is a consideration. Some accesses have room for one or two cars, others for a half-dozen, others for none. On busy days the lot at the chosen start may be full up, forcing a switch to an alternate.

Blyth Park to Norway Hill, ½ mile, elevation gain 450 feet

The initial stretch of trail is not yet officially open. But notice must be taken of Blyth Park rising from the banks of the Sammamish River at an elevation of 25 feet up the lovely wooded hillside of Norway Hill. Here the Sound-to-Mountains Trail will come in via the Burke-Gilman Trail (which see).

From Main Street in old Bothell drive the 102 Avenue NE bridge over the Sammamish River. Past the railroad tracks turn right on Riverside Drive to the park, which abuts the Wayne Golf Course.

Whether or not hiking the Tolt Pipeline, one easily can spend an hour or two poking along the riverbank and wandering paths on the hillside. One of these informally intersects the pipeline swath, where the official trail eventually will go.

Norway Hill to Highway 405, 1 mile, elevation gain 50 feet

To drive to the present official trail start, cross the Sammamish River from Bothell, and turn left. In ½ mile turn right on a road signed "Norway Hill." In ½ mile pass a road to the right, signed "Norway Hill"; this leads to 104th and the present official trail start, but at a point with poor parking. So continue ⅓ mile on 112th to the pipeline and parking for three-four cars.

Now, to back up and describe the route in sequence: From Blyth Park the (future) trail switchbacks ½ mile to the 480-foot top of Norway Hill and the official (present) trail start at 104th. Superb views down to the Sammamish, out Bothell Way and the valley to Kenmore, Lake Washington, and Olympics. From 104th the trail descends by houses, through woods a long ½ mile to 112th and parking. In ¼ mile more is the concrete jungle of Highway 405.

To cross the freeway, from the trail turn left up a farm road to a freeway access. Follow footpaths plainly marked on the pavement. Pass a Pool It Parking Lot (to get here to dump your car, take Exit 22 from 405 and cross the freeway on NE 160th to the lot on the west side). Beyond the freeway the route turns right to rejoin the pipeline, all this crossing business taking about ⅓ mile.

Highway 405 to Sammamish River, scant 2 miles, elevation gain 125 feet

Backyards. A good rest stop in tall firs of East Norway Hill County Park. Climb to cross busy 124th (some parking). A nursery marsh-field left, houses right.

Ascend to 400-foot top of East Norway Hill. Fields. Acreage estates. Horses. Broad view east to Cascades. Descend to Sammamish valley. At bottom, cross railroad tracks to limited parking by Woodinville-Redmond Road.

The short stretch of trail to the Sammamish River is not officially open. And there's no bridge. So, to continue onward a detour is necessary.

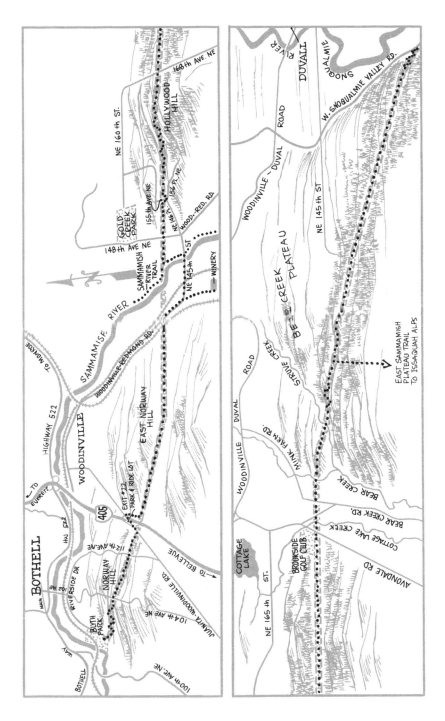

OVERLAKE: MERCER ISLAND TO EAST SAMMAMISH PLATEAU

Sammamish River to Bear Creek Valley, 4 miles, elevation gain 650 feet

Until a bridge is built, detour south to 145th. For compensation, at that point take a sidetrip into park-like grounds of Chateau Ste. Michelle Winery. Walk the trails. See the duck ponds. Have a sip of the juice.

Cross the river and turn north on the riverbank path (see Sammamish River Trail). Alternatively, if driving, go north on 148th to the swath and good parking. From the riverbank to 148th the trail is in undeveloped Sammamish Valley County Park; nice fields, marsh grasses, river, waterfowl. Total distance of this detour is 1 mile.

Ascend steeply from 148th to a 350-foot crest. Horse ranches. Nice woods. Views back down to the Sammamish and over to East Norway Hill.

Where the pipeline makes an air crossing of the deep gulch of 155 Avenue, find a path to the right down in woods. On the far side of the gulch climb steeply to a subtop hill at 350 feet. Big stable here. Horse estates.

Drop to a tangled ravine, then begin a steady uphill in big-fir forest. Pass a pleasant vale to left—pastures, barn, horses, sheep. Climb to the 545-foot summit of Hollywood Hill and a road, 168 Avenue NE; limited parking. Grand views west to downtown Seattle, Puget Sound, Olympics. Continue through pastures, cows, horses, old barns. Then into forest. At the east edge of the high plateau, views of Pilchuck, Haystack, Index, Phelps.

Descend in wildland to remote quiet. Continue on the flat, by pastures, marshes, to the green valley bottom of Bear Creek and Brookside Golf Course. Here at Avondale Road is good parking.

Note that all along this Hollywood Hill stretch are paths taking off this way and that. What marvels lie hidden in these woods?

Bear Creek Valley to Snoqualmie Valley, 4 miles, elevation gain 350 feet

Cross the splendid flat bottom of Bear Creek Valley, which actually has three creeks and tributaries, plus marshes, pastures, woods. In succession cross Avondale Road (parking), Cottage Lake Creek, Bear Creek Road (parking), Mink Farm Road (parking), Bear Creek, and Struve Creek. Passing houses secluded in woods, start upward in wildwoods, climbing to the summit of Bear Creek Plateau (Novelty Hill) at 525 feet.

Stay high nearly 2 miles, all in woods, mostly wild. Trails take off every which way over the plateau; not being posted, they may be open to exploration for miles.

Views out to the Cascades, down to Snoqualmie pastures. Then the descent on a switchbacking service road to the West Snoqualmie Valley Road at 50 feet, close to the Snoqualmie River. Very cramped parking here.

To continue the Sound-to-Mountains Trail, turn south ½ mile, then east on Novelty Hill Road (NE 124th) 1 mile across the river and valley to join the Snoqualmie River Trail (which see) at Novelty.

To pick up the Tolt Pipeline and follow it east into the Cascades, see **Footsore 2.**

One-way trip 11½ miles, allow 8 hours
High points 480, 400, 545, and 525 feet, elevation gain 1600 feet
All year
Bus: many Metro lines to Bothell, walk ½ mile to Blyth Park

Fog-filled Sammamish valley from the Tolt Pipeline Trail. Mt. Phelps in distance

ISSAQUAH ALPS

Remnant of the "Old Mountains" that stretched from Yakima to Cape Flattery before there were such places, and before there were Cascades and Olympics, the Issaquah Alps are a finger of highlands reaching 20 miles out from the Cascade front and poking Puget Sound City right in the eye. Steep topography and cruel climate have kept most development on the lower, outer slopes, preserving for this generation magnificent social opportunities — chances to set aside spacious wild parks and long forest trails in the very middle of the megalopolis now a-building, to shape the overall personality of the agglomeration of urban-suburban centers as crucially as do the area's lakes and saltwaterways.

The existing trail system, all built and maintained purely by local hikers and horsemen, and much of it on private land, dependent on the traditional "tolerated trespassing," is liberally sampled in these pages. For a fuller description and detailed maps see the booklets published by the Issaquah Alps Trails Club: **Guide to Trails of Tiger Mountain,** by William K. Longwell, Jr., and **Guide to Trails of Cougar Mountain and Squak Mountain,** by the author of this here book.

Cougar Mountain lifts from the shores of Lake Washington to a highest peak of 1595 feet — an amazing elevation so close to Seattle, as tall an 3½ Queen Anne Hills piled one atop the other. Despite intense suburbanization of the western flanks, interior uplands still are open and green (in winter, white), and so wild that deer and bear and coyote abound and a cougar visits periodically to crop the rabbits.

Social Opportunity #1. In the early 1980s the people of King County will decide whether to permit a city of 45,000 people to be built high in the snows and wetlands and cliffs of Cougar, on top of old coal mines, or whether to establish a Cougar Mountain Regional Park, a 2400-acre wildland that for a million people (and in another generation, double that?) would be less than a half-hour away via Metro bus.

Next in the line is Squak Mountain, 2000 feet high, so cliffy on east and west that large stands of virgin forest survive. Given to the people by the Bullitt family, the undeveloped Squak Mountain State Park occupies the summit ridge.

Social Opportunity #2. Adjoining the park are forest lands equally beautiful and wild, too high and steep for residential or other development, and uneconomic in acreage and location for tree-farming. By trading public lands elsewhere for private lands on the mountain the park could be doubled or tripled in size — which in the mathematics of wilderness means a quadruple or ninefold increase in esthetic value.

Tiger Mountain — actually a range of peaks, the highest 3004 feet — is the most "mountainous" in elevation and climate (snows can pile deep any time from October to May) and the most "alpine" in plant communities (silver fir and mountain hemlock, lupine and paintbrush and tiger lily and queen's cup), and has much the most extensive trail system.

It also has much the most extensive system of roads, built to service radio towers and manage the forests. For years the rude roads were shared amicably by four-wheelers and two-wheelers, horses and hikers, because everyone came to enjoy forests and creeks, flowers and birds, sunsets and city lights. However, in the 1970s arrived a new breed of infants, morons, and crazies, the gymnasium wheel-spinners whose sport is speed, noise, gouging soil, smashing plants, and muddying waters. If the sport has any proper arena this side of Hell it is **not** Tiger Mountain, ringed by residential communities which are asked to tolerate a thousand motorcycles in their backyard. Some of the invaders are hoodlums whose special subsport is terrorizing peaceful citizens, giving them the distinct impression they are about to be mugged, or worse.

Social Opportunity # 3. Following is the plan proposed for Tiger by conservation groups: (1) Trade private owners (principally, Weyerhaeuser) off the inner, upper wildland of the mountain, block up ownership in hands of a public agency, to permit unified, coherent management. (2) Manage much of the mountain with a new (to America) method of **urban tree-farming** that maintains an output of cellulose while protecting water quality (for domestic use and fisheries), wildlife habitat, historical sites, and appropriate wildland recreation. (3) Exclude from the timber harvest certain major streams, selected trail corridors, and unique ecosystems. (4) Rationalize the existing road system: improve some roads to let passenger vehicles easily drive to streamside picnic grounds and high viewpoints; confine public vehicles to specified roads, closing all others to use except by the land-managers. (5) Set and enforce speed and noise regulations that would maintain an atmosphere in which families could picnic, and young lovers drive up to see the sunset, without trembling in fear as gangs of thugs rumble by, leering and throwing bottles and firing pistols.

These are the three core mountains of the Alps. Completing the province are Grand Ridge and Mitchell Hill, glanced at herein, and Taylor Mountain-Brew Hill, largely in the off-limits Cedar River Watershed. Beyond the valley of the Raging River, that intriguing stream which belongs wholly to the Old Mountains, rises the easternmost of the Alps, Rattlesnake Mountain, discussed in **Footsore 2.**

USGS maps: Mercer Island, Issaquah, Maple Valley, Hobart, Fall City, Snoqualmie

Coal Creek Park (Map-page 114)

The peaks of Cougar Mountain—the Newcastle Hills—wrap in a horseshoe around the basin of Coal Creek. Seattle's first railroad was built to a deadend here in 1878; the Newcastle mines then were King County's major industry, surpassing timber and even real-estate speculation, and in the years around 1880 the valley's population rivaled that of Seattle. Physical evidence of those bustling times is seen only by the sensitive eye. The sensitive soul feels the presence of the ghosts who walk the woods—in company of coyote and deer and bear.

The central section of the stream flows in a deep, narrow gorge incised in an older, broader valley. Though Coal Creek County Park is amid suburbia, the tall, steep walls and lush forest block out sights of civilization and soak up the noise, making room for the babble of creek and chirping of birds.

Coal Creek Parkway to Scalzo Creek

Exit from Highway 405 onto Coal Creek "Parkway" (engineers' euphemism) and follow it southeasterly 1¼ miles to the dip where it crosses the valley on a fill. Park on the shoulder, elevation 175 feet.

Undeveloped and unsigned, the park extends downstream to Highway 405 but the best is upstream. Drop to the trail on the true right bank. Shortly cross on a rustic bridge and shortly recross, hopping in summer when hop-rocks are exposed, wading in winter when the creek runs deep. (The recommended footgear is rubber boots—or tennis shoes that quickly get soaked and so what.) Man's intrusions soon are left behind for a wildness of giant cottonwoods and maples, smaller hemlocks and cedars, vine maple and skunk cabbage, outcrops of sandstone, and gravel bars featuring lumps of coal. In the winter spawning season watch for salmon—and the herons and kingfishers and eagles and raccoons that also are on the watch.

Coal Creek

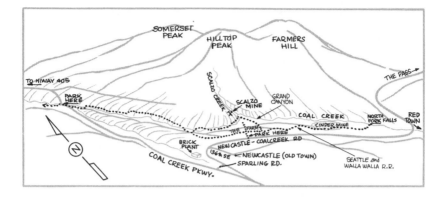

The trail goes up on the valley wall and comes down, crosses the creek four times to dodge this cliff or that bog or tangle of mossy logs, finishing on the true right bank. Decent enough so far except for water and mud, the path now dwindles to naught at the tributary ravine of Scalzo Creek, where rusty algae color the oozy seepage from the Scalzo Mine, a minor operation of the 1930s.

By fording Coal Creek just downstream from Scalzo Creek the route can be continued up through a splendid slot gorge, the walls 175 feet high, but The Farm provides pleasanter access.

Round trip 3 miles, allow 2 hours
High point 300 feet, elevation gain 300 feet
All year
Bus: Metro 210 to Coal Creek Parkway and Newport Way; walk the parkway ¾ mile to the dip

The Farm to North Fork Falls

The cows left in 1977 and the buildings have been removed, making more space for deer to gambol in the pastures and bears to harvest the apple crop. Farm lanes descend to the most spectacular section of Coal Creek and lead to the Seattle & Walla Walla Railroad (1878-1930).

From the dip (see above) drive Coal Creek Parkway 1¼ miles south. Turn left on (unsigned) Sparling Road, then left onto Newcastle Road. Follow it ¾ mile (passing 136th, entry to the Old Town of Newcastle, settled in 1863 and still inhabited) and spot a gated lane on the left. Parking here for about two cars; more space to the east on the shoulder. Elevation, 550 feet.

Three walks can fill a happy afternoon. For the first, follow the main farm lane to the tip of a curious long peninsula ridge that juts out in the valley and gives views of Seattle towers and Cougar peaks—and straight down to Scalzo Creek. Roam pastures and orchard. Descend game traces to a connection-via-wading with the Coal Creek trail.

For the second, a short bit from the gate turn right through a cut and walk lanes down the slope past a cattail pond (frogs and ducks) to a petite Grand Canyon where the creek cuts the foot of a wall of tawny sandstone and tumbles over tawny blocks. Peer into tawny-bottomed pools for trout.

For the third, when the lane from the cut descends, contour off right on a grassy fill—the century-old grade of the railroad. A strand of rusty barbed wire announces the boundary of the park, which, however, is proposed for extension upstream. The grade is obliterated for ½ mile by the Cinder Mine, where waste rock from the coal mines, cooked by the spontaneous combustion of coal into pink and yellow clinkers, is being excavated and processed into material for running tracks and cinder blocks. Resuming at pit's end, the grade proceeds a final ½ mile past apple trees and rose bushes that once graced the yards of miners' homes. Just out of sight up the slope is the site of the Newcastle School (1914-1969). The railroad deadends just out of sight of the site of the hotel. Push on a few yards beside the creek to North Fork Falls, a jolly good splash in the rainy months.

For a sporty return, stick with the creek all the way to The Farm. Distance, 1 mile; time, about 3 hours. The going is never dangerous or unusually cruel but demands a lot of pondering—and the trailfree jungle gorge gives as much solitude as a person can get without actually going underground.

Round trip (all three walks) 4 miles, allow 3 hours
High point 575 feet, elevation gain 300 feet
All year

Coal Creek continues and in a Cougar Mountain Regional Park oo would the trail: across Newcastle Road to the Ford Slope, an incline that descended at an angle of 42 degrees a vertical distance of 850 feet, to depths where 11 locomotives worked to deliver coal to the steam hoist; through Red Town, the center of Newcastle population in final decades of Pacific Coast Coal Company's operation; to one trail branch through the Long Marsh to the Far Country; to another branch up Coal Creek to Klondike Swamp and the High Marsh and Anti-Aircraft Peak.

Far Country Creek-Far Country Lookout-De Leo Wall (Map-page 121)

A trail from Licorice Fern Wall along Far Country Creek, by Surprise Wall and Trog Swamp, is planned as the major southern entry to the Cougar Mountain Regional Park.

From Exit 15 on I-90 drive Highway 900 south a long 4 miles and turn tightly right on narrow and twisty May Valley Road. In 1¼ miles park on the shoulder by May Valley School, elevation 325 feet.

Ascend the schoolyard to the courtyard between Buildings B and C and take the path up the bank into the woods and a T with a major trail. Turn right in mixed forest, a flower riot in early spring, ¼ mile to a Y. The two forks rejoin later; the nicest way is left, steeply up to Licorice Fern Wall, a vertical 50 feet of ferns and moss, and upward more to the top (600 feet). Vistas of green pastures and brown horses. Blossoms of twinflower and pipsissewa, pink wintergreen and honeysuckle, miner's lettuce and seablush.

The path turns right along the brink ¼ mile and drops to the reunion.—And as of publication in late 1981, total confuson where a half-section of wildwood is being short-platted in 5-7-acre lots. However, the developer has given King County a trail corridor and in early 1982, when the trees stop toppling and the

Licorice Fern Wall

bulldozers gouging, the Issaquah Alps Trails Club will build a new trail. From Licorice Fern Wall, watch for flags. Once the trail is established, the horse traffic from May Valley ranches quickly will make it easy to follow.

Aside from the lovely creek, the trail will feature the magnificent fern drapery of Surprise Wall, the chunks of fallen andesite that form The Trogs, the broad ookery of skunk cabbage and cottonwoods, vine maples and frogs, of Trog Swamp. The way will climb to an ancient woods road-path (775 feet), about 1½ miles from the school, and follow it left ½ mile to emerge from green dusk into the big sky of a 1974-75 pulpwood clearcut.

This is the Far Country, once upon a geologic time a single basin and still a unity, though drained by three branches of May Creek, and still, though mangled by logging, a glory of in-City far-ness, secluded from the faraway outside world by guardian ridges.

At about 2½ miles is Lookout Junction, 750 feet. The route can continue from here to either of two great destinations. Or both.

Round trip 5 miles, allow 3 hours
High point 775 feet, elevation gain 800 feet
All year

To Far Country Lookout

Spot red flags climbing steeply right in the jungle of young alders. Once found the trail is obvious and short, gaining 200 feet in ¼ mile, emerging on the open nose of a ridge at Far Country Lookout, 950 feet. Look out far to Enumclaw, Rainier, Tacoma Smelter stack, Puget Sound, I-5, Sea-Tac Airport, and the vacancy where St. Helens used to poke whitely above Bald Hills.

From the Lookout the Cougar Ring Trail proceeds into The Wilderness, connecting at Shy Bear Pass to Wilderness Creek Mainline (see below).

Round trip from Lookout Junction ½ mile, allow ½ hour
High point 950 feet, elevation gain 200 feet

To De Leo Wall

From the junction continue on the main lane ¼ mile to Far Country Corner (750 feet), an andesite outcrop bright in season with alumroot, rock cress, and columbine; close by is Far Country Falls, loud in season with tumbling waters of Long Marsh Creek. A few yards past the falls turn left on a sideroad. (The main road, approximately on the route of the prehistoric Indian Trail, proceeds to Red Town and Coal Creek.)

Across Long Marsh Creek on the sideroad is a Y; go left on a flagged pulp-logging road. Dense young alders and and mixed-conifer woods begin and the flagged path crosses the delicious cool ravine of Dave's Creek and goes upsy-downsy along the side of Marshall's Hill, passing secret camps of local youngsters. At 950 feet, a devious 1 mile from the falls, the path emerges on a sky-open buttress.

This is De Leo Wall, plummeting 600 feet from the 1125-foot summit of Marshall's Hill to the slopes in May Valley, some of its naked cliffs as many as several hundred feet tall. Sit on the buttress and gaze over pastures where cows graze and dogs bark, to Renton and Southcenter, Lake Washington and the southern Olympics, Rainier and the Tacoma Smelter and the steam plume of the St. Regis pulpmill. In spring the rocky bald is brightened by Indian paintbrush and blue-eyed Mary and strawberry.

The airy-scary path beyond the buttress is not recommended. However, a major access trail on a slightly different line is planned as a major access from Lake Boren to the Cougar Mountain Regional Park.

Round trip from Lookout Junction 2½ miles, allow 2 hours
High point 950 feet, elevation gain 300 feet

Wilderness Creek-The Boulders-Long View Peak-Wilderness Peak-Clay Pit Peak-Anti-Aircraft Peak (Map-page 121)

Much of Cougar Mountain carries manifold marks of man—mining for a century, several waves of logging, roads built and abandoned, homesteads reclaimed by forest, forests felled by advancing suburbia. But in The Wilderness man passed swiftly through a long time ago and never returned; in the wake of the loggers who in any one place spent a day or two, there have walked, since then, only bear and cougar and deer and coyote—and latterly, hikers.

Working cooperatively, animals and hikers have developed a Wilderness system of trails and routes totaling perhaps 20-odd miles—enough to bewilder a newcomer. An experienced wildland navigator, equipped with compass and the Trails Club guidebook maps, and with plenty of time and a good sense of humor, can enjoy hours and hours of the confusion that exhilarates yet doesn't terrify. The inexperienced hiker still can venture safely into The Wilderness but is advised to keep looking over his shoulder and to scatter plenty of bread crumbs.

From Exit 15 on I-90 drive Highway 900 south 3¼ miles, to ½ mile south of Sunset Quarry and a scant ¼ mile north of Issaquah Highlands Camping Club. Park on the shoulder, elevation 365 feet.

Spot the path that climbs the cutbank and trenches a hellberry thicket, then ascends a straight-up cat-logger's gouge of the 1940s. This gypo operation cut only a few trees and the remaining forest has so thrived in the lush valley as to seem a virgin splendor of large maples and cedars. Close left sounds waterfalling Wilderness Creek; sidepaths lead to nooks for sitting and musing.

In ⅓ mile, at 800 feet, is Boulders Junction. Wilderness Cliffs Mainline goes right, climbing steeply to Big View Cliff and Wild View Cliff, virgin forest of Douglas fir, and eventually Wilderness Peak. The best introductory route is left, on Wilderness Creek Mainline, which contours a short bit to The Boulders,

Wilderness Creek

huge blocks of andesite tumbled from the cliffs, covered with ferns and moss. It is enough. Picnic here amid the green gloom of handsome big trees, beside the splashing creek, notably delectable on a hot summer afternoon.

The Mainline splits, one piece on either side of the creek, a nice little loop. For distant destinations the best path is on the left (the creek's true right). At 1200 feet, 1 mile from the highway, the trail intersects Ring Road; turn right. In a few feet, as Ring Road bends left, go off right on a sideroad a few more feet to the Section Corner, marked by cobbles heaped around a stump. Several steps beyond is a Y; go right ¼ mile to Long View Junction, 1250 feet.

To Long View Peak. Ascend the left fork ¼ mile to a Y; go left a few final steps to the summit, 1450 feet, finely forested by Douglas fir. From the brink of a precipice gaze out over green wilds of Cabbage Creek to green pastures of May Valley and long views to Renton, Sea-Tac Airport, Tacoma Smelter, St. Regis steam plume, Black Hills, and Rainier.

To Wilderness Peak. Take the right fork—obscured at the start by fallen trees—¼ mile to Shy Bear Pass, 1310 feet, at the head of Wilderness Creek. A flagged path descends the other way, down Cabbage Creek, to Far Country Lookout. The Mainline follows an ancient logging road from the pass ½ mile to Penultimate Plateau, 1575 feet, and Clay Pit Junction, 2 miles from the highway.

The trail proceeds straight ahead—but now takes the name of Wilderness Cliffs Mainline, offering a superbly confusing loop back to Boulders Junction (keep smiling).

The Ultimate Plateau, summit of Wilderness Peak, 1595 feet, Cougar's highest, is a short beat up through salal to a splendid stand of Douglas fir; beyond the summit on the east ridge the forest is perfectly virgin. There is the satisfaction of conquest, of wilderness solitude—but no view.

Round trip (including Long View Peak) 5 miles, allow 4 hours
High point 1595 feet, elevation gain 1500 feet
All year

To Clay Pit Peak

From Clay Pit Junction a flagged path goes north across the plateau and steeply drops to Blackwater Pond, 1450 feet. The way follows trenches dug during prospecting for fire clay; twice it leaves a trench to climb left to another. Beware on the right of the gaping hole of the ventilation shaft of the old Newcastle Queen Mine. Just beyond the summit of Clay Pit Peak (1525 feet) the way emerges from alder forest on the upper edge of the Clay Pit, a giant scoop that supplies the Newcastle Brick Plant. Mining occupies only a few days a year; usually the pit is deserted except for the deer and coyote, whose tracks are everywhere. Enjoy broad views over headwaters of Coal Creek to Anti-Aircraft Peak and Radio Peak, out to Seattle and the Olympics, and over the Sammamish-Issaquah valley to the Cascades.

Round trip from Penultimate Plateau 1½ miles, allow 1 hour
High point 1575 feet, elevation gain 350 feet

To Anti-Aircraft Peak

Slip and skid down the Clay Pit westerly toward the entry road, 1400 feet. A short way into the pit from the entrance spot flags descending alder forest. In a long ¼ mile is West Fork Tibbetts Creek, 1225 feet, formidable amid brush and muck but easily crossed on a large log. Flags lead across the broad, swampy flat of Cougar Pass, clearcut for pulpwood in 1976, climb into alder forest, and at 1400 feet, ¾ mile from Tibbetts Creek, intersect a woods road, closed to vehicles. Turn left a short step to the gate of "Radar Park."

For the summit, turn left through the gate and wander rolling meadows to the top, 1450 feet. Near here in War II a battery of anti-aircraft guns defended Issaquah against sneak attack. In Cold War I this was the location of the command radar for Nike missiles located in silos a mile away down the mountain. The undeveloped King County park gives a sky-high feeling, especially when southerly gales are driving clouds over the meadows or northerly gales are drifting the powder snow.

For the best views turn right from the park gate to Cougar's greatest viewpoint, Anti-Aircraft Vista, on the brink of the precipice that plummets to Lake Sammamish. Look north along blue waters to the Sammamish valley, and north more to Mt. Baker and the San Juan Islands. Look left to Lake Washington and the Olympics, right to the Snoqualmie Valley and the Cascades.

Round trip from the Clay Pit 3 miles, allow 2 hours
High point 1500 feet, elevation gain 600 feet

Lakemont Gorge-Bear's Orchard (Map-page 122)

It was the plot to build Lakemont "Boulevard" (engineers' euphemism) that ushered in turbulent modern times on Cougar Mountain, causing formation of the Residents Association and, later, contributing to organization of the Trails Club as well. The "boulevard" cannot be built because Nature has designed the structure of rock and soil to forbid it; it should not be attempted because this is the largest wildland gorge on Cougar's north slope, a corner of God's good green earth that has written all over it, "FREEWAYS AND HOUSES STAY OUT."

Turn off I-90 on Exit 13 and park at the stubend pointed like a pistol at the heart of the gorge. Elevation, 200 feet.

Follow flags across the soggy meadow to the boot-beaten path on the valley wall. In a short bit it hits the lower end of a cat road gouged in 1975 in preparation for boulevard construction. The strolling is easy on road-become-trail, up through lovely mixed forest that in a hot summer afternoon is 20 degrees cooler than outside. Ferns drape mossy maples and steep valley walls. Hemlocks and cedars are large. Peltola (Lewis) Creek makes music tumbling through a jungle of salmonberry and devils club. A walker feels magically transported to an Olympic rain forest. Sidepaths lead to the creek (one continues to the Bear's Orchard—see below).

Deep forest yields to young alder grown up in the 20 years since the fizzling of a premature development scheme. At ¾ mile, after a final slope of slippery clay, the pilot road tops out on the brink of a broad plateau, 600 feet, and Ts with a woods road; go left. Still incised in a gorge but not so deeply, the creek is

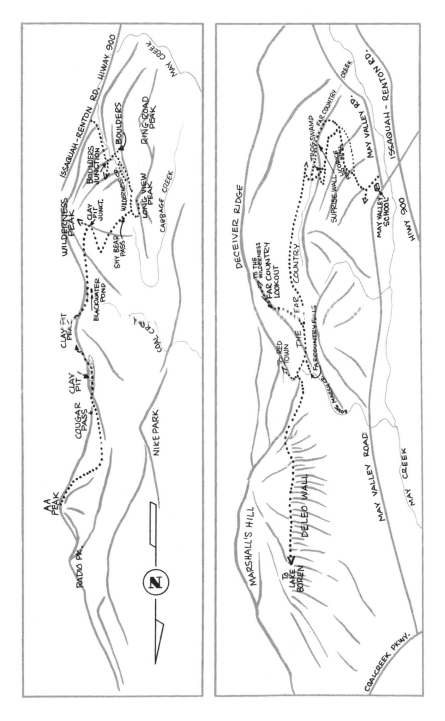

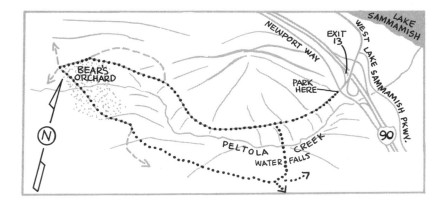

easily scrambled to for picnics in wild splendor beside the babble. From the woods road's deadend a path leads a few steps to the other road from the brink Y; turn left. At a scant ½ mile from the brink turn left ⅛ mile on a mucky track to Peltola Creek, no longer in a gorge. The trail crosses, climbs a bit, then goes along the flat. At 650 feet, 1½ miles from Exit 13, the path enters a clearing that from 1912 to 1940 was a farm—and sometime moonshine factory. Naught remains but tangles of hellberry and dozens of gnarled, lichen-gray fruit trees. Many a little brown jug was filled with the fermented, distilled squeezings, a "grapa" of villainous local reputation. Nowadays the delicious apples of some old-fashioned variety annually fill many a bear—or a single bear many times. Hikers in the harvest season are advised to place their feet carefully.

Round trip 3 miles, allow 2 hours
High point 650 feet, elevation gain 450 feet
All year
Bus: Metro 210 to stop just beyond Exit 13, walk ¼ mile back to trailhead

The main trail turns uphill at the orchard edge, branching ultimately into a network much used by local walkers and horseriders but for outsiders complicated by NO TRESPASSING signs.

The loop return starts from the upper edge of the middle of the orchard. Follow flags up to an old railroad grade, 700 feet, and turn left and contour ¾ mile of grand forest to a junction. Flags lead up right to many adventures. For the loop follow the flags left to a series of spectacular waterfalls in a tributary gorge, then precipitously (but safely) down the wall of the main gorge to Peltola Creek. A short ascent to the pilot road closes the loop at 400 feet, 1¼ miles from Bear's Orchard.

Squak Mountain State Park: Central Peak-Northeast Face Loop (Map-page 125)

The Canadian glacier that squeezed through valleys on either side made Squak Mountain the steepest of the Issaquah Alps, a thin ridge so formidably cliffed that loggers of the 1920s mainly high-graded, leaving large stands of virgin forest, and no subsequent human activities have seriously molested the wildland. Nature made the motion and the Bullitt family seconded it, bestowing upon the people a square mile of cliffs and forests and creeks for a state park. Development and formal dedication of the park must await appropriation of funds for a trailhead in the city of Issaquah and an easement from there to the boundary. Except for measures to exclude the vehicles that now break the law by entering the park, that is about all the development there will be—terms of the Bullitt gift require the park to be machine-free, forever wild.

Adjoining the park are other lands of equal beauty, and equally high and steep, that offer the opportunity for a park several times the present size. The Northeast Face Loop is a classic of the Alps, on everybody's list of favorites, superbly sampling both park-as-is and park-that-could-be.

From Exit 15 on I-90 drive Highway 900 south 2½ miles to just beyond Milepost 19. Spot a narrow woods road turning in to the powerline. Park on the highway shoulder, elevation 425 feet.

Ascend the steep, deeply rutted West Face Road, which begins on "pass through" land of Burlington-Northern and is a favorite midnight playground of four-wheel sports, whose vehicles often fall off the road and go smash. Peace is quite secure in daylight—sober drivers rarely venture high.

The lane ascends steadily in a splendid forest of big old firs and hemlocks and maples and alders. Creeklets waterfall down green gulches. The mountainside drops steeply off, opening interior panoramas through a sky of green leaves. Fairy bells and columbine line the way, and swordfern and lady fern and licorice fern and maidenhair fern.

At 1¼ miles, 1090 feet, the road switchbacks right, and soon left, and in a scant 1½ miles passes close by the North Ridge Road, on the left; a few steps

Telephoto of Seattle and the Olympic Mountains from Squak Mountain

up the latter is Issaquah Junction, 1275 feet, where the East Side Road goes off left—remember it, it's the return leg of the loop.

Continue up the West Face Road onto the North Ridge Road. For the simplest route to the summit, at 1400 feet, ¼ mile from the junction, go off left on Lower Summit Road, which curves south, in and out of forest vales, around spurs, a joy. At 1700 feet, 2¼ miles, a sideroad climbs right a short distance to the Bullitt Fireplace, all that remains of their summer home. Continue straight ahead to Central Peak, 2½ miles, 2000 feet, decorated with a thicket of radio towers.

Views would be meager were it not for slots cut in the forest to let microwaves in and out. One gives views of May Valley, Cougar Mountain, Renton, Lake Washington, Puget Sound, Vashon Island, and the Tacoma Smelter. Another shows Lakes Sammamish and Washington, Bellevue, the Space Needle, and Mt. Baker. To the south is a screened view of the Cedar Hills Garbage Dump, Enumclaw, and Rainier.

Don't quit just because you've bagged the peak—the best of the loop lies ahead. Descend the service road a short bit to 1925 feet and turn left on the Summit Trail, a lovely wildland path down a ravine of lush mixed forest. At a scant 3 miles, in the notch between Central Peak and Southeast Peak, is Thrush Gap Junction, 1500 feet. Turn left, north, on a trail that in the 1920s was a narrow road that barely held the primitive Mack trucks and chain-drive Reos. At little A Creek are stringers of an old bridge, fern gardens in the air. The road contours, blasted from andesite cliffs, a wonderful stroll in ginger, solomon's seal, and oak fern, with screened views out to Issaquah and Tiger Mountain.

At a scant 3½ miles the road-trail abruptly ends on the crest of a spur ridge, 1600 feet. Traces of grade go out on the spur a few feet to a strange clearing. Sawdust! The whole slope is sawdust, partly covered with a gorgeous sprawl of twinflower. Here, high above the valley, a portable sawmill operated—a "tie mill," carted around on a truck, that squared small trees into railroad ties. Another surprise: a view—not of the expected Issaquah but over Cougar Mountain to towers of downtown Seattle.

Plunge down the sawdust into woods, quickly hitting the East Side Road-Trail at 1300 feet. Turn left and contour around tips of spur ridges, deep into an alder-maple ravine, by windows out on the valley. At 4¾ miles the East Side Road completes the loop at Issaquah Junction.

Loop trip 6 miles, allow 5 hours
High point 2000 feet, elevation gain 1600 feet
All year

Squak Mountain: West Peak Loops (Map-page 125)

Squak has a big classic and a pair of little classics, offering the same variety of forests and the same intriguing wanderings. The difference is that these loops are not within the park-as-is but the park-as-it-must-become.

From Highway 900 at 425 feet (see Central Peak-Northeast Face Loop) ascend the West Face Road to the second switchback, at 1¼ miles, 1220 feet. Go off the end on the Chybinski Trail, a 1920s logging road that hasn't seen wheels since. The grade runs to the edge of a deep ravine and seems to end. Stringer logs of the old bridge span the gap, sprouting hemlocks. Admire. Then

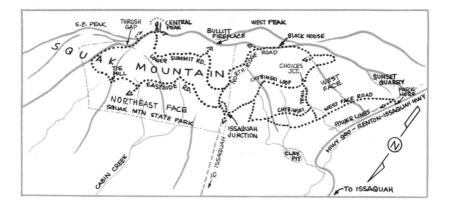

backtrack to the bypass trail down over an admirable trickle-creek and up again to the grade. Gently climbing by holly and trillium, then contouring the steep mountain wall in columbine, selfheal, and coltsfoot, the road passes large barrier logs that halt midnight marauders coming from the other direction. At Choices Junction, 1¾ miles, 1525 feet, a decision must be made between two loops.

Chybinski Loop

Turn right, down a steep, washed-out cat track. In ¼ mile it gentles at 1070 feet. The cat track also completes a loop but the much better option is to turn right, up the bank, onto an old grade with sufficient logs to bar wheels, not so many to mar pleasure in alder, fir, and hemlock, the trickle of a creek, the windows (in winter) out on Cougar Mountain. At ⅓ mile from Choices Junction the grade obscurely joins the West Face Road at 1025 feet, a scant 1 mile from the highway.

Loop trip 3 miles, allow 2 hours
High point 1525 feet, elevation gain 1100 feet
All year

West Peak Loop

From Choices Junction continue on the road as it starts south, bends north, steadily climbing. At a Y switchback right, up, to the summit plateau, 1750 feet; the lower subsummit, 1785 feet, lies to the left. Pass a short spur road to the Block House and continue to a saddle at a scant 2½ miles. To the right, with no trail access and no views but much green solitude is West Peak, 1950 feet. Stick with the road as it drops steeply to hit the North Ridge Road at 2¾ miles, 1575 feet. Proceed downhill to the West Face Road and go left to square one.

Loop trip 4 miles, allow 3 hours
High point 1750 feet, elevation gain 1350 feet

Round Lake

Issaquah Watershed — Tradition Lake Plateau (Map-pages 127 and 133)

No other municipality of metropolitan King County has more wildland within city limits than Issaquah. Though broad swaths of powerlines and a gas line cut through the trees, on either side are enclaves of deep woods. Two lakes nestle in bowls and several swamps hide in secret glooms. Bands of elk tramp the trails, bald eagles roost in snags. This is the quintessential "wilderness on the Metro 210," a place to spend winter afternoons or summer evenings or full days in any season, the wildness counterpointed by history — old logging, old homesteads, old waterworks, old golly-knows mysteries.

The easiest entry, in terms of energy output, is from the east. Leave I-90 on Exit 20, turn right on SE 70th, and follow it west to the turnaround at the gate, elevation 450 feet (noticeably higher than Issaquah, and that's why this is the entry preferred by toddlers and saunterers). Walk the service road, barred to every sort of public vehicle, ¼ mile to the powerline. Directly across is the woods road that leads to West Tiger 3, West Tiger Caves, and other wanderings. A short way to the west on the powerline is the woods road that is the eastern end of the Tradition Lake Loop. A scant 1 mile from the gate is Three-Way Junction, hub of routes discussed in following paragraphs.

The neatest entry is from downtown Issaquah. Park anywhere on the streets — or get off the Metro 210 — and walk Sunset Way east from the town center, the Front Street intersection, elevation 90 feet. As Sunset begins to rise to become an I-90 onramp turn right, steeply uphill, on a gravel track that climbs to the old Northern Pacific Railroad grade at 200 feet, just where the trestle used to cross the valley.

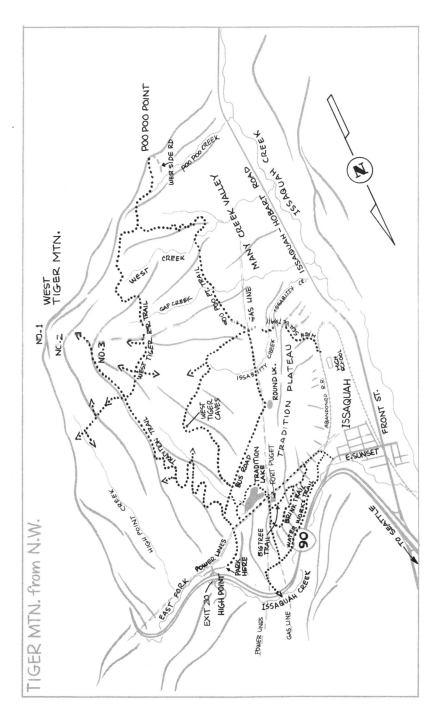

Immediately turn sharp left on what seems an extension of the grade but actually is the remnant of a road to the old Issaquah Waterworks. In several steps a trail strikes directly up the forest slope. Here, at a very scant ¼ mile from Sunset, is Waterworks Junction.

Waterworks Trail-The Springs

Continue on the road remnant to the first Springs and a pair of reservoir tanks, an ancient one below the grade and a merely old one above. Until the State Highway Department agrees to move its danged fence down the slope, the route beyond will be a bit of a struggle. Worth it. But not to every Sunday stroller. The service road had a chunk bitten out by freeway construction. An animal path climbs along the fence, steeply, then drops, steeply, to regain the resuming road. Another trail crawls under the fence, contours the freeway cut, and crawls back under the fence to the road—which hasn't seen a wheel in decades.

The fence mess behind, joy reigns supreme—supremer, in summer, if walkers carry nettle sticks to fight off the stingers. Down left is East Fork Issaquah Creek, where all year the water ouzels dip and in winter the salmon spawn and die, to be eaten by eagles. Up right is a wonder of a virgin forest steeply climbing hundreds of wild feet. And there are The Springs...

In Pleistocene time the Canadian glacier dammed up great big Issaquah Lake, then filled much of it with deltas of sand and gravel and clay. Abundant rainfall and snowmelt from West Tiger flows to the old delta—the Tradition Plateau—and mostly sinks in, forming a vast underground reservoir. Though Issaquah now pumps water from wells, it holds a large share of the plateau as a "watershed in reserve" that in case of need could readily be returned to service, and meanwhile is a heritage treasured by the citizens and freely shared with hikers from throughout the region.

The bulk of the water from West Tiger flows in underground aquifers to the scarp cut by East Fork Issaquah Creek and there seeps out, trickles out, and gushes out—one Spring after another for half a mile. The larger ones pass through concrete collection-filtration boxes that once were connected to the reservoir. Visitors from cities whose water is chlorinated, rusted, and altogether chemicalized come here for cold, clean, delicious drinks.

At ¾ mile from the railroad grade is the last collection box and the end of the road. A steep but good game trail continues up and down a scant ¼ mile to the gas line. Turn right, steeply and meanly up, to the Lower Plateau, 450 feet. In a final ¼ mile from the Waterworks outlet, and past the outlet of the Brinks Trail, is the outlet of Big Tree Trail.

One way from Sunset Way to Big Tree Trail 1¾ miles, allow 1½ hours
High point 450 feet, elevation gain 600 feet
All year
Bus: Metro 210 to downtown Issaquah or High Point

For a sidetrip or a loop, follow the game trail over the gas line into woods, out again on a freeway cut, and down to East Fork Issaquah Creek where it is crossed, side by side, by a little old 1920s bridge of old Sunset Highway and the behemoth 1970s mass of I-90. Pause to reflect. Then follow the creek bank

1,100-year old Douglas fir on Dig Tree Trail

under I-90; note the myriad stompings by animals, who take this route from Tiger Mountain to Grand Ridge. On the far side climb a short bit to the Issaquah-High Point Trail and loop on back to town.

Lower Plateau-Big Tree Trail

At Waterworks Junction take the trail steeply uphill in glorious forest logged so long ago, and so sparingly, it seems perfectly virgin. The way passes splendid large Douglas firs, skirts the ravine of a Spring, and joins a gravel path from the railroad. At 425 feet, a scant ¼ mile from Waterworks Junction, is the lip of the Lower Plateau, a magnificent viewpoint. Many folks climb here in sunset or twilight for the Christmas-card vistas over the little town of Issaquah, the green plain of Pickering Farm and the Issaquah Skyport, where sailplanes soar and parachutes float, and Lake Sammamish.

Walk the service road east a scant ¼ mile, to where it begins to climb to the Upper Plateau, and turn left into the woods on a well-beaten path. In several hundred feet is Big Tree Junction. The Brink Trail goes straight ahead, meandering along the plateau brink with looks down ravines of The Springs, at length emerging on the gas line.

For the sylvan spectacularity, turn right on Big Tree Trail. Though less than ¾ mile long, an afternoon is not enough. Examine the path for tracks and sign of coyote, cougar, deer, elk, bear, raccoon. Sit on a mossy log beside the luscious swamp, through which water moves ever so slowly and quietly, enjoy the blossoms of lily-of-the-valley, and fill lungs with skunk cabbage. See eight species of fern and scores of mosses and lichens and liverworts. Hear the winter wren and varied thrush. The wildland arboretum has two unique features, as well. A stretch of cedar puncheon dating from the 1880s is the area's only known surviving bullteam skidroad, along which oxen dragged the "big sticks." So much time has elapsed since then that trees too small to interest the loggers have grown to noble dimensions, a rain-forest mix of Douglas fir, Sitka spruce, hemlock, cedar, and fern-hung maple. Some Douglas firs were too large for the bullteams—one measures 24 feet in circumference and has been found by coring to be 1100 years old!

Emerge on the gas line—and perhaps turn around and do it all again. To the left on the swath are the outlets of Brink Trail and Waterworks Trail. To the right ¼ mile is the lip of the Upper Plateau, 500 feet, and the intersection of north-south gas line, north-south powerline, and east-west powerline—Three-Way Junction. Just to the west are concrete ramparts of Fort Puget.

One way from Sunset Way to Three-Way Junction 1¼ miles, allow 1½ hours
High point 500 feet, elevation gain 300 feet

Tradition Lake Loop

Tradition Lake is a body of water to dismay trout fishermen and other water purists, to delight bass fishermen, frogs, and birders. Fed by surface and subsurface flow from West Tiger and draining underground to swamps of the Lower Plateau, its level rises in winter to the edge of superb fir forest, drops in summer to expose acres of marsh grass, and more in fall to permit fields of mint to flourish, providing a most aromatic walk.

Both ends of the loop trail start from the east-west powerline. One, a path, enters the woods by a power pole a few steps east of Three-Way Junction; the other, a woods road, a few steps east of the lake and a few steps west of the woods road opposite the High Point entry road. Beaten out by beasts and birders and fishermen, the path goes up and down, sometimes on the shore through creek dogwood and ninebark, usually up the slope in forest of fir or alder. In winter-spring look for bald eagles perched in snags. In any season walk softly and sneak up on the ducks. In summer admire the green pads and yellow flowers of pond lily. When the water is low, spot remains of two lodges abandoned by the beaver colony in the early 1970s or so; see their ubiquitous chewings of stumps and logs.

A maze of paths offers alternative walks. One leaves the shore to cross Tradition Creek to the orchard of an old homestead, scene in fall of raids by apple-plundering bears. Another stays with the shore to the delta of the creek, then climbs to the orchard, whence the old woods road goes a short bit to the powerline. Walk west to complete the loop, on the way enjoying views of West Tiger above the lake foreground.

Loop trip from Three-Way Junction 1½ miles, allow 1 hour
High point 500 feet, elevation gain 100 feet.
Round trip from Sunset Way (Big Tree Trail and Tradition Loop combined) 4 miles, allow 3 hours
High point 500 feet, elevation gain 400 feet
Round trip from High Point gate (Tradition Loop only) 2¼ miles, allow 1½ hours
High point 500 feet, elevation gain 100 feet

West Tiger Caves (Map-page 127)

Since their 1980 rediscovery (local kids had known where they were all along but organized cavers had misplaced them) the West Tiger Caves, described by the recognized archivist of such matters, Dr. William Halliday, as the "largest known talus caves in the state," have become exceedingly popular. Apparently formed by giant blocks of andesite tumbling from glacier-oversteepened slopes above, the caverns intrigue Tom Sawyers and Becky Thatchers. Even claustrophobics who refuse to go underground enjoy the remarkable architecture of rock and fern, tree and moss. Even without caves the walk would be a woodland delight.

As with most Tiger hikes, there are a dozen good ways to skin the cat, such as from downtown Issaquah (best for bus-hikers) and Issaquah High School. The least energy expenditure and routefinding problems, and the most greenland variety, are provided by a loop from High Point. Leave I-90 on Exit 20, turn right on SE 70th, and drive west to the turnaround and gate, elevation 450 feet.

Walk the service road ¼ mile to the powerline and cross to a woods road. In ¼ mile is a Y. The left is the way to West Tiger 3; go right, straight ahead, on Bus Road, in ¾ mile passing the return outlet of the loop, crossing Tradition Creek, passing the mysterious Greyhound Scenicruiser, and emerging on the gas line. Continue a few steps to the powerline, beyond which lies Round Lake. This point is 1¼ miles from the High Point gate and the same distance (but 350 more feet of elevation gain) from the Metro 210 line in downtown Issaquah, via Sunset Way and Three-Way Junction (see Tradition Plateau).

West Tiger Caves

Follow the powerline south a scant ½ mile to where the High School Road climbs up from the right (another approach—see Poo Poo Point). Turn left up a knoll of bare andesite and cross the gas line to the forest edge, 510 feet. Two old woods roads take off side by side, the High School Trail to Poo Poo Point angling up right, the Section Line Trail angling up left.

Take the left, climbing steeply in splendid mixed forest, a garden of woodland flowers in spring, in bare-tree winter offering screened views out to Issaquah. In a long ½ mile from the gas line the switchbacking way crosses Round Creek, 1020 feet, swings around a tributary vale, and turns even more steeply uphill. At 1320 feet, 1 mile from the gas line, watch on the left for blazes and flags and a beaten path; if you miss it on the way up, the skidroad ends close above, so look more closely on the way down.

The rude path trends down a scant ¼ mile that seems more, what with muck-slithering and log-crawling, to the magic spot, 1230 feet. Take off your pack, pull out your flashlight—you didn't **forget**, did you? Prowl. Between great blocks are narrow chasms with walls of cascading ferns. Atop are mossy old trees. All around are tall Douglas firs filtering sunshine/fog. Don's Cave is a walk-in, large enough for a hundred hikers at once. Equally large, O'Brian's Cave requires a short squeeze down a rabbit hole that opens to a great room. Peer into other darknesses—new discoveries may await.

For the loop, follow flags and boot tracks steeply and delicately down to the end of caves and blocks, where the slope gentles out in alder-maple forest and masses of swordfern. The path picks up an old logging grade, wends on down a ridge between Cave Creek and Tradition Creek, and crosses the latter in a babbling gully. At 1 long mile from the caves the flagged route passes a huge, fire-blackened stump and emerges on the Bus Road, 550 feet, closing the loop.

Loop trip from High Point gate 4½ miles, allow 3½ hours
High point 1320 feet, elevation gain 900 feet
All year
Bus: Metro 210 to downtown Issaquah, walk via Sunset Way and powerlines; or to High Point

West Tiger 3 (Map-pages 127 and 133)

The views from West Tiger are unreal as an aerial photograph, a surpassing lesson in the geography of Puget Sound country, spread out like an enormous relief map all around. Virtually the entire **Footsore** world is in sight, from Black Hills, Rainier, and the remnant of St. Helens south, to Olympics west, to San Juan Islands, Baker, and Shuksan north, and Cascades east. There is salt water from The Narrows to Elliott Bay to Admiralty Inlet to Skagit Bay, and cities from Tacoma to Bremerton to Seattle to Everett.

Of the West Tiger peaks, 3 is the lowest—and the best. It juts out farthest, seeming to hang in air over downtown Issaquah a swandive away from blue waters of Lake Sammamish, just as sailplanes from the green plain of Pickering Farm often hang in air over the peak. It has no over-communication towers and—though a Boeing bulldozer ran amok here in 1980, burying a power cable that could just as well have come from another direction—no permanent tracks touch the summit, which thus is razzer-free even on loud summer Sundays. Burned naked by the fires of many decades ago, blasted by

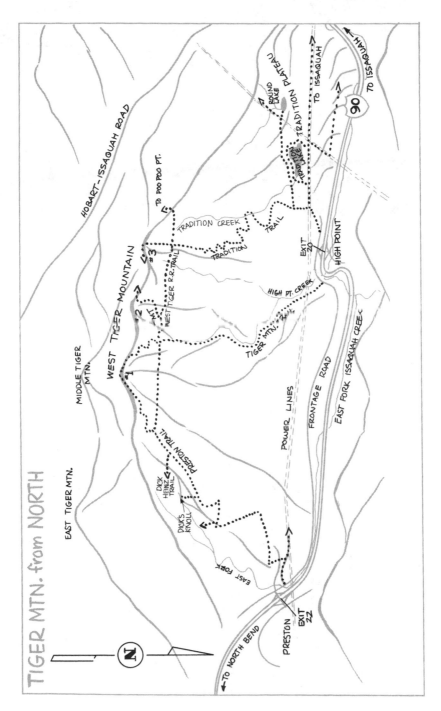

TIGER MTN. from NORTH

Star tracks (from time exposure) and night lights of Seattle from East Tiger Mountain

cold storms in winter and hot sun in summer and vicious winds the year around, the thin soil barely covers andesite slabs and supports only a skimpy crop of trees stunted to a pseudo-alpine look; spring brings a mountain-meadow-like coloring of spring gold, lupine, tiger lily, and ox eye daisy.

The easiest and simplest of the many routes to the summit is the Tradition Trail, ascending from near the lake. The two simplest approaches to the trail are from downtown Issaquah and High Point.

For the latter, leave I-90 on Exit 20, turn right on SE 70th, and drive west to the turnaround and gate, elevation 450 feet. Walk the service road ¼ mile to the powerline.

For the former, from Metro 210 bus stop or parking place in downtown Issaquah, elevation 90 feet, walk via Sunset Way, powerlines, Three-Way Junction, and Tradition Lake (see Tradition Plateau), reaching the same place in 1½ miles (1¼ miles longer and with 350 feet more elevation gain but with bus service; also, parked cars are safe overnight).

Go off the powerline on the woods road directly across from the High Point entry road. In ¼ mile is a Y, Bus Road Junction. Go left, soon leaving the plateau flat and turning steeply up in mixed forest. The way winds and switchbacks, passes spurs left and right, and in one stretch was mucked up by Boeing's unnecessary 1980 bulldozer; the rule is, stay with the most-used and steadiest-up way. The only really confusing spot is a switchback just beyond a crossing of Tradition Creek, which runs most of the summer; take the switchback left, recrossing the creek.

At 1370 feet, a scant 1½ miles from Bus Road Junction, the old logging road ends. Constructed trail turns straight up the fall line. Once all wheels have fallen down and hurt themselves badly the grade relents and in a long ½ mile attains West Tiger Railroad Grade, 1900 feet.

The trail crosses the grade and continues up, shortly emerging from forest into views over Grand Ridge and the Snoqualmie valley to the Cascades, and then proceeding through shrubs, over andesite rubble (or when winter winds blow from the North Pole, in drifted snow) up the ridge crest, at ½ mile from the railroad grade reaching the summit, 2522 feet.

Talk to the sailplanes. For a special treat, stay for the sunset over Puget Sound and the Olympics. And then for the city lights.

Round trip from High Point gate 6 miles, allow 5 hours
High point 2522 feet, elevation gain 2100 feet
All year
Bus: Metro 210

Round trip from downtown Issaquah 8¼ miles, allow 7 hours
Elevation gain 2500 feet
Bus: Metro 210

Poo Poo Point (Map-page 127)

In the winter of 1976-77 there was heard in downtown Issaquah the haunting call of the Yellow-Shafted Talkie Tooter, the "poo! poo!" and "poo-poo-poo-poo-poo" by which the choker-setter talks to the yarder. Thus was ushered in the Second Wave of clearcutting, the cleanup of patches of virgin forest ignored by the First Wave of the 1920s. The loggers proudly declare that mowing down the ancient trees on Poo Poo Point opened one of Tiger's finest views. Well, give them **that.**

Of the many routes, the High School Trail has the best combination of woods and creeks. Drive (or if getting off the Metro 210 bus, walk) south from Sunset Way in downtown Issaquah 1 mile on 2nd Avenue to Issaquah High School and park on the shoulder, elevation 160 feet.

A short way south of the school the Northern Pacific Railroad made its gigantic Issaquah Switchback; the grade, now an unmarked road-trail, can be seen on either side of 2nd Avenue. Turn left and follow it north behind the football stadium. As the grade proceeds north, turn off right onto the Old State Road. Gated to keep out public wheels, this road ascends left around the sidehill, levels out to cross Issabitty Creek, and at a long 1 mile from 2nd Avenue intersects the powerline. Climb andesite slabs to cross both powerline and gas line to the forest edge, 510 feet.

Two side-by-side roads angle upwards, diverging. Take the right, the High School Trail, and ascend steadily into wondrous Many Creek Valley. At 1200 feet, 2½ miles, the way in quick succession crosses a summer creek, all-year Gap Creek, and the deep, richly-forested ravine of West Creek. A jumble of rotted logs tells of the one-time logging-truck bridge. Sit beside the sparkling waters under marvelous big cedars and think of many things, of log exports and subdivision, and whether pigs have wings. Many folk escape here from city madness on hot summer afternoons and eat a picnic supper in the wildness and the cool.

A bit beyond still another ooze of a creek the old road ends, at 1280 feet, and a trail sets out straight up the slope, going through a stand of old-growth Douglas fir at 1500 feet, amid paint splashes marking a proposed timber sale. In a long ½ mile from the road-end, having gained 700 feet, the trail intersects West Tiger Railroad Grade, 1900 feet, 3¼ miles. Turn right a short bit to the end of the grade and follow a trail down across Poo Poo Creek, up, then steeply down to near the end of West Side Road at 1720 feet, 3½ miles.

Walk the road a long ¼ mile left and up to Poo Poo Point, 1775 feet. Four-wheelers grind heavy rubber. Two-wheelers spin little minds. Hang-gliders fling frail wings and flesh into the valley. When school is in session there is peace and solitude here, in views straight down to green pastures of Issaquah Creek and the row of yellow schoolbuses by the high school, south to May Valley and Rainier and Renton, west over Squak and Cougar to Seattle and the Olympics, north to Issaquah, Lake Sammamish, and Baker.

Round trip from 2nd Avenue 7½ miles, allow 5 hours
High point 1900 feet, elevation gain 1900 feet
All year
Bus: Metro 210

In midweek, before school lets out, Poo Poo Point can be pleasantly attained by walking the West Side Road, either by driving as far as desired from Highway 18 before parking, or by parking on SE Tiger Mountain Road and walking a short bit through the woods to the West Side Road (see Grand Canyon). The latter route is 5½ miles round trip, elevation gain 1100 feet.

West Tiger Railroad Grade-Many Creek Valley (Map-pages 127 and 133)

Between the era of logging that used oxen and horses as pulling power, and modern logging with trucks, for several decades the railroad dominated the industry and tracks were laid throughout lowlands and foothills. Most grades have been converted to truck roads or otherwise obliterated. The longest remaining unmolested near Seattle is the West Tiger Railroad Grade, running 4 miles—the entire distance at an elevation of 1900 feet—from the north side of West Tiger Mountain around to the west, then south, in and out of the enormous amphitheater of Many Creek Valley. Logging concluded here in 1929. When hikers arrived in large numbers in the late 1970s they found the clearcuts grown up in handsome large alder and maple or mixed conifers, interspersed with patches of virgin forest ignored by the loggers. Moreover, they found that except for fallen bridges the grades were just as they were when the rails and ties were pulled up for use elsewhere. The West Tiger Grade is proposed for preservation as an Historical Landmark, a chapter in the history of the forest industry—and a delightful stroll, winter and summer.

A glory in itself, the grade is central to the looping for which West Tiger is famous. Trails go off both ends, climb from below, and climb above. Hikers doing West Tiger 3 or Poo Poo Point and finding themselves with extra time and energy commonly give the day a serendipitous conclusion, a loop return through Many Creek Valley. The number of possible loops approaches infinity. The following end-to-end description will stimulate the imagination.

The south end is the ravine of Poo Poo Creek. A trail connects to Poo Poo Point, the quickest, easiest access to the grade, via the West Side Road. Very near the terminus is the top of the High School Trail from Issaquah's 2nd Avenue. From here the grade rounds a ridge into Many Creek Valley on steep sidehill that gentles out in the squishier, creekier center of the amphitheater.

Whenever the grade runs out in empty air, backtrack to find the path down and up to a resumption. Note stringers of old bridges, mostly broken-backed and fallen, a few still intact, nurse-bridges growing ferns and hemlocks and

Hang-glider sailing off Poo Poo Point

candyflower in midair. Watch for railroad ironware, logging ironware—rusting history.

Having crossed West Creek at 1 mile and Gap Creek in ¼ mile more—the two largest of the eight or so (many) creeks—the grade curves onto steep south slopes of West Tiger. Now for something completely different: virgin forest of nobly large and tall Douglas firs, too small to interest loggers of the 1920s but such that 1980s loggers carry towels to sop up their drooling. These trees are on public land, owned by King County, managed by the state DNR. Can the public afford to preserve not only an historic logging railroad but a stand of historic left-behinds?

A rude sidetrail up to West Tiger 3 and the Tiger Mountain Trail is passed, and then the mean Section Line Trail down to the Tradition Plateau and up to West Tiger 3. At 2¼ miles is the intersection with the lovely and easy Tradition Trail that drops left to the lake vicinity and climbs right to West Tiger 3.

The grade bends around the ridge to the north side, at 3¼ miles joining the Tiger Mountain Trail where it descends from West Tiger 2. The united way crosses headwaters of High Point Creek, then splits at 3¾ miles, the TMT descending left, the grade contouring on to a powerline swath. This swath goes straight up to the summit of West Tiger 1, gaining 1000 feet in less than ½ mile—a genuine mountaineering experience when under a foot of snow! A much nicer way to climb the peak is to follow the grade a short bit to its end at 4 miles, still at an elevation of 1900 feet; a trail continues to the Preston Trail.

One thing mightily puzzled the discovering hikers of the late 1970s. The railroad connected to nothing. At both ends, deadends. The mystery was explained by Professor Fred Rounds, who told how the "Wooden Pacific Railroad," or "Western Pacific Railroad," joined the lumber mill at High Point, elevation 450 feet (all remains obliterated by I-90), to the railroad. Steam donkeys lifted rails and railroad cars and locomotives and loggers up this tramway, and lowered tramcars loaded with the "big sticks" whose stumps are gaped at by hikers of today.

One way 4 miles, allow 2½ hours
High point 1900 feet, elevation gain (missing bridges) 300 feet
All year
Bus: Metro 210 to Issaquah or High Point
Sample loop combining Tradition Trail and High School Trail, 10 miles from High Point gate, allow 7 hours
Elevation gain 1800 feet
Round trip from Poo Poo Point 9 miles, allow 5 hours
Elevation gain 500 feet

Tiger Mountain Trail (Map-pages 133 and 139)

On October 13, 1979 was held the official opening of the Tiger Mountain Trail, by then 7½ years in the thinking and 3½ in construction, occupying close to 300 person-days, costing a total in public funds of $0.00, and resulting in a 10⅓-mile route that surely is among the supreme classics of near-city wildland trails in the nation. The route includes varied and grand viewpoints, plant communities ranging from virgin fir to alder-maple to pseudo-alpine andesite barrens—a luxuriant sampling of the good and great things of Tiger Mountain. The trail is a masterpiece, a monument to all who contributed hard labor— above all to the project boss, Bill Longwell, "Chief Ranger of the Issaquah Alps."

It presently is not a walk for every casual stroller. The continuing menace of motorized marauders still requires trailheads to be kept obscure and many defenses of wheelstopping rock and log left in place. In winter the trees blow down and in summer the brush grows up and Longwell's Volunteer Rangers are hard-pressed to keep the path clear. And also in winter the snow may pile deep, concealing every evidence of the route, and as clouds blow wildly by in twilight the heroic mountainclimbers are seen to grin with delight and humble hikers to look very sad.

An inexperienced hiker can best learn the route on a trip guided by the Trails Club or other outdoor group. Experienced wildland navigators, however, can buy "Longwell's Guide" with its detailed map and trail log and forge ahead fearlessly. The following description is not enough to tell how to do the trail—but suggests why one should want to.

The favorite method of hiking the whole trail in a day is one-way, starting at the south end (higher, thus with 1000 feet less elevation gain), having first placed a car at the north end to permit a shuttle around the mountain. (A party needs at least two cars; hitchhiking isn't practical.)

The most-used sections of the trail are the two ends: the north part is an excellent forest walk up High Point Creek and a popular route to summits of West Tiger; the south part, also with superb deep woods, offers the nicest way up Middle Tiger.

For the north trailhead, leave I-90 on Exit 20 and turn left on the frontage road to the turnaround and gate, elevation 490 feet. Walk past the gate and High

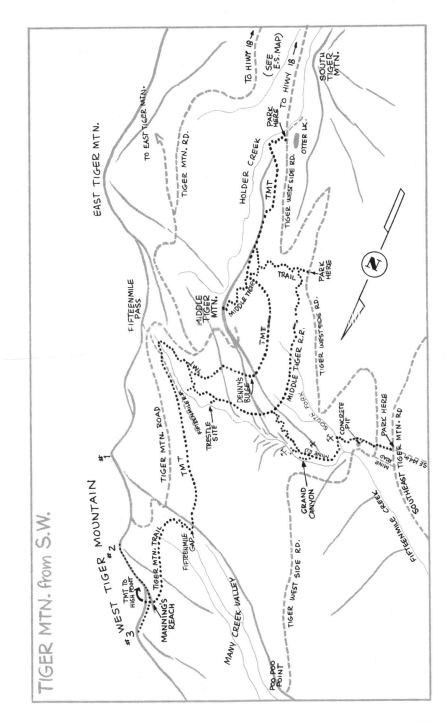

TIGER MTN. from S.W.

EAST TIGER MTN.

TO EAST TIGER MTN.

TIGER MTN. RD.

TO HIWY 18

(SEE E.S. MAP)

TO HIWY 18

SOUTH TIGER MTN.

HOLDER CREEK

PARK HERE

OTTER LK.

TMT

TIGER WEST SIDE RD.

FIFTEENMILE PASS

MIDDLE TIGER MTN.

MIDDLE TIGER

TRAIL

PARK HERE

N

TMT

TIGER WEST EDS RD.

TMT

DENNYS BULGE

TMT

MIDDLE TIGER R.P.

SOUTH FORK

TIGER MTN. ROAD

TRESTLE SITE

FIFTEENMILE R.

MINE RD.

CONCRETE PIT

PARK HERE

#1

TMT

GRAND CANYON

MINE ROAD

SE 164 ST

SOUTHEAST TIGER MTN. RD.

WEST TIGER MOUNTAIN

#2

TMT TO HIGH POINT

Tiger Mtn. TRAIL

FIFTEENMILE GAP

TIGER WEST SIDE RD.

FIFTEENMILE CREEK

#3

MANNING'S REACH

MANY CREEK VALLEY

POO POO POINT

139

Above a sea of clouds on West Tiger 2 (Photo by Harvey Manning)

Point Pond, cross a bridge of the old Sunset Highway over High Point Creek, and turn sharp right up a service road to the powerline and across the swath. As the road turns steeply uphill left at 690 feet, a long ½ mile from the gate, watch closely for boot-beaten track going under obscuring branches of a hemlock into the woods, right. If you've found the correct hemlock you'll soon see "TMT" markers.

For the south trailhead, drive Highway 18 to the summit of the pass between Tiger and Taylor Mountains and turn off across the broad gravel expanse of "The Staging Area," as wheel-spinners used to call it. Two logging roads enter the woods side by side, Tiger Mountain Road right, West Side Road left. Take the left and drive a long 2 miles. At 1500 feet, just past a sideroad left, and just across from the swampy secrets of Otter Lake, also on the left, spot an unmarked trailhead on the right. Once in the woods it becomes plain, confirmed by the "TMT" markers.

To proceed from the south:

Alternating at first between constructed tread and railroad grades of 1920s logging, the TMT wanders through a splendid mix of forests 1¾ miles to intersect the Middle Tiger Trail, 2120 feet, which drops left to Middle Tiger Railroad Grade and the West Side Road, climbs right to Middle Tiger.

The TMT rounds open, broad-view slopes of Middle Tiger and swings into the valley of Tiger's major stream, Fifteenmile Creek. At 1960 feet, 2½ miles, watch for an obscure sidepath left to Denny's Bulge, a fine viewpoint over the valley. A short bit beyond is a flagged route down to Middle Tiger Railroad Grade. At 3¾ miles, 2000 feet, the TMT crosses Fifteenmile Creek on a crude bridge and climbs to Fifteenmile Railroad Grade, which connects up right to Tiger Mountain Road and Fifteenmile Pass, down left to Hidden Estates Trail. The TMT continues climbing to Lone Rock, 4½ miles, 2160 feet, then winds in and out of gullies, up and down to a ridge saddle and brief views at 2200 feet, 5¼ miles, the halfway point. In another ¼ mile the way intersects Hidden Estates Trail, which climbs right to the Tiger Mountain Road, a route to summits of West Tiger.

The way wends onward through woods, over West Tiger Creek and Issaquah Gap Creek high in the amphitheater of Many Creek Valley, then at Rick's Rock emerges into a magnificent alpine-like traverse in dreamlike vistas of intermingled civilization and wilderness, climaxing at Manning's Reach, 6¾ miles, 2600 feet, highest point of the TMT.

A path climbs right to West Tiger 2, another drops left to West Tiger 3 and the West Tiger Railroad Grade. Views end in dark woods leading to West Gap, 7 miles, 2500 feet. The way descends and climbs to a final scenic spectacularity on the open north ridge of West Tiger 2 at 7¼ miles, 2570 feet.

Thence the way is down through shrub into forest, intricately and deviously switchbacking to the West Tiger Railroad Grade at 8 miles, 1900 feet. In another ¼ mile the TMT leaves the grade to descend High Point Creek, following the route of the old "Wooden Pacific Railroad" past relics of logging operations, through luscious forest. The TMT goes right, off the tramway grade, and at 9¾ miles, 690 feet, hits the powerline service road. Continue (see above) to the north trailhead, 10.3 miles, 490 feet.

**One way from Otter Lake (south) trailhead to High Point (north) trailhead
   10.3 miles, allow 8 hours
High point 2600 feet, elevation gain (ups and downs) 1200 feet
All year
Bus: Metro 210 to High Point**

West Tiger 1 (Map-page 133)

Highest of the three peaks, West Tiger 1 is not the pleasantest, cluttered as it is with sky-trashing towers and reeking on sunny Sundays with slack-jawed wheelspinners; WT 3 is more pristine and serene — and has better views, too. However, WT 1 has the Preston Trail, most professional in the Alps, crafted over the years by Dick Heinz, so plush that hikers usually suppose the government did the job, and wonder when and why.

Unfortunately, this wonder of the Alpine world is not a cinch to find at the bottom; the surveyor originally did so only by walking from the top to see where he came out. Moreover, many tricky offshoots lie in wait to befuddle and mislead. The surest introduction is on a guided trip scheduled by Mountaineers, Trails Club, or other group.

The foolproof route to the summit of WT 1 is a combination of Preston Trail and Tiger Mountain Trail (which see). Start at the latter's High Point trailhead, elevation 490 feet. At a scant 2 miles, 1750 feet, just before a mucky creek, the

TMT veers right from the cat road; continue straight up to 1900 feet, where a path goes left to hit and follow the West Tiger Railroad Grade. (If impatient, take the powerline swath directly up the cruel fall line, gaining 1000 feet in a scramble of less than ½ mile, to the summit of WT 1.) Better, take the path left from the end of the grade, at a scant 1 mile from the swath intersecting the Preston Trail at 2250 feet, and follow it ¾ mile up to the summit ridge.

Ah, but thusly one misses the forest magnificence of the lower Preston Trail. Well then, do a loop. Ascend from High Point, descend to Preston Way (see below), walk it several hundred feet to where the powerline crosses, follow the powerline service road 1¾ miles to the Tiger Mountain Trail, and descend a final ½ mile to the High Point trailhead.

Experienced hikers frequently find and climb the Preston Trail. To make the attempt, leave I-90 on Exit 22 and park on a shoulder of SE Preston Way, elevation 550 feet.

Walk SE 82nd ¼ mile to SE 297th, turn left a rather scant ¼ mile up a gravel road, and watch on the right for flags entering the woods; a decent trail on an ancient road sidehills lush greenery and fine old trees. In ½ mile, at 900 feet, Dick's excellent trail joins on the right—climbing from private homes and loud dogs, not for thee and me.

Partly on old logging grades, partly on constructed tread, the way ascends in glorious forest whose 4-foot cedars and hemlocks and firs simulate virginity. At 1¾ miles, 1700 feet, turn right from a rail grade (which continues ahead to Preston horse pastures) and climb right, passing more feeder paths from the left—every horse in town has its own access.

At 2 miles, 2000 feet, the trail turns sharp left to the crest of the north ridge of Tiger, topped by big old firs prominent from afar west, backlighted by the sunrise sky. Watch for the sidepath to Dick's Knoll, a rubbly andesite knob with remains of an old cabin and the hike's first views.

The trail follows on and near the crest of the east containing ridge of High Point Creek to a junction at 2½ miles, 2150 feet; a newer Dick Heinz Trail goes off left 1½ miles to Fifteenmile Pass, a segment of the Grand Tiger Traverse from the Grand Canyon to Preston. In ¼ mile more, 2250 feet, a trail goes right to the West Tiger Railroad Grade and High Point (see above).

The way swings from the ridge over a slope of alder forest with winter views to the Cascades, enters dense small-conifer woods (blueberries in season), and at 3½ miles attains the summit ridge and the first of the blabbermouth towers. A mucky motorcycle runway leads ¼ mile along the flat to the main scene of electronic pollution, the aluminum mines, and the views.

Round trip from Preston trailhead 8½ miles, allow 6 hours
High point 2948 feet, elevation gain 2400 feet
All year
Bus: Metro 210 to Preston, walk to interchange

Round trip from High Point trailhead 8 miles, allow 6 hours
Elevation gain 2500 feet
Bus: Metro 210

Loop trip from High Point trailhead 11½ miles, allow 8 hours
Elevation gain 2800 feet

Grand Canyon of Fifteenmile Creek-Middle Tiger Railroad Grade (Map-page 139)

Rising in the broad saddle of Fifteenmile Pass, which separates the bulks of West Tiger and East Tiger, Fifteenmile Creek is the central watercourse of the mountain, the longest and largest completely **within** the mountain. Beautiful and wild and exciting for all its deep-forested miles, the stream scenically climaxes in the Grand Canyon, where falls tumble down a slot steeply and gaudily walled by green trees and shrubs, gray and brown and yellow sandstone and shale, and black coal. Poking about old mines and searching for yellow amber add interest.

Walkers wanting a bit more exercise commonly do a loop combining the Grand Canyon with the Middle Tiger Railroad Grade, proposed to be designated as an Historic Site and preserved from modern bulldozers and trucks.

Drive Issaquah-Hobart Road south 4 miles from Issaquah and turn east on SE Tiger Mountain Road 1¾ miles; park on the shoulder near SE 144 Place, elevation 861 feet.

Across the road from SE 144th enter a forest on what in 1979 was a foot-horse trail, in 1980 a motorcycle runway, and by 1981 a jeep wallow—an example of what governmental neglect has permitted to happen on Tiger Mountain. In several hundred feet intersect the West Side Road at a point 4¾ miles from Highway 18.

Turn left on this mainline logging artery several hundred feet and note an old woods road joining from the left—the Tiger Mountain Mine Road. In a few steps the West Side Road diverges left and the Mine Road goes obscurely right, straight ahead, through a borrow pit into the forest.

At ½ mile is a large field; wander off left to peer down into a concrete pit containing a device with large steel teeth that were meant to chew up the coal that wasn't mined by a stock operation of the early 1960s. The road returns to forest and gently ascends along the sidehill of a splendid green valley, the creek roaring far below. At ¾ mile, 950 feet, the road bends in and out of the ravine of the South Fork, a delicious creek; look for a hole in the bank, either a coal prospect or an amber-miner's dig.

Around a corner at 1 mile is a Y, 980 feet. For the picnic trip take the left fork, contouring to concrete artifacts and rotten timbers and the end of the mining railroad; dating from around World War I and sporadically active in the 1930s, this operation produced little coal. A slippery path leads to the slot of the Grand Canyon, where water sluices through trenches in the rock and swirls in potholes and splashes hikers' hot faces. In winter the slot is totally occupied by raging furies; in late summer a person can scramble and slither in, startling the water ouzels as they flit by.

The right fork passes the mine (rusty algae ooze out, maidenhair fern hangs over the black mouth), sternly climbs past the slot, then levels out at creek level and at 1½ miles, 1200 feet, deadends. Note timber footings of the vanished bridge; in low water hop across and investigate ironware and the collapsed tunnel, which was timbered only with alder poles and went in just far enough to extract cash from the investors.

Round trip 3 miles, allow 2 hours
High point 1200 feet, elevation gain 350 feet
All year

Now for the loop return.

From the deadend scramble strenuously up the bank past a large stump. Steep but easy flagged path ascends 300 feet in ¼ mile to the Middle Tiger Railroad Grade, 1500 feet. Though not as long as the West Tiger Railroad Grade, this survival is just as superbly historical and scenic. Professor Fred Rounds tells us the grade came from the lumber mill at Hobart, where the millpond still can be seen beside the road, crossed Fifteenmile Creek valley on the famous Horseshoe Trestle, and via a switchback continued up the valley to Fifteenmile Pass. He and fellow loggers, based at the bunkhouse in Hobart, rode a speeder to work each morning. The logging ended with the crash in 1929.

Before doing the loop, turn left on the grade ½ mile to Fifteenmile Creek, 1780 feet, a bully site for a picnic in the wildwoods beside the splashing stream, watching the dippers dip. On the way note where the ¼-mile Horseshoe Trestle spanned the valley; a few of the uprights still are. Note the 2-inch cable, the skyline that was rigged between spar trees to carry the big sticks high in the air over the valley for loading on rail cars.

(To do a variant loop, near the creek a flagged path climbs 200 feet in a scant ¼ mile to the Tiger Mountain Trail, which leads to the Middle Tiger Trail.)

Returned from the sidetrip, follow the grade 1 mile in peaceful woods to the Middle Tiger Trail at 1300 feet. At several spots the trail detours around vanished bridges. This rail line was built by "Trestle" Johnson, noted for his fanatic devotion to trestle bridges. By contrast, that other self-taught Swede engineer who with double-bitted ax and jawful of snoose laid out the West Tiger Railroad Grade was equally devoted to stringer bridges. Whatever the comparative merits, it must be said that trying to bridge Fifteenmile Creek with a stringer design would've demanded the ingenuity of more than one Swede—maybe even of a Norwegian.

Descend the Middle Tiger Trail a short bit to the West Side Road at 1200 feet; in the gully of the large creek at the trailhead note fallen timbers of another of "Trestle's" masterpieces. Complete the loop by walking the West Side Road 1 mile back to the turnoff to SE Tiger Mountain Road.

Loop trip plus sidetrip 5 miles, allow 4 hours
High point 1500 feet, elevation gain 1000 feet
All year

Middle Tiger Mountain (Map-page 139)

Located way out in the middle of the air between the deep valleys of Fifteenmile and Holder Creeks, equidistant from the hulking ridges of West Tiger and East Tiger, Middle Tiger is the best vantage for studying the architecture of the "Tiger Range." It further is one of the supreme viewpoints of the Alps, still another smashing chapter in the Tiger Mountain textbook on the geography of Puget Sound. Finally, in common with West Tiger 3 it simulates true alpinity with shrubby trees and flowery andesite barrens.

Of the several ways to the summit (which include a short motorcycle trench up from an offshoot of the Tiger Mountain Road, more's the pity), two are best, each for a different reason.

Grand Canyon of Fifteenmile Creek

Most popular, requiring the least energy and providing the most deep woods, is the ascent via the Tiger Mountain Trail (which see). From the Otter Lake trailhead, 1500 feet, walk 1¾ miles to intersect the Middle Tiger Trail and turn right ½ mile to the top.

Best in snows of winter and mucks of the rainy season, when the West Side Road may be difficult or impassable for ordinary automobiles, is the approach from the SE Tiger Mountain Road (see Grand Canyon). From the parking shoulder at 860 feet walk through the woods the short bit to the West Side

Road, turn right, and climb 1 mile to the start of the Middle Tiger Trail.

This trailhead is reached by car by driving the West Side Road 3¾ miles from Highway 18. After switchbacking down an enormous clearcut, park where the road crosses a deep gully, elevation 1200 feet.

Obscured at the start by logging slash and grass, the path scrambles straight up the ravine wall from babbling creek and fallen timbers of a railroad trestle to join an old trail from Mirrormont that was mangled below here by road construction and clearcutting. As the grade relents in the woods, at 1300 feet, spot the Middle Tiger Railroad going off left from the trestle site. The way ascends steeply in (mainly) alder forest to ¾ mile, 1760 feet, where a sidetrail goes off right to hit the Tiger Mountain Trail; at 1 mile, 2120 feet, is the intersection with the Tiger Mountain Trail. Continue up into patches of bracken and stands of young firs, pass windows out on lowlands; pause to admire lichen-green granite erratics dropped by the glacier from Canada. The way switchbacks from a gully to a sky-open ridge and the summit, 2607 feet, 1½ miles.

Burned bare by fires, new growth discouraged by cold of winter and heat of summer and loud winds that blow the year around, the half-naked, mountain-meadow-like summit is bright in season with lupine and spring gold, paintbrush and daisy and goldenrod.

Look through Fifteenmile Pass to a long row of Cascades. Look over summits of Squak and Cougar to Seattle and Puget Sound and Blake Island and the Olympics. Beyond green pastures of Fifteenmile Creek and May Valley, and raw dirt of the Cedar Hills Garbage Dump, see valleys of the Cedar River and Green River and the Pleistocene's Big River, waters of Lakes Young, Kathleen, Wilderness, and Tapps. Discern Vashon Island and The Narrows and the Tacoma Smelter stack and the steam plume of the St. Regis pulpmill and the Black Hills. Look across the Osceola Mudflow to the volcano (Rainier) it came from and to the ruins of a volcano that in July of 1980 scattered some of itself on Middle Tiger.

For flowers and views do the climb on a sunny day of spring or summer. For mystery do it in a soft autumn fog that mayhap settles into valleys to become a shining cloudsea. For arctic adventure come in winter when billions of flakes swirl around the summit—or billions of sun-sparkling crystals are flung in your eyes by a northerly gale. Ascend (carefully!) when dramatic cloud castles are drifting, drifting nearer, nearer, slanting gray rainlines to earth—and suddenly zapping each other and shaking the mountain and impelling your feet hastily downward. And don't forget the light show at night.

Round trip from SE Tiger Mountain Road 5 miles, allow 4 hours
High point 2607 feet, elevation gain 1800 feet
All year

Round trip from West Side Road via Tiger Mountain Trail 4½ miles,
**   allow 3 hours**
Elevation gain 1100 feet

Round trip from West Side Road via Middle Tiger Trail 3 miles, allow
**   3 hours**
Elevation gain 1400 feet

*Mount Rainier from Middle Tiger after a late October snowstorm
(Photo by Harvey Manning)*

East Tiger Mountain from Middle Tiger

East Tiger Mountain-Silent Swamp (Map-page 149)

East (Main) Tiger used to be hikers' most popular peak by far, and the standard "trail" was the service road that led to the summit fire-lookout tower and, when that was removed in the mid-1960s, to the blabber towers. Even now, in these darkest days of the Invasion of Wheelspinners from Outer Space, the views are so different from those on other peaks that the ascent can be warmly recommended—but only on weekdays before school lets out.

However, even on razzer-loudest Sundays the Silent Swamp is a gorgeous walk by itself—and combines beautifully with another wheelfree haven, Beaver Valley (which see).

Drive Highway 18 to a point 3 miles from I-90's Exit 25 and 1¼ miles from Holder Gap, the pass between Taylor and Tiger Mountains. Turn north off the highway on the narrow but obvious East Side Road and follow it up to and across the powerline and along the deep-forested Raging River slopes. At 1282 feet, 1½ miles, the road dips into the valley of Trout Hatchery Creek just where the two forks join. It then climbs and levels out on an old railroad grade. At 2¼ miles spot the inconspicuous trailhead, usually flagged, and park, elevation 1400 feet.

Ascend a short bit to a railroad grade. To the left it meets the East Side Road (for a reason to be explained below). Turn right on the grade, which makes a sweeping U-turn around the end of a low ridge, goes through a wide saddle at

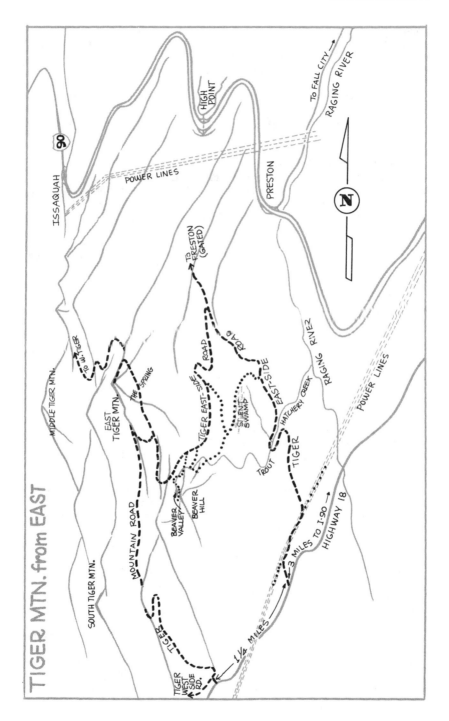

TIGER MTN. from EAST

1550 feet, and enters the valley of Silent Swamp. Hark! What is that new sensation that smites the ears? It is the sound of silence. The ridge has blocked out the din of I-90. Listen now to frogs and wrens. Gape at huge stumps of cedar and fir. Admire devils club and skunk cabbage of the lovely swamp, headwaters of North Fork Trout Hatchery Creek.

The grade sidehills from the swamp to a junction at 1 mile, 1700 feet, and a lesson in railroad history—and the reason this railroad grade, as well as those of West Tiger and Middle Tiger, is proposed for preservation as an Historic Site.

Whereas the Hobart mill engineered its rail approach to Middle Tiger forests with a long, gradual sidehill ascent, and the High Point mill built a tramway up West Tiger, the Preston mill that operated on East Tiger employed switchbacks in this manner: A stretch of grade angled up a slope to a deadend. At the distance of one locomotive and a train of cars back from the deadend, the next stretch of grade took off uphill at an acute angle in the opposite direction. A train climbing the mountain proceeded past the junction to the deadend, pulled by the locomotive. A switch was thrown and the train went into reverse and backed up the next stretch, pushed to another deadend by the locomotive, which on the next switchback again took the lead.

On the route thus far, the Silent Swamp trail where first intersected had just completed a switchback from the stretch of grade now occupied by the East Side Road. The sweeping U-turn was used to obviate the need for one switchback. Here at 1700 feet is the next switch.

The grade reverse-turning to the right leads ½ mile in lovely woods to the East Side Road at 1850 feet—and another switchback. For the best walking, though, continue straight ahead to the deadend at the deep-woods ravine of South Fork Trout Hatchery Creek, 1¼ miles, 1720 feet. Why go on? No dandier spot for a picnic than by the splash of the creek. Watch dippers flit from boulder to boulder.

Round trip 2½ miles, allow 1½ hours
High point 1720 feet, elevation gain 320 feet
All year (East Side Road may be impassable in winter)

To continue to higher destinations, follow constructed (meagerly) trail along and across the creek,then up the fall line to the deadend of an old logging road. Turn right, back over the creek, to the East Side Road at 1950 feet, 1¾ miles.

Note: A few steps up the road is the turnoff to Beaver Valley (which see).

For the summit, stick with the road all the way, nice sociable side-by-side walking, with rarely a vehicle on weekdays. The road climbs steadily, swinging around the side of the 2786-foot satellite peak of East Tiger; views begin to open through young firs whose crowns are leaping up to block views. The road tops the saddle between the peaks and drops a bit to join an offshoot of the Tiger Mountain Road at 2670 feet, 1½ road miles (3½ miles from the start of this walk).

The final ¾ mile is packed with entertainment. One item is the interesting Spring, source of the Spring Fork of Raging River; ponder where it gets its year-round flow, here so near the summit. The other is the sky, which now grows enormously as trees shorten. Though there is never a single 360° panorama, views extend in every direction as the road winds south, west, north, west, and south again—so confusingly that a hiker needs a compass to avoid mistaking Duvall for Seattle. At one time or other there are views over the Raging River to Rattlesnake Mountain and the Cascades, views over I-90 to Lake Alice Plateau, Snoqualmie Valley, Glacier Peak, and Baker, views south to Rainier and the ruins of St. Helens, and over Middle Tiger to Seattle and Puget Sound.

At 4½ miles, 3004 feet, the road flattens on the bulldozer-leveled summit. The ground is littered with aluminum and shriveled french fries. The sky is trashed with metalwork. A forest of huddled hemlocks blocks views north and east but horizons are open a hundred miles south and west. When civility returns here, maintained by law enforcement, East Tiger will again be, as it was before, a famous place to come at night for the city light show. At present the only group that could safely enjoy this place at that hour would be a regiment of Marines armed with tactical nuclear weapons.

Round trip 9 miles, allow 6 hours
High point 3004 feet, elevation gain 1600 feet
All year

Trout Hatchery Creek

Beaver dam in Beaver Valley

Beaver Valley (Map-page 149)

A tiny blue dot on the USGS map caught the surveyor's eye and drew his feet—to a scene that made him feel as did those explorers prowling jungles of Yucatan who stumbled upon ruins of the Old Empire of the Mayans. Inspecting with the archeologist's eye, one deduces that soon after the loggers moved out, in the late 1920s, the beaver colony moved in to harvest the second-growth salads springing up green and luscious. Over the years they dammed not merely the single blue dot seen by the GS camera in the sky but 20-odd, building dams as tall as a hiker and up to 50 feet long. Some of the ponds are silted in and meadowed over, others are open water, their dams showing signs of repair quite recently. However, the teeth marks on large conifers, which aren't a beaver's notion of holiday feasting, tell of the hunger that led them to migrate, probably in the late or middle 1970s, in search of lettuce and tomatoes.

During nearly a half-century of residence they so remodeled this headwaters valley of North Fork Trout Hatchery Creek as to create an ecosystem unique in the Alps; other elements of uniqueness derive from the unusual microclimate here in an odd nook between "Beaver Hill" and the main mass of East Tiger. The place must be preserved.

From Highway 18 drive the East Side Road (see East Tiger) past the lower Silent Swamp trailhead to a junction at 3¼ miles, 1468 feet. Take the switchback uphill left to the upper Silent Swamp trailhead at 4½ miles, 1950 feet. (To combine Beaver Valley with Silent Swamp, see that trail description.) A few feet farther the East Side Road turns right, sharply uphill. The route to Beaver Valley is the railroad grade, overgrown and brushy, that goes obscurely straight ahead. Elevation, 1960 feet.

Don't complain about the blowdowns and weedery—they exclude motorcycles. At a flat below the grade, and also above, the curious can find artifacts of an ancient booze factory that may not have had a federal license. In ¼ mile, 2000 feet, is the lip of the ravine of North Fork Trout Hatchery Creek.

Here, at a landing with much evidence of donkey and yarder and railroad, look across the gap to resumption of the grade. Look down to tumbled ruins of the trestle and to the first beaver dam.

Turn right, uphill, on a non-rail road. Log-hauling in this vicinity apparently was by a peculiar combination of lokie and truck—rusty chunks of truck are scattered along the many roads that radiate from rail landings. The ingenuity of those Swede engineers knew no bounds.

In a short bit cross the creek on remnants of a fill and battle upward through devils club and other evils. The flagged path turns off the road, right, through dense, choked forest and down to the creek and the first of the big dams, ½ mile, 2080 feet.

Downstream there is only one major dam; most of the action was upstream. Allow hours for exploration and inspection and musing. The dams are a study in themselves, the way the sticks are woven together, the way sedimentation by the creek gradually made them watertight, then filled in ponds, requiring new dams elsewhere. See if you can find where the beaver lived, in lodges or perhaps creek-bank burrows.

The insect community is outstanding, waterskates skating, mosquitoes whining, spiders lying in ambush. The varied thrush nests hereabouts, and possibly the golden eagle.

Classified as an ecotone, a transitional plant community, the forest features an unusual combination of Sitka spruce, here near its far-east limit, and Pacific silver fir, here near its closest approach to Seattle. Other conifers mingle, and old snags—one or more may have been sparpoles during the logging. Shrubs include fool's huckleberry, Alaska huckleberry, bearberry. Flowers include queen's cup and St. Olav's candlestick. Mosses, lichens, and liverworts are amazingly various and profuse. Please walk softly, stay on paths established since discovery of the valley in 1980, don't stomp the scene to death.

At a long ¾ mile from the East Side Road is Salamander Lake, 2140 feet, in the saddle where the creek heads. The loggers seem to have had a landing here. The beavers did themselves proud, damming a pond that caught the eye of the GS in the sky. In spring the pond is a mass of egg sacs of frogs and rough-skinned newts, who for months put on a gaudy show.

Round trip 1½ miles, allow 1½ years
High point 2140 feet, elevation gain 200 feet
All year (in winter the East Side Road may be impassable)

Issaquah-High Point Trail (Map-page 155)

Nigh onto a hundred years ago the railroad was completed from Issaquah eastward to Snoqualmie Falls and beyond. A decade ago the tracks were ripped up and grass began to grow. Happily, in obedience to a law that required it to maintain a non-freeway (non-I-90) connection between Issaquah and Preston, the state Highway Department purchased the grade; in its own sweet time it will fully obey the law by constructing a foot-horse-bicycle path that will be a link in King County's Issaquah-North Bend Trail. In the interim the stretch from Issaquah to High Point is a splendid walk from either end; sidetrips climb Grand Ridge to grand vistas, drop to the creek to see the six species of salmon that swim by toward spawning grounds, and cross under I-90 to Tradition Plateau.

To start from Issaquah, leave I-90 on Exit 17 and almost immediately turn east on Gilman Boulevard (old Highway 10) to Boehm's Candy Shop; park somewhere near, elevation 100 feet. If coming by Metro 210, walk to this point via Sunset, 3rd Avenue, Creek Way, and a footbridge.

To start from High Point, leave I-90 on Exit 20, turn left, and park in the wide space left of the road to Preston, elevation 450 feet. Begin on the gated bridge over Issaquah Creek.

From Issaquah, after stocking up at Boehm's, walk Gilman to the deadend at Liberty Lanes, a bowling alley, and continue on a path squeezed between the freeway fence and East Fork Issaquah Creek, the greatest salmon-spawning stream so near Seattle. (Come to Issaquah for Salmon Days, the first weekend in October.) Cross under thundering concrete of I-90 and climb the grassy bank to the railroad grade at a scant ¾ mile from the candy; from here, at 250 feet, the timber trestle spanned the valley to the Issaquah Switchback.

Turn east and lolligag leisurely 2¼ miles east, passing creeks in cool ravines, artifacts of an old coal mine, and in spring about a hundred species of madly blooming flowers. In winter watch for kingfishers and herons and eagles and whatever else on two wings or four feet that fancies dead fish.

Round trip from Issaquah 6 miles, allow 4 hours
High point 450 feet, elevation gain 350 feet
All year
Bus: Metro 210 to Issaquah or High Point

The basic walk has infinite variations and embellishments. From the High Point end, for example, there is no elevation gain and the lack of obstructions makes the stroll eminently suitable for toddlers and seniors.

Though the state Highway Department obliterated most of the railroad grade eastward, narrow old Preston Way—much of it none other than the Sunset Highway of the 1920s—is a pleasant stroll, so little traveled and mostly so removed from I-90 as to seem to be still **in** the 1920s. At 3 miles from the High Point interchange is the village of Preston and a Metro 210 stop. A delightful hike for non-autoists is to take the bus to Preston and walk back the 6 miles to the 210 stop in downtown Issaquah.

For sidetrips and loops in sequence from the Issaquah end:

#1. Immediately upon hitting the rail grade turn left, past one of the two most enormous erratics known in the Alps, a chunk of granite that Canada ought to

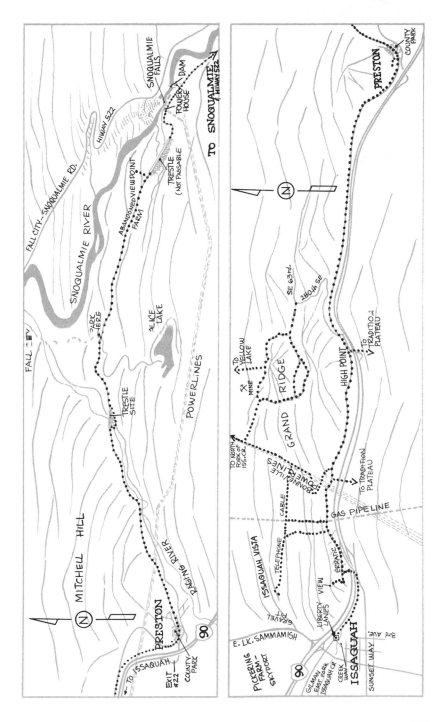

Nurse stump on Grand Ridge trail

bill us for. Go off the grade onto the freeway cut and contour to views of the Little Town of Issaquah, the Pickering Farm where sailplanes soar and parachutes drift.

#2. At ⅓ mile turn steeply uphill on an obscure woods road through old gravel pits. At 525 feet the road tops out on the glacial-lake delta-plateau. At ⅓ mile from the railroad is a T with a telephone-cable road. Turn left to an enormous clearing, preparation for ultimate expansion of the Lakeside Gravel Mine. Continue some ½ mile to the brink, Issaquah Vista, the area's finest views of Issaquah, Squak Plain, Pickering Farm, Issaquah Skyport, sailplanes, and Lake Sammamish.

#3. At a scant 1 mile note, below, a crossing of the creek by I-90. Descend near a freeway fence to the creek, follow the animal migration route under the concrete roof, and connect to the Waterworks Trail (see Issaquah Watershed) for a loop back to town.

#4. At the swath of the Northwest Natural Gas Pipeline, climb to the East Sammamish Plateau Trail (which see).

#5. At 1 mile turn uphill on a woods road that switchbacks through coal mine artifacts, up to the Bonneville powerline, and ultimately to the brink at 700 feet, with views over East Fork Issaquah Creek to West Tiger and Squak. The powerline service road leads north to intersect the telephone-cable road, which connects to the gas line. There also are connections to the Hour Trail (which see).

#6. Walk the High Point interchange under I-90 and loop back to Issaquah via Tradition Lake.

Grand Ridge-the Hour Trail (Map-page 155)

Cedars and firs and hemlocks so big one wonders they weren't logged in olden days—until one goggles at olden-day stumps. An exuberance of vine maple and salmonberry and devils club. Creeks and swamps. Tracks of—maybe meetings with—deer and coyote and bear. A deep experience of the insides of a second-growth wildland at lowland's edge, suburbia's edge.

Leave I-90 on Exit 20, turn north to Preston Way, and drive east to 280 Drive SE. Turn steeply uphill ¾ mile. Where the road turns sharp east and is signed SE 63, "Private Road, Dead End," park on the shoulder, elevation 880 feet.

Take the obvious, unmarked horse trail along the fence into the woods. Cross a nice creek and ascend its lush valley ½ mile to a Y. Here are the two ends of the Hour Trail, so called because on horseback it is 1 hour all the way around from the Black Nugget Stables.

For short up-and-back walks, take either fork. For the loop, also take either. The clockwise, more moral for the right-handed majority, will be here described.

Ascend a vale to a ridge crest, a glory of alder forest, and a Y; go either way, it doesn't matter, both are wild and nice and they rejoin in ½ (right) and ¾ (left) mile, at 1½ (about) miles from the road.

Gently descending slopes of Grand Ridge northward, the path enters confusion. If that is your pleasure, and you have plenty of maps and Boehm's Alpine Candy in your pack, and the day is young and bright, keep taking lefts; you'll find routes to the Bonneville powerline (see Issaquah-High Point Trail) and the Black Nugget Road (see East Lake Sammamish Plateau Trail).

To approximate the horse's hour, keep taking rights. Thus you will stay on public land in superb forest, swing into and out from a marvelous creek that drains to North Fork Issaquah Creek, and maintain a safe distance from houses below. After about ½ mile near residences the trail joins the route up from Canyon Creek (see Yellow Lake-Reynolds Mine-Hour Trail) and curves around a steep and rocky slope above the gulch of another North Fork tributary. A final scant 1 mile completes the Hour Trail—this leg, with windows through big firs to Snoqualmie Valley and the Cascades, is the most outer-scenic.

Round trip 4 miles, allow 3 hours
High point 1100 feet, elevation gain 600 feet
All year

Preston-Snoqualmie Falls Trail (Map-page 155)

On the Fourth of July of 1890 Daniel Gilman celebrated completion of his railroad from Seattle to Woodinville to Issaquah (then called "Gilman," as was only just) to Snoqualmie Falls by running an excursion train to the falls. The line, later that year completed to Salal Prairie, east of North Bend, was successful for a time, hauling coal to Seattle and serving a farmland whose prosperity is suggested by the fact the trains killed 198 farm animals in a single year. However, in the 1920s passenger service was discontinued and several decades later the Northern Pacific, by then the owner, stopped the trains altogether. Using Forward Thrust funds, King County Parks acquired the right-of-way and in 1982 will formally open a hiking-biking-horse (no machines) trail from Preston partway to Snoqualmie Falls (to the Lake Alice Road). Cool forests and splashing creeks, flowers and birds and views, and peace, all are here, on short strolls and long rambles.

Leave I-90 on Exit 22 (Fall City-Preston) and drive the short bit north to Preston County Park, elevation 500 feet.

Walk by the community building and up a path to the railway grade and turn right. Beyond a few houses the mood becomes totally woodsy-secluded. Now and then glimpse barns and houses down by the Raging River. Pass a fine wild creek with a path to the cool babble, and a powerline swath with a path inviting a long exploration up slopes of Mitchell Hill—also ascended by ancient woods road become game trails. At 2 miles a picturesque timber trestle used to span the Raging River valley. The railroad perversely sold it for salvage and hikers thus must backtrack from the vista point, descend a detour trail to the highway, follow it downvalley, and switchback up to the (former) far end of the trestle.

Back on grade, the trail bends east, passing a window to the Raging River quarry, then leaves the Raging for the Snoqualmie. At the old Fall City Siding the way crosses the Lake Alice county road (alternate start for a walk) 380 feet. Remember, only the right-of-way is public; logging has savaged much of the once-lush second-growth forest and for a stretch there now are homes and barking dogs. However, wildness resumes, tangled gorges are crossed on fills and trestles, a powerline-horse path is passed that leads to miles of roaming on Lake Alice plateau. Watch for an old farm, the foundation of the house hidden on the right by a tall hedge, the barn and fields sloping down left.

At 5 miles a long, high trestle spans a deep gorge. A few steps before it is a knoll on the left, logged in the 1970s; find an overgrown logging track out to the brink and splendid views over valley pastures to the white tumult of Snoqualmie Falls, Big Si towering in the background.

A final 1 mile cannot be done until the airy trestle, an architectural treasure, is planked and guardrailed. Beyond, the grade slices along the rock wall of the falls scarp. A scramble-path plummets to the Snoqualmie River at the base of the falls. (Beware!) A perilous brink gives straight-down looks to the plunge basin. (Watch it!) Beyond a Puget Power installation the grade reaches Highway 522, 400 feet—an alternate start for the hike as far as the airy trestle and the route of the Metro 210.

For description of the route continuing east to Niblock Spur and the Puget Sound Railroad Historical Museum, the town of Snoqualmie (known until Gilman's railroad arrived as the "Hop Farm"), headquarters of the steam trains of the Snoqualmie Valley Railroad (the spirit of Daniel Gilman lives!), and North Bend, see **Footsore 2.**

Round trip to airy trestle 10 miles, allow 6 hours
High point 500 feet, elevation gain 300 feet
All year
Bus: Metro 210 to Preston or Snoqualmie

Snoqualmie Falls and Mount Si

Cedar River Park in Renton

CEDAR RIVER

Which river of the Seattle area is the most frequently used by the most people? No, not the Green-Duwamish, nor the Snoqualmie. It's the one that runs through the mains, gushes from the faucets, of all the south portion of the city and of neighboring communities served by Seattle City Water. It's the one that folks swim in and sailboat and hydroplane on as it flows through Lakes Washington and Union to Puget Sound.

Which river flowing from the Cascades is the shortest, recreationally speaking? The one that Seattle City Water, still smarting from the scandal of the hushed-up typhoid epidemic of the Alaska-Yukon-Pacific Exposition, locks up tight at Landsburg, permitting the purity eastward to the Cascade Crest to be sullied only by deer, fish, ducks, and loggers.

Despite truncation, the Cedar provides many miles of pleasant walking in and near the city, some on bus lines. Eventually, when the watershed management is changed from "closed" to "regulated," hundreds more miles of trails can be built on south slopes of the Issaquah Alps and on front peaks of the Cascades.

USGS maps: Mercer Island, Renton, Maple Valley, Black Diamond, Hobart

Cedar River Trail (Map-page 163)

A trail from Lake Washington eastward through Renton and Maple Valley to the Cascade front. A connection via Beacon Ridge to downtown Seattle and the Puget Sound Trail. Another up Lake Washington to May Creek, Coal Creek, Issaquah Alps, and Bellevue. A second link to the Alps via Walsh Lake. Routes south along Big Soos Creek to Auburn, along the railroad past Lake Wilderness to Black Diamond and Green River Gorge. Loops within loops... The Cedar River Trail is planned as a key arterial in the ultimate Urban Trails System of King County. Meanwhile it offers a variety of walks, short to long, in city park and country jungle. And always there is the river.

Lake Washington to Cedar River Park

In this age when Growth is coming to be seen as not worth it if it adds only flesh, no spirit, many a community is engaged in a quest for identity, a search for soul. Renton found part of its soul right in the heart of town—the Cedar River—and built a splendid trail where citizens can walk and jog close to home, and where visitors can learn what Renton is all about.

Drive Logan Avenue North from the city center north past Renton Stadium to the entry of Boeing Renton Plant. Turn left on North 6 Street, signed "Cedar River Trail," and proceed to a deadend at Lake Washington, elevation less than 25 feet.

A Boeing fence unnecessarily blocks access to the absolute mouth, a few feet distant, but doesn't shut off views to Mercer Island, Beacon Ridge, Queen Anne Hill, and another element of Renton's soul (if the city would lift up its eyes), Cougar Mountain.

The wide trail—blacktop, then cinders—parallels the channelized river in lawns amid new-planted trees and shrubs. The water floats fleets of ducks and gulls; thickets shelter flitter-birds. On every side are big tin pots sicklied o'er with the pale cast of watercolor — Boeing jets built on the trail side of the river and trundled across a bridge to Renton Airport to make maiden flights from which they never return because the field is too short for jets to land.

Listening to the thundering present, ponder the wild past. Primevally, the Black River drained from the lake hereabouts and flowed close beneath the steep slopes of Beacon Ridge to join the Green River; on the way, somewhere in the middle of the plain that until recently became part of the lake during the rainy season, the Black was joined by the Cedar River, which later was diverted into Lake Washington.

Note the future opportunity — the Seattle City Light powerlines descending Beacon Ridge, the potential link to Seattle and the Puget Sound Trail.

The park lane passes Renton Stadium, crosses under Logan Avenue, and goes by a massive pier of the long-gone railroad bridge to Renton Senior Center. The path enters a residential section, crosses under Williams Avenue, Wells Avenue, and Bronson Way to Renton Public Library — which bridges the river!

Past the baseball field, by the swimming pool, cross the street and go under the railroad and Highway 405 to Cedar River Park, mainly noted for Carco Theater. Here the river debouches from Maple Valley onto the Renton Plain, part of the Big Valley. At 1¾ miles from the lake, Stoneway Concrete presently halts pleasant progress.

Round trip 3½ miles, allow 2 hours
High point 25-odd feet, insignificant elevation gain
All year
Bus: many Metro lines to downtown Renton, 110 to Renton Library

Cedar River Park to Maplewood Golf Course

Renton plans to extend its trail to the golf course, 4½ miles from the lake. Sidewalks already follow Maple Valley Highway most of the distance. However, one hopes the official trail will be on the other side of the river — quieter, greener.

Drive Highway 169 (signed "Enumclaw") from Renton under the railroad and Highway 405 to Carco Theater-Cedar River Park. Park on the west edge, elevation 25 feet.

Ascend the embankment to the railroad, cross the bridge over the Cedar, and at the junction turn left, leaving the Big Valley for Maple Valley. Industry and cars are quickly left behind. The rusty, silent rails cut the foot of the valley wall, green and rugged and wild for 350 steep feet.

The best part starts at 1 mile from the junction, just past a gaudy cliff of sedimentary strata. Go off onto a river terrace once inhabited, now quiet fields lined by tall poplars and great cottonwoods. Mountains of lilacs, a juniper 50 feet tall, and blossoms of garden escapes recall vanished homes. A plank bridge, closed to vehicles, crosses the river at SE 5 Street to this joyous spot one hopes is owned by the public, held for a park. At ⅓ mile as the tracks go (past a swamp and lily pond), and ½ mile as the river runs, railroad bridge #1 makes a logical turnaround.

Round trip 3 miles, allow 1½ hours
Bus: Metro 110 to Renton Library

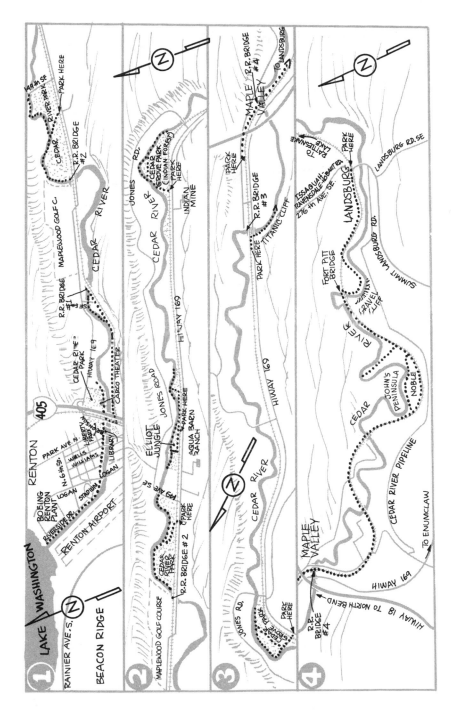

CEDAR RIVER

Maplewood Golf Course to Maple Valley Junction

The bad news for a hiker is that folks hereabouts are so tired of fishermen tromping through their petunias and agitating their dogs that they've fenced, posted, signed, and almost totally privatized the Cedar, both along the Maple Valley Highway and on Jones Road, across the river. The so-so news is that the railroad tracks continue straight through, but are mostly beside the noisy highway, rarely by the river. The good news is that King County Parks owns several large, undeveloped chunks of floodplain and floodway fields and forests where vehicles and guns are prohibited but feet can romp as they please.

Note: The walker will see many new dikes and rejoice at the thought of easy strolling. But the news on dikes is between so-so and bad: most are accessible only via private property that is devoutly defended; when you manage to get on one, it generally ends quickly and usually has no connection to trail or gravel bar. However, this isn't **always** the case...

Maplewood Wildwood

At railroad bridge #2 commences a gloryland of an old farm acquired by King County Parks.

Drive Maple Valley Highway a long ⅓ mile east from bridge #2 at the end of Maplewood Golf Course. Note on the right a two-storey, mossy-roofed, white farmhouse (very handsome). Just beyond, on the left, spot a gate barring a lane out into the field. Parking space for several cars, elevation 75 feet.

The entry lane winds to the river through fields that grow only grass, broom, tansy, and hellberry—toured by hawks, so something lives there, scurrying around in the weeds. The width of the fields so softens highway noise that the river readily drowns it out. From the far bank steeply rises a 325-foot wildwood wall. Peace.

The lane turns downstream on a short stretch of dike to a place where the state Department of Fisheries annually, October-November, installs a weir in the river to divert spawning sockeye salmon to a holding pond where eggs can be stripped—part of the Cedar River Enhancement Program, which has been so successful that in spawning months a person can hardly see the river bottom for the big red fish—and can hardly take a step along the banks without stirring up a gang of ducks, herons, gulls, and other fishers.

The downstream way enters a forest distinguished by monster cottonwoods; sidetrails lead out on gravel bars. Across the river are a magic grotto where a creek falls free into the green, and a tall wall of sandstones and shales with a seam of coal at the foot. In low water one can wade...

The upstream way prowls through more cottonwoods to a river meadow with a look across the water to a sand wall pocked by swallow holes.

Round trip (upstream and down) 2½ miles, allow 2 hours

Elliot Jungle

This chunk of King County parkland runs along 1 mile of river—with just about zero easy walking. However, you can't beat it for privacy.

Drive a long ⅓ mile east from the entrance to Aqua Barn Ranch and spot a wide turnout on the north side of the highway, at the railroad's Mile 16.

Walk the tracks back west toward Aqua Barn, looking for a chance to bust

Cedar River near Maple Valley

through the snowberry and wild rose (a colorful duet in winter fruit) to the cottonwoods, onward to the river.

Then walk the tracks south. Beside a highway turnout take the old road-path over a field, down to an ancient gravel mine, and to the river.

Round trip both ways 2 miles, allow 2 hours

Indian Forest

Just east of a sprawl of buildings occupied by Advanced Roofing System, on the site of the old Indian Mine, park on a wide turnout on the north side of the highway.

Find a gated woods road into the columnar cottonwood, to a dike that runs ½ mile upstream. Paths continue on, steadily more obscure. Between railroad and river lie nearly a square halfmile of floodway sloughs and floodplain forest, a wild tangle, a grandeur.

Round trip 2 miles, allow 2 hours

Titanic Cliff

From railroad bridge #3 to Maple Valley Junction the houses are too frequent and the river and highway too adjacent to please the walker. However, the Titanic Cliff cannot be ignored.

Just before reaching #3 from the Renton direction spot a tiny road going off right. Follow it to the river and park, elevation 275 feet.

A riprap bulwark keeps the Cedar from undermining Titanic Cliff. Stroll ⅓ mile to the foot of the neckbending wall, naked and terrific and 200 feet to the impossible top. Goggle and retreat, because just beyond is the gulch that drains Lake Desire-Shady Lake-Otter Lake-Peterson Lake, and it surely is a wild magnificence, but you could sink into the ook and nevermore be seen. However, if that fate can be avoided a pathless mile of jungle awaits exploration.

Round trip ¾ mile, allow ½ hour

Maple Valley to Landsburg

Now for something completely different—wild river flowing through lonesome wildwoods, beside gravel bars to delight and under gravel cliffs to astound.

The railroad distance from Maple Valley Junction to Landsburg is 5½ miles, a nice distance for an easy day's round trip. Park near the rail line, elevation 343 feet, and hit the tracks.

However, since the best of the trip is near Landsburg, the description will start at that end. Drive Issaquah-Hobart-Ravensdale Road 3 miles south of Hobart to the Landsburg Bridge over the Cedar River. Park near the railroad tracks, elevation 560 feet.

Fisherfeet have beaten a trackside path for 1 mile, and paths every few yards to overlooks of dippers and ducks, mossy nooks among the maples, and bars fit for a picnic. On the survey in early October there were a gull or heron on

Abandoned tracks near Black Diamond

every boulder, squadrons of ducks patrolling the avenue, raptors circling above, and backwaters and pools were so full of sockeye salmon you could walk across and never get your feet wet.

Where the tracks enter an odd little valley, turn off left on a riverside path that follows the river around a big loop for ⅔ mile (the railroad gets to the end in ⅓ mile). Enchantment! Virgin-looking forests of big old conifers. Groves of giant cottonwoods. Understory of vine maple in flame (in October). Camps on the gravel. And across the river the Great Gravel Cliff rising an absolutely vertical 150 feet from the gulls. At first the way follows what appears to be an ancient railroad grade, then becomes a mixture of mucky woods roads and fishing paths, a bit brushy at spots. The segment concludes at a bridge signed "Fort Pitt Bridge Works Pittsburg PA 1908." It's a beauty and absolutely must be placed on the State Historical Register before B-N scraps it to earn a dirty nickel.

Across the bridge are more deep-shadowed wildwoods, more sunny bars, but this area is suggested as the turnaround for a neat little walk from Landsburg—what with all the sidetrips you easily could be the whole day at it, especially if the kids have anything to say.

Houses now enter the scene, across the river. And there are no more easy paths to the water. However, at a long ½ mile (as the rails run) from the first bridge is the Cedar River's most exciting moment, a pair of peninsula ridges enclosed by giant meanders. John's Peninsula, on the far side, only can be explored when the river is wadable. The one on the near side, a skinny ridge with cliffy walls, is strictly for the doughty.

Though wildwoods continue, excitement diminishes. At ⅓ mile from the start of the peninsulas is a crossing of SE 248 Street, entry to the hideaway homes of Noble. Public feet are pretty well excluded from the river. The survey stopped at the second bridge, 1 mile from the Noble road, because suburbia thickened. However, the long 2 miles (with two more bridges worth photographing) to Maple Valley Junction would be superb prelude to the climax upstream.

Round trip (with a few sidetrips) from Landsburg to first bridge 4 miles, allow 3 hours
High point 560 feet, minor elevation gain
Round trip (no sidetrips) from Maple Valley Junction to Landsburg 11 miles, allow 6 hours
Elevation gain 300 feet

Landsburg to Rattlesnake Lake

At Landsburg begins the Seattle City Water Cedar River Watershed, in all the 25 air miles to the Cascade Crest closed to humans except a handful of city employees, several scientists, and a few thousand loggers, each of whom signs a pledge to drop chainsaw and run to the Sanikan in case of need, in order not to pollute the city's chlorinated, fluoridated, limed, asbestosized, pipe-eating water.

Rumor hath it that phantom hikers have walked the railroad east from Landsburg by the light of the moon, risking deportation to a penal colony, but meeting no vocal objection except from the coyotes. At something like a dozen miles from Landsburg they are said to have been picked up by confederates lurking in the shadow of Rattlesnake Ledge. They are reported to have been enraptured by the river, the railroad bridges, sites of vanished logging villages and sawmills, the broad delta flat of Green Valley, the creeks flowing from Taylor and Rattlesnake Mountains and nameless peaks of the Cascade front. However, these phantom scofflaws must stand condemned by society. If you want to enter the watershed, do it legally—with chainsaw in hand.

Maple Valley to Black Diamond (Map-page 171)

A river, a lake, a marsh, and lots of second-growth woods. And a coal mine that as recently as 1977 was operating, a poignant memory of the past and glimpse of the future. All this on a low-key tour along the bed of the abandoned branchline railroad on the height of land between the Cedar and Green Rivers.

The tour is suggested as two hikes from Lake Wilderness. Take a short walk one way to the Cedar River, a longer one the other way to Black Diamond, or both.

Drive the Maple Valley-Black Diamond Road, Highway 169, south 1¼ miles from the Maple Valley bridge over the Cedar, turn right on Witte Road ¾ mile, then left and left again ½ mile to Lake Wilderness County Park, 475 feet.

From the parking lot walk north and east around the shore, through the University of Washington Continuing Education Center, and up woods to the rail grade on the wilder side of the non-wilderness lake, featuring a fine grove of large firs. Do not hasten, take time to savor the best part of the whole trip—the interlacing trails in this 40-acre arboretum of native plants.

For Maple Valley turn left, in woods and then pastures, under and along highways and across the Seattle City Water pipeline. In 2½ miles is the gap where the railroad used to cross the Cedar River. The bridge now gone, transfer to the adjacent highway bridge to join the active (well, still with rails in place) railroad at Maple Valley Junction. Along the way are views of McDonald and the many peaks of Tiger.

For Black Diamond turn right and, mostly in woodland, passing large marshes, briefly near the highway but usually some distance off, follow the grade 5 miles to the outskirts of Black Diamond and the end of the line. Along the way are looks out to McDonald and Rainier, looks in to creatures of wildwoods and wildmarshes. At the end is the big show: heaps of old cinders from the spontaneous combustion of waste rock, now being quarried for road ballast, running tracks, and building blocks; antique machinery that in 1977 was busy washing and sorting the black diamonds precisely as was done here 50 and 80 years ago. Next time OPEC gives our tail a twist, look for the machinery to crank up one more time.

Round trips 5½ and 10 miles, allow 3 and 6 hours
High point 600 feet, negligible elevation gain
All year

Lake Youngs (Map-page 171)

The fourth-largest lake in lowland King County never will have swimming beaches or hydroplane races, rarely will even be seen by the general public—except from Tiger Mountain. Yet most everybody in the southern half

Lake Wilderness from the old railroad grade

of Seattle takes a bath in it now and then because this is the holding reservoir between the Cedar River and Seattle City Water mains. The shores are not for recreation, nor are the forests that cover three-quarters of the 4 square miles of Lake Youngs Reservation. But outside the fence...

The 9-mile Fence Run is popular with joggers, who don't mind traffic on arterials. Walkers and horse-riders prefer the several stretches where the fence deviates from roads, followed by a broad city-owned trail closed to vehicles, the way quiet and delightful and deeply green—inside the fence because the city keeps it that way, outside because the folks who live there do so specifically to be neighbors to a wildland.

Trailheads are readily recognizable by the white gates barring vehicles, happily signed NO MOTORCYCLES, and citing the statute under which razzers may be fined, jailed, and exiled to Lower Slobbovia.

CEDAR RIVER

Segment 1
Drive SE Petrovitsky Road (the main Renton-Maple Valley speedway) to where Old Petrovitsky Road loops off to the fence, elevation 500 feet.

Walk east. This is the least-wild segment since it several times jogs to hit the road. However, these are brief intrusions in 1¼ miles of peace.

Round trip 2½ miles, allow 1½ hours
High point 670 feet, elevation gain 400 feet

Segment 2
From the same place walk west. How quiet it is. How green. How tall is the green. The way drops to a bog aromatic with Labrador tea, then climbs a bit and goes onward to hit 148 Avenue SE in ¾ mile.

Round trip 1½ miles, allow 1 hour
High point 533 feet, elevation gain 150 feet

Segment 3
Drive 148 Avenue SE to SE 216 Street, elevation 500 feet.

The trail drops a bit to a wetland—note the large Sitka spruce. Then the large hemlock. Admire the tall Douglas fir. In October be dazzled by the vine maple. Humanity intrudes, but gently, at a creek dammed to be a duck pond. At a fence corner look sharp for a glimpse of the lake near its overflow outlet, Little Soos Creek. The 1¼ woodland miles end at SE 224 Street.

Round trip 2½ miles, allow 1½ hours
High point 500 feet, elevation gain 150 feet

Segment 4
Drive SE 224 Street east from the vale of Little Soos to still another gated lane, elevation 555 feet.

The ups and downs, zigs and zags, proceed 1½ miles to SE 184 Avenue.

Round trip 3 miles, allow 2 hours
High point 600 feet, elevation gain 250 feet

Round trip all segments 9½ miles, allow 6 hours
Elevation gain 950 feet
All year
Bus: Metro 155 to 140th and Petrovitsky

Discussions are underway that could culminate in a trail, similar to the Tolt Pipeline Trail, from Landsburg to Lake Youngs. From the lake to Maple Valley the pipeline mainly is beside Petrovitsky Road, excellent for horses and perhaps bicycles, less interesting to walkers. From Maple Valley to Landsburg the pipeline is mostly in wildwoods, sociable and peaceful strolling, though not as exciting as the railroad (see Cedar River Trail).

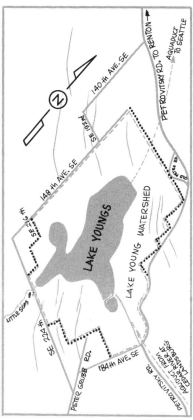

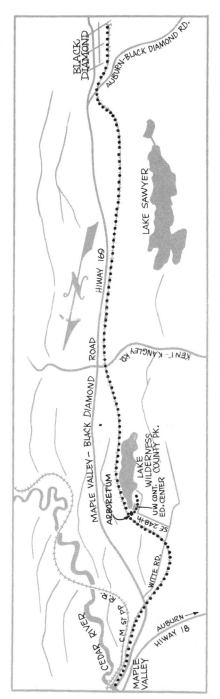

Mount Rainier and industrial plants along Green River

DUWAMISH-GREEN RIVER

Old Coyote, he was always up to something. He taunted the volcanoes into erupting at him, then stole the godly fire and gave it to the Indians, who before that had to eat their fish raw and shiver all winter. He bought an extra-long drink of water from the Frog People and while at it dug a sneaky hole in the dam and the water ran out into rivers and lakes and everybody forever after could drink as much as they liked without paying.

The White River used to flow from Mount Rainier to Elliott Bay, joined at Auburn by the Green and at Tukwila by the Black, which on its way from Lake Washington was joined by the Cedar. Old Coyote, he thought it would be fun for Tacoma to be able to say that Rainier (Tahoma) was none of Seattle's business, so he dug a ditch that carried the White south to the Puyallup. Next he decided Kirkland might enjoy being a port for ocean-going ships, so he dug a ditch west from Lake Washington that in a WHOOSH lowered it to the level of Lake Union and dried up the Black River. Finally, Old Coyote felt Jim Ellis would need help in cleaning up Lake Washington, so he diverted the Cedar up the abandoned channel of the Black to give the lake a regular supply of pure mountain water. Old Coyote, he was a crazy guy.

He played these pranks in the Big Valley, the heavy-throbbing (if frenetically, erratically) heart of Puget Sound City. Where once the Big River flowed from the Big Glacier, trying to escape to the ocean, freeways now rumble over the unfruited plain and thunder up the valley walls, jets rocket cloudward like so many Flash Gordons headed for Mongo and plummet forestward like so many gaudy baubles seeking Christmas trees. A person may pray for Someone to stop the music, so everybody would have to stay where they are and settle down to grow corn.

Year by year the industry and commerce of Puget Sound City bulldoze south from Elliott Bay and north from Commencement Bay. The brown-black alluvium that once fed Tacoma and Seattle garden truck and dairy products now produces a crop of concrete and prefab and fumes and noise. Sadder still, in a way, is the no man's land between two worlds, surveyors' ribbons fluttering in the thistle and tansy.

Oddly, the Duwamish-Green never has been as footful as now. Hastening toward self-destruction by starvation if not irradiation, the folks hereabouts seem hotter to walk than ever. Nerves, perhaps.

Upstream past the heavy industry, the Duwamish-Green is almost continuously walkable, through the Big Valley to Auburn. The Green Valley that there diverges eastward presently has a discouraging density of mean-it fences and hostile signs. But soon begins the Green River Gorge, a book in itself. Further, plans are in works (or at least in heads) to hook together a continuous Duwamish-Green Trail—and link it at Auburn to the White River Trail to make Rainier, again, Seattle's business.

The walking (not the logging) presently stops at the Cascade front. Mt. McDonald gives broad panoramas over the lowlands, and long looks up the Green toward Howard Hanson Dam, whose reservoir waters Tacoma (thus keeping feet out of the mountain valley, lest they foul the waters) and holds back floods (thus permitting the Big Valley to switch from corn to warehouses).

USGS maps: Renton, Maple Valley, Black Diamond, Cumberland, Eagle Gorge, Auburn, Des Moines, Poverty Bay

Duwamish River-Green River Trail (Map-page 175)

The Tacoma-to-Tahoma Trail leads (or could, see **Footsore 4**) from Commencement Bay up the Puyallup River to The Mountain. So, too, a Seattle-to-Rainier Trail could go from saltwater to glaciers, ascending the route the glacier waters ran when Europeans arrived. To do the trip a hiker need only transfer at Auburn from the Green River to the White and continue as described in the next chapter.

The subject here is the riverbank way from Elliott Bay to the mouth of the Green Valley. The parks departments of King County and Big Valley cities have a plan for a continuous river trail from Tukwila to Auburn, and much already exists. In the blue-sky department is a scheme to extend the route up the Green Valley through the Green River Gorge to the mountain front. The following description is partly a prospectus for the dream, but a wonderful lot of it is already real, awaiting your feet (bicycles, rollerskates, rubber raft, canoe...).

Duwamish Waterway

Seattle's old waterfront, from the Skidroad north, is now used mostly for play; fish and chips are much bigger business than cargo. The working waterfront, the world port, is mainly up the river—though because of all the dredgings and straightenings and widenings the map properly calls the first 6 miles the Duwamish "Waterway." The docks and ships are here and also the Northwest's densest concentration of heavy industry.

Strictly speaking, there's no room for pedestrians lacking hardhats. Rarely seen, here, are the rucksack and camera. Yet the esthetics of the scene, the (if you'll excuse the expression) ecology, and the history have an appeal. Some of America's industrial machinery is as mammothly powerful and youthfully brawling as Carl Sandburg's Chicago. And some is as rickety as the England of "I'm aw right Jack." One gapes at how much mass of Earth was manhandled to shape such complex engines. One smiles at oddments of ramshackle houseboats, rotten little vessels, and beautiful junk.

Though the Port of Seattle has not marked a self-guiding industry trail complete with worker-watching blinds, the walker who is properly brash (and cautious) can poke about on industrial streets and find lanes to the water. Generally one will be assumed to have legitimate business. Especially if wearing a hardhat.

Duwamish River: Mt. Motorcycle, Allentown, Foster Golf Course, Black River, Fort Dent

After 6 miles of "Waterway" the blue lane on the map narrows and begins meandering and the map hails the transformation by calling it Duwamish "River." The widening spaces between industrial plants contain houses and surviving farms and even parks.

A fitting start for a walk is the ascent of Mt. Motorcycle, elevation 110 feet, what's left of a larger mass of basalt after the quarrying.

Park on the shoulder of S 115 Street where it turns east from E Marginal Way, elevation 15 feet. Following paths of Yamahas and Kawasakis, scale the beetling crags to the bald summit. Gaze north along the industrial Duwamish to the tall orange cranes of the working waterfront, towers of downtown Seattle. Gaze south along the tree-lined Duwamish to Rainier. Listen to the roar of I-5

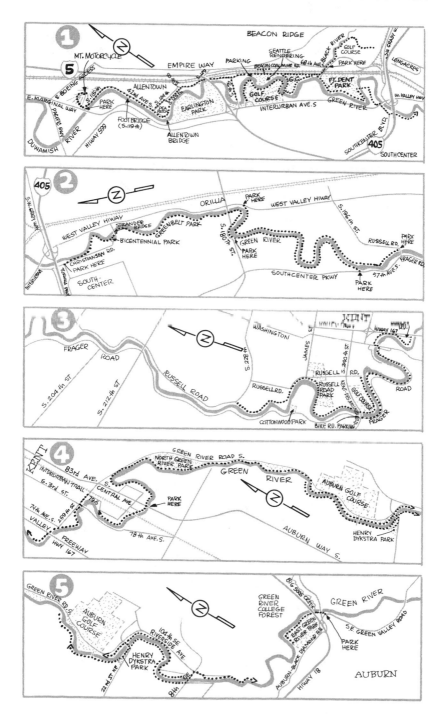

Footbridge over the Duwamish River at South 119th Street

and Old 99 and 599 and 509 and 181 and 900 and, in the sky, Route 666, where the beasts bellow as they plummet into forests of Riverton Heights.

Round trip up Mt. Motorcycle ½ mile, elevation gain 100 feet

Descended from the mount, walk out on the Marginal Way bridge to look down to (but not through) olive-green waters flowing between steep mud "beaches" (the river here is still tidal). Ponder rotten pilings and bulkheads, slimy riprap, and ducks. This is the quintessentially multiply-mangled lowland stream of the Inland Sea, with all sorts of history to absorb if your skin is thin enough. The marvel is how much swimming, and floating, and diving, and flying continues.

Now commences the upstream march. It must be on the road shoulder, not on the "beach" nor in the hellberry thickets, but views are continuous up and down the water corridor framed by tall trees and across to homes of folks whose lives are quieter and more rural than out in the suburbs, and cheaper too, and with more wildlife to watch while reclining at ease in a backyard hammock.

A happy spot is South 119, where a footbridge provides vistas of wooded, tangled banks, miles and miles of critter refuges. Think canoe.

Allentown Bridge gives more views of the water, and of fisherpeople, some of whom slide cockleshells in the river and paddle about. One ponders the possibility (and wisdom) of a rubber-raft float to Elliott Bay.

Allentown (King County) Pea Patch announces the farming frontier and permits riverbank walking. In September, hereabouts, a hiker can bag a dozen ears of corn for a dollar.

One way from Marginal Way to Allentown 1¼ miles

The river route continues on 124 Street. (A jog onto 125th gives a view across the water to a mudbank from which fishers wade, and also their dogs, and also cows from the glebe.) The river road changes to 50 Place South, passes under viaducts of South 129 Street and I-5 and becomes single-lane. Off right, 56 Avenue deadends at rooted pilings that once supported a bridge. The river road ends at the Seattle Rendering Works, where overaged fish, horses, dogs, and cats are made into soap or something. A bit short of the plant entrance is a turnout-parking area beside the railroad tracks. In the next stretch the pedestrian has no competition from automobiles — but must keep an eye to the rear, lest Amtrak's annual passenger train comes through.

The rendering works flavor the start of the walk. Across the tracks is a fine, large marsh, splendidly birdy, vividly contrasting with the violence of Empire Way, high above on the side of Beacon Ridge. The marsh also is accessible via South 129 Street viaduct and little old Beacon Coal Mine Road South, a 19th century survival worth a visit in its own right.

Across the river sprawls a greensward that would gratify a Whig lord of the reign of good Queen Anne, and one considers taking up golf in order to walk there. Then the greensward is beside the tracks and paths through the hellberries tell that non-golfers **do** walk there, at such season and hours and in such weather as not to disturb the game. In fact, canny non-golfers have beaten paths down from fairways to mudbars to compete with herons and gulls and ducks. A graceful footbridge connects the two sections of the Foster Golf

Duwamish River

Course (public links, City of Tukwila), which with all the meanders runs along nearly 2 miles of riverbank—the greenest and quietest remnant of the Old Duwamish. A walker who chooses stormy days is unlikely to meet another soul. Stick to the weedy rough. Perhaps carry an old golf club.

"Black River Junction," says the railroad sign. And there it is, by golly, a drainage ditch beneath the bridges.

One way from Allentown to Black River 2 miles, not counting sidetrips

The Black River is a mandatory sidetrip, but only in good skulking season. Again, don't interfere with the game.

Immediately south of the 68 Avenue South bridge over the Black, park at King County G-1 Pump Plant, elevation 20 feet. Walk service road the short bit down the Black to a Truly Momentous Spot, the confluence of the Black River and the Green River, the start (and end) of the Duwamish River.

Visualize the Green when it also contained the White. And the Black when it carried the waters of Cedar River, Sammamish River, May Creek, Coal Creek, Kelsey Creek, Juanita Creek, Thornton Creek, and dozens more. See the Indian canoes paddling up the Black on their all-water way to Issaquah. And the barges carrying coals from Newcastle to Elliott Bay.

Return to the pump plant, where floodplain floodwaters are pumped from the Black (now merely the sum of local oozings) into the Green, lest the dikes meant to keep the Green from overwhelming the plain prevent oozings from draining off the plain. Slink under or around the fence onto the greensward and creep along the edge of the Black River Jungle, a grand huge wetland wildland between golf course and the foot of Beacon Ridge. Look for a hundred species of birds and a dozen mammals, including some that go bump in the night. Imagine steamboats. Or the **African Queen.**

Round trip up and down the Black River 2½ miles

For non-skulkers a public park offers an alternate approach to the confluence. Southcenter Boulevard crosses Interurban Avenue to the bridge over the Green River, the entry to Fort Dent, mainly consisting of soccer, football, and baseball fields. Hellberry hedges line the river, but paths trench through for close looks at birds and canoes, and the wild condos on the far bank. Views of the Black River Quarry eating into Beacon Ridge are impressive. A pleasant path circles a Storm Water Retention Pond, signed "Ducks Only." Canada geese picket on the lawns, simply furious. The path connects to the mouth of the Black River.

Loop trip around Fort Dent 1½ miles

Green River: Tukwila, Southcenter, dikes, farm roads
A scant ¾ mile from Fort Dent via Southcenter Boulevard, at the Highway 405 bridge over the Green, begins the most-walked river path in the region, thronged on nice noons by lunchers from offices and factories and shops of Southcenter, busy morning and night with joggers and bicyclists. (Much of the

way there is a cinder lane for the one, blacktop for the other.)

The northernmost parking spot is near the intersection of Christiansen Road and Tukwila Parkway, just south of the 405 bridge. A path briefly goes beside the road, then swings away to lawns and cottonwood groves and picnic tables of an office park. At Strander Boulevard the path enters Tukwila's Bicentennial Park, featuring a little log-cabin picnic shelter. It crosses under Strander bridge and becomes Tukwila's Christiansen Greenbelt Park. Trees have been planted that in time will augment the shade of old cottonwoods. The storage pond behind King County Pump Station No. 17 gives the ducks good feeding, though not such feeding as the tens of thousands who wintered or nested in the vast marshes that became Southcenter, when the area also fed Seattleites a cornucopia of garden truck.

The southernmost parking spot for this stretch is at the end of the formal public trail at South 180 Street, just across the river from Orillia.

One way from Highway 405 to Orillia 2 miles

Green River at Southcenter

Kayaking in the Green River near Kent

The story now is of dikes with broad gravel paths atop. All are gated against vehicles. Some are signed "No Motor Vehicles" or "Don't Block the Gate." Others say "Private Property No Trespassing"—but one notes well-beaten paths around the gates. The fact is, a quiet and respectful walker isn't going to be hollered at and chased away. Actually, there's hardly anybody to do any hollering. Southcenter is advancing steadily southward but has only begun to establish bridgeheads beyond Orillia. Meanwhile, the farmers have mostly sold out to the developers and moved away; the rich alluvium grows naught but lonesome fields of tansy and thistle and mullein.

It's rather sad walking. But always the river flows. And the views grow across the Big Valley to the Issaquah Alps, back north to Beacon Ridge, and south to Rainier. Here and there fields still grow food. But the main crop is surveyor stakes, ribbons fluttering in the breeze.

Both sides of the river are diked. On the true left bank the northernmost parking is at South 180 Street, the southernmost where the dike meets Frager Road. On the true right bank the northern start is the divergence of the dike from West Valley Road, the southern end where the dike meets Russell Road. Other accesses are apparent as one drives by.

One way on true left bank from South 180 to Frager Road 2 miles
One way on true right bank from West Valley Road to Russell Road 2¼ miles

Ah, the fragrance of fresh manure. Ah, the cows, the corn, the berries and cukes, sagging barns and paint-flaking farmhouses, America the rural beautiful, not yet subdivided for warehouses and office parks, still feeding our American faces without benefit of long-distance trucking, refrigeration, and irrigation. For how long? Don't ask. Enjoy. Also enjoy wild greenery of the nearby valley wall, reminder of the Really Big River. When will the glacier return? Whisper a prayer.

Nevertheless, the river route here is better bicycling and canoeing than walking because roads closely follow both banks most of the way. Old-timey farm lanes, narrow and twisty (all the better for the Grand Prix, my dears) go past the Al Davis Farms and horses of the O C Corral.

The true left bank is the route of Frager Road, which passes many pastoral sideroads and Kent's Cottonwood Grove Park to the start-end of the Kent Bikeway Loop at Kent-Des Moines Road. An underpass permits safe biking-walking under the road to a resumption of Frager, which continues to South Washington Street. Here turn north, over the river, to the true right, and then right on Hawley Road, which shortly deadends. The bike trail continues close beside Highway 167, under whose bridge it passes. When the bikeway turns left, keep right on the dike to a junction with the Interurban Trail at a railroad bridge. A jog up onto South 259 Street finishes this segment at 79 Avenue.

The route along the true right bank follows Russell Road past a square mile of Boeing in a part and continues by farms until Russell swings away from the river. Dike carries on, briefly rejoining Russell but diverging again, meandering around a golf course, underpassing the Kent-Des Moines Road, ending where Russell deadends at the river.

One way on true left (then right) bank from Frager Road to 79 Avenue in Kent 7 miles
One way on true right bank from Russell Road to deadend 4½ miles

Green River: Kent

Having come so far it is meet to pause and see what's happened to river and valley. As for the channelization, nothing has changed since Mt. Motorcycle. But the water... It's transparent! Not absolutely clear, yet boulders in the bed can be seen. There are rapids! And mudbanks of the tidal area have yielded to fine sand. The elevation of downtown Kent is something like 35 feet.

Often called "Kent Valley," at this point the Big Valley is more than 2 miles wide from forested scarp to scarp, largely occupied by freeways, increasingly less farmed as speculators-assessors force out agrarians, more and more industrial-crummy. The city is a mixture of the industrial and commercial, old-residential detached houses with yards, newer-residential trailer courts with communal asphalt, and new-new semi-high-rise condos that face their little lawns and minute decks out upon the Green River where wild things swim and fly, creep and crawl, and across to farms.

Where Central Way South crosses the Green River to become Auburn Way is a handy start from parking lots and bus stops.

The downstream way hooks up via 79 Avenue to South 259 Street (see above), an important link for hikers coming from Seattle. However, though an old red barn and a line of poplars are nostalgic, and coveys of quail explode and the horses are friendly, and in summer the crickets sing, the most interesting feature is the across-the-river row of AAA Auto Wrecking, Bison Auto Wrecking, Rock's ditto and finally Budget.

Upstream is very different, the most popular stroll in Kent. The dike from Central Way bridge passes Oakhurst Office Park, then apartments and other residences, some with canoes or truck innertubes for going right out in the middle of the kingfishers and the fish and the twitterbirds. The "No Trespassing" signs don't really mean it, if you're afoot and polite and quiet and behave like you live there.

At the tip of a great meander the apartment houses end, and so does the dike, at Green River Road South—exactly where North Green River Park begins.

One-way from South Central downstream to South 259 Street 1 mile
One-way from South Central upstream to Green River Road 1 mile

Green River: North Green River (King County) Park

Lovelier and lovelier, happier and happier, so the river grows as it progresses backward and upward toward where it came from, trailing clouds of glory. The ultimate total subdivision of the Big Valley is now at least half out of mind because the river runs close against the wild wall of forests, as much as 400 feet tall. And in all this stretch there's nary a NO TRESPASSING sign along the river because the public has it all, miles and miles. And the public loves it—the green wilderness above, the green river below, the green farms (now) beyond, and the country lane following the stream.

A person can walk the whole way beside the road, bothered by few cars, delighted by cottonwood colonnades, fields across the river (or the road), and friendly fishermen and cows. The best walking, though, is where the road cuts

Footbridge across the Green River at Auburn's Dykstra Park

off meanders and paths lead out to quiet bars for sunning, wading, picnicking.

The northernmost access is Kent; from Central Way South, South 259 Street turns off east and becomes Green River Road South. At the end of the apartment houses an unmarked path leads out across a field, drops to an old woods road, and spins off many paths to the river, where a low-water route along banks and bars connects south again to Green River Road.

Parking shoulders and paths are everywhere south. It's holiday country. At Auburn City Limits begins, on the valley-wall side of the road, the Auburn Golf Course. On the river side of the road a path proceeds around the meander bend into a stupendous grove of cottonwoods with a parking area and picnic grounds and a sandy bar where children swim and wade. A delightful footbridge crosses the river to Henry Dykstra Park. This belongs to the City of Auburn, and so, a change of venue.

One-way from Kent's South 259 Street to Auburn's Dykstra Park 3¾ miles

Green River: Auburn

From Auburn Way follow 22 Street East to Henry Dykstra Park and the start of four riverside walks. Two begin across the footbridge in the cottonwoods. Walk north to Kent, as described above. Walk south via 104 Avenue SE to the Green River College forest, described below.

Two are on the city side of the river. Throughout this section of town large signs announce, "Riverbanks closed to motorized vehicles and horses." What they mean to say is the dikes are freely open to human feet.

The dike gate on the north side of Dykstra Park is gated but not posted. Lovely homes and landscaped yards line the way on the left, and the river is just below on the right. Houses yield to a playfield, then a farm. In 1½ miles the dike ends at Auburn city limits. The river, and the open fields, continue to Kent.

The dike gate on the south side of the park says "Public Fishing Easement." Be quiet and polite as you walk beside the lovely homes and yards 1½ miles to the 8 Street NE bridge over the river. Cross and continue to the Green Valley mouth.

One-way north from Dykstra Park to dike's end 1½ miles
One-way south to 8 Street NE 1½ miles

Green Valley Mouth (Map - page 185)

The Green River flows in the Big Valley, which is called the Green River Valley. But it's not. The true Green Valley starts at the exit of the Green River Gorge in Flaming Geyser State Park and extends some 7 air miles (more as the water flows) downstream, in all this distance having a cozy floodplain barely ½ mile wide at most. Only then does the river leave its homey little valley to wander out in alien vastness. A riverside walk samples the transition zone.

Drive east from Auburn on Highway 18 and just before its bridge over the Green River exit onto the Black Diamond Road. Shortly, just before this road's bridge over the river, turn right on the Green Valley Road and immediately pull off left on the fishermen's riverside parking area, elevation 75 feet.

Walk downstream under the Black Diamond road bridge, the railroad bridge, and the Highway 18 bridge. Across the Green is the mouth of Big Soos Creek, babbling from the woods. Sit on the gravel bar and admire. Note that the river, at journey's start a pea soup, by Kent become a clouded limeade, now is clean and clear elixir—well, not for drinking, but inviting hot feet.

A broad dike guards the park-like pasture to the left. In low water the hiker will prefer to leave its road and walk gravel-sand bars, the river's width away from the wild valley wall rising from streambank willow-cottonwood to Douglas fir of the Green River College forest (which see). Swallows flit, ducks quack, hawks circle, and pterodactyl-like herons implausibly lift off from the gravel and ponderously flop to treetops. Remote, peaceful, idyllic.

The dike road swings left and fades out in woodland paths between a murky pond and the river. At 1 mile from the start a path reaches railroad tracks. Along them to the right a short bit another road leads right to another dike. More pastures and birds and river. Now, as the Green River is entering the Big Valley, snuggling the foot of the bluff for comfort, houses begin and the hike is best ended, 2 miles from the start.

For another experience of the Green Valley mouth, cross the railroad bridge at Big Soos Creek and explore the other side of the river, as described in Green River College Forest, below.

One way from Green Valley Road to start of houses 2 miles

Green Valley

The 10-odd (river) miles from the mouth of Green Valley upstream to the mouth of Green River Gorge are as cozily old-barn, broad-pasture, prettily-

Steelhead fishing in Green River

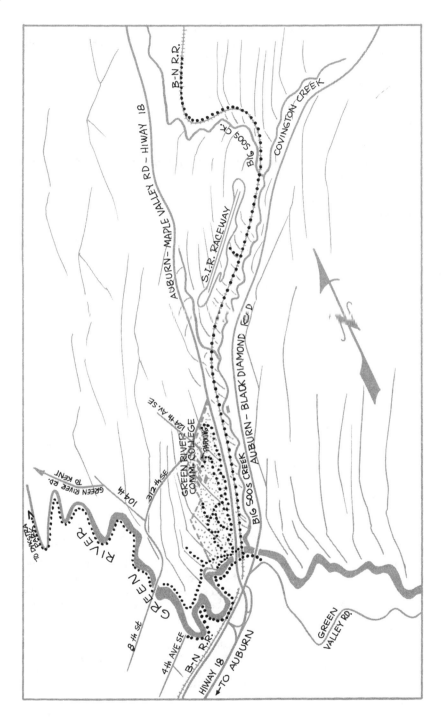

pastoral as can still be found so near the core of Puget Sound City, and may the program to preserve agriculture in places other than California and the Columbia Plateau hold this vale sacred. When (if) the food is saved, then will be time enough to add recreation of the footing sort—a river trail to savor the cows and the corn, the enclosing valley walls (green, green, very green), and the water (green, too) wherein the fish swim.

For now, a person wishing to visit the fish-bird freeway will find the Green Valley Road assiduously and sternly fenced and signed, except...Except at several inconspicuous signs, "Public Fishing Easement," or "Please Use Stiles and Trails Provided." There **are** ways to the river, at least three. The explorer might find lanes to the dikes, the gravel bars, the dippers and herons.

Watch this space.

One-way trip 1-50 miles, allow minutes or days
High point 75 feet
All year
Bus: Metro 123 to S 115th; 154 to Allentown; 150 to Fort Dent; 123, 145, 150, 155 and others to Southcenter; 150 to West Valley Road, Kent, and Auburn

Interurban Trail (Map-page 187)

Accentuate the positive. This is a grand stroll for railroad buffs, closely paralleling busy-working lines. And little wild pockets amazingly survive—drainage-ditch creeks a-swimming with ducks, bits of unfilled marsh with blackbirds a-nesting, pastures of as-yet-unsubdivided pastures with cows a-grazing. And views are long up, down, and across the Big Valley, from one forested bluff to the other.

Eliminate the negative. Forget if you can, as the energy crisis deepens, that until killed by the Pacific Highway in the late 1920s, for a quarter-century the Seattle-Tacoma Interurban Railway offered quick and convenient transit.

The old interurban right-of-way, owned by Puget Power and used for power-transmission lines, is now—through granting of permission by the company—a public trail. The city of Kent opened 6½ miles in 1972 and King County another 8½ miles in 1979, completing a route from Tukwila on the north to the Pierce County line.

Unlike locals, who can walk or bicycle from home, outsiders have a parking problem—unless they come by bus. For that reason, though there are many possible starting points for many different trips, a sample introductory trip is suggested which goes south from Orillia and returns.

From Highway 405 at Tukwila, exit to the West Valley Road, then exit from that to the quaint little old hamlet of Orillia on S 180 Street (formerly a train station was a major reason for its existence) and park, elevation 50 feet. At the east town edge find the sign, "Interurban Trail Park. Open Daylight Hours. Bicycles Horses Hiking." Here, 1½ miles from the north end of the trail at Tukwila, begins the Kent-maintained segment.

Closely paralleling the Union Pacific and Burlington-Northern tracks, the trail proceeds south, now in heavy industry, now in surviving fields. At 3¾ miles (from Tukwila) the way crosses 212 Street (parking possible) and at 5½ miles, just after crossing under Highway 167, is James Street, site of a Metro Park and

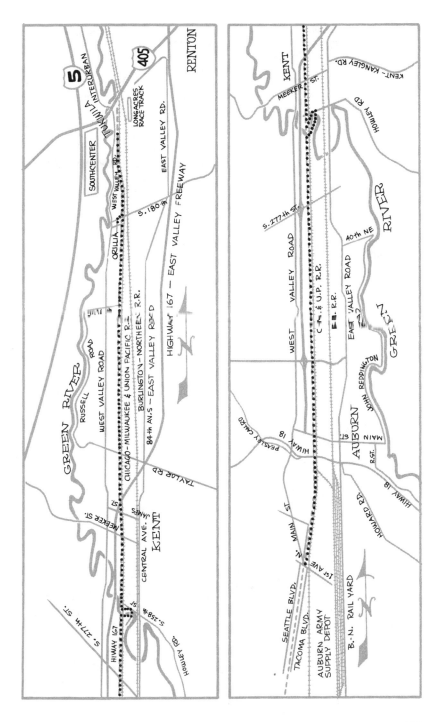

Ride Lot that provides good access. At 6½ miles is Meeker Street, in Kent; the downtown section east a block has handy parking and buses. At just short of 7 miles it is necessary to jog east to cross the Green River on a highway bridge (the interurban bridge long gone), then west to resume the trail. Parking is possible here. This is suggested as the turnaround for the sample introduction; enjoy the Green River, which has been nearby but unseen the whole way south.

At 277 Street, 8 miles, the Kent stretch of trail ends; parking is chancy here, though hikers can park at a distance with ease and walk the street to intersect trail. At 10 miles is Auburn's NW 15 Street, a crossing under freeways, and after a quiet rural stretch, increased industry. At 11 miles is the center of Auburn, with plentiful parking plus bus service. Having all the way to here followed a perfect north-south line, now the route turns southwest, passing Algona at 13 miles, Pacific at 14, and at 15 miles leaving the Big Valley and swinging west into the valley of Jovita Creek, ending (for now) at the county line.

Sample round trip (Orillia-Green River) 11 miles, allow 7 hours
High point 50 feet, no elevation gain
All year
Bus: Metro 150 to Kent

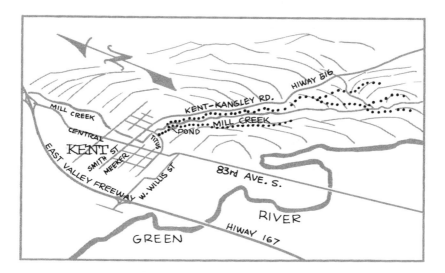

Mill Creek Canyon (Map-page 188)

A green gash in the valley wall of the Green River, creek and forest preserved in a Kent city park the full length of the canyon from its beginning as a mere gulch in the upland down to its debouchment on the broad floodplain of the Big Valley.

From Central Avenue on the east side of Kent turn east on Smith Street (Highway 516, the Kent-Kangley Road) to a stoplight. Turn south a few feet on East Titus Street (confusingly signed "Jason Avenue" at the light) to the parking area of 100-acre Mill Creek Park, elevation 50 feet.

Walk past the vehicle-barring gate to a fish pond. From here a trail leads up each side of the creek. The one on the right (south) presently doesn't extend to the canyon head, though trail-building by volunteer youth groups continues. For an introductory tour, take the north-side trail.

Now down by the creek, deep in shadowed depths, now slicing the steep sidehill, now high on the rim, the path proceeds up a valley in forest of fine big cottonwoods and other hardwoods, then mixed forest with cedars, hemlocks, firs, and a rich understory and groundcover. Street noises fade. Glimpses of houses on the rim diminish. Feeder trails join from surrounding neighborhoods, sidetrails drop to creekside sitting spots, the main trail splits and unites, in a scant 2 miles ending at a paved road on the rim. However, by taking a sidetrail down to the creek and up to the opposite rim, the trip can be extended a bit to a field (and private property) where Mill Creek is no longer in a wide wild canyon but a narrow gulch fouled with farmers' garbage.

Round trip 4 miles, allow 3 hours
High point 350 feet, elevation gain 300 feet
All year
Bus: Metro 150 to Kent, walk to park

Mill Creek in Kent

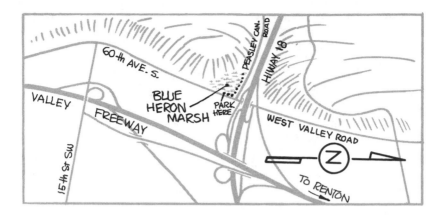

Blue Heron Marsh (Map-page 190)

The walk is short. But plan to spend a long while, especially if you come in spring when flowers are fresh and songs loud and herons active. Look for some 88 species of birds, 16 mammals, 7 reptiles-amphibians—and all within the roar of Peasley Canyon's and the Big Valley's freeways!

From Highway 18 go off south on Highway 181, the West Valley Road, at the canyon mouth. Drive south past the first stoplight and turn west into the parking area, elevation 75 feet.

The central significance of the place is that it survives. Along about 1968 a few folks noticed that the abandoned 1950s gravel mine had evolved into a marsh and been adopted by some two dozen pairs of great blue herons as a place to hatch and raise their young. Scarcely had the heronry—one of only two known in urban King County—been discovered when the Highway Department announced plans to obliterate it. However, citizens showed the engineers how they could build their highway to let the marsh be and so the herons survive, as of 1981.

Maintained by the Rainier and other chapters of the Audubon Society, the trail rounds the marsh in willow woods and ascends Peasley Canyon to an end close by Mill Creek in remains of an old orchard. The herons come to the nests in January or so and in February can be observed rebuilding the nests. The youngsters hatch out by April and leave on their own in July or so. During this period herons can be observed going off in morning to hunt fish, frogs, snakes, rodents, and insects.

Round trip 1 mile, allow hours
High point 100 feet, elevation gain 25 feet
All year

Green River College Forest (Map-page 185)

On the high promontory whose bluffs fall west to the Big Valley, south to the Green Valley, and east to Big Soos valley lie the Green River College campus and its contiguous forest, used in an instructional program that encompasses the planting and tending and harvesting of trees and the building and

Hiking trail on the Green River College campus

maintenance of trails. Totalling 4 miles in length, the trails sample big-tree wildlands on the plateau, forests on the steep bluffs, tanglewoods of birdland sloughs along the Green River.

In various conditions of repair from plush to overgrown, the trails offer a range of experiences from leisurely strolls to sweating, face-scratched, shin-bruised, boot-soaked adventures. While crashing around in the brush it's hard to believe the campus and forest cover only some 300 acres. The trails are unsigned, no problem when spending a full day poking about to see where every path goes. The following route is reasonably easy to stay on and samples the varied terrains and ecosystems.

Drive Highway 18 east from Auburn and shortly after crossing the Green River turn left and follow signs to the main campus entrance, elevation 425 feet. Buy an all-day parking permit at a vending machine and park in any unreserved space. Find one of the many locator maps placed around campus and with its help navigate to the street bounding the south edge of the campus. Spot an unmarked trail into the forest. (There are four other trailheads on the campus edge and if you're lucky enough to get lost you may return on any of them.)

Walk over a bridge and by a pond .07 mile to a junction and turn right. Continue in superb big-tree forest, ignore a sidetrail right at .23 mile, descend from the plateau to a bench, and enter a 1976 clearcut and plantation, these obscuring a junction at .11 mile with a sidetrail right—the return trail of the route described here. Beyond the clearcut the way drops in lush forest .23 mile to the Green River. The path upstream leads to Big Soos Creek (which see). Turn downstream. A path on the bank attracts, but deadends at a slough; backtrack to a more inland route deep in cottonwood-willow floodplain woods. In .41 mile is an obscure junction beside a slough; note aluminum bits on an alder and a middling-large cedar a few feet along the uphill trail to the right, the route of the return.

But first make a sidetrip downstream, out of the college trail system, onto an old road with more forest, many ways to riverside, gravel bars, duck-watching spots, and ending at a public streetend (104 Avenue SE) in about 1¼ miles. As a sidetrip off the sidetrip, partway along take an old road-trail that climbs ½ mile to the top of the bluff and a broad view out to Auburn and the Big Valley.

Returning from this 3½-mile round-trip sidetrip, at Obscure Junction go uphill on the most spectacular part of the trail system. The way ascends steeply in stupendous forest to the crest of a spur ridge between two tanglewood gulfs, then completes the climb (.37 mile from the river) to a junction on the bluff rim. Turn right on the flat, then angle across the sidehill, drop to a ravine and creek crossing, climb to the clearcut, and in .40 mile rejoin the trail of the trip start. Return .41 mile to the campus edge.

Or say the hell with it. You may not be able to follow these directions anyhow as new trail-clearing or logging confuse the issue. The best idea is to devote a whole day and plan to get lost.

Suggested round trip 5¾ miles (college forest loop 2¼ miles, off-campus sidetrip 3½ miles), allow 4 hours
High point 425 feet, elevation gain 800 feet
All year
Bus: Metro 153 to campus (weekdays only); 150 to Auburn, walk Main, M, and 8 Streets 1½ miles to Green River bridge, on far side walk the bank road to campus

Big Soos Creek (Map-page 185)

The Three Bears came in assorted sizes. So do these three valleys that also live together: the rather-too-broad-for-comfort Big Valley, the spacious but not overpowering Green Valley, and the petite (despite the name) Big Soos valley, partly miniaturized pastures, partly cool-shadowy wildwoods through which babbles the creek.

Farther upstream, north of Lake Meridian, King County owns and is holding for future recreational development 6 miles of Big Soos; farming continues there for the interim and barbed wire makes walking messy. But never mind, the best part of the valley, the Big Soos Gorge, is the route of a railroad that hobos and locals have walked since the tracks were laid.

Park as for Green Valley Mouth (which see), elevation 75 feet. Walk downstream to the railroad bridge over the Green River. (Alternatively, especially if coming by bus, approach from Green River College, which see.) Most of the way paralleled by a walker-horse path, the tracks pass cows in pastures, fish in a hatchery, and soon swing away from Highway 18 into quiet forest. Note: This is a mainline railway so keep a sharp lookout for speeding trains.

A deep, nameless tributary valley is crossed on fill. Then, out of sight but on Sundays not out of sound, is passed the Seattle International Raceway. Farms are left behind for a remote-feeling wildland. At a scant 3 miles the tracks cross Big Soos at its junction with Covington Creek, along whose valley is a woods road. A path to the creek gives a look at the handsome old fern-draped masonry arch of the Soos culvert; they don't build 'em like that anymore. Subsequent paths give further access to gravel bars and rapids.

At 4 miles the tracks return to farms, the gorge dwindles to a mere gully, and Jenkins Creek, larger than Big Soos, enters. A sand-cliff swallows' apartment house is the last sight to see before turning around. From here the tracks leave Soos for Jenkins Creek and proceed to points east in less interesting country.

Round trip 8 miles, allow 5 hours
High point 300 feet, elevation gain 225 feet
All year
Bus: see Green River College, Green River Mouth for two approaches

Green River Gorge (Map - pages 197, 201, 203)

For some 6 air miles, or 12 stream miles, the Green River flows in a narrow canyon whose walls rise as much as 300 feet, always steep and often vertical or overhanging. Its meanders are intrenched in solid rock, slicing through some 9000 feet of tilted strata of shale and sandstone, with interbedded coal seams and imbedded fossil imprints of shells and vegetation. From the mid-1960s proposal by Wolf Bauer for "a unique natural showcase of free-flowing wild river and primeval canyon" came the plan for a Green River Gorge Conservation Area now being implemented by the Washington State Parks and Recreation Commission. The long-range intent is to acquire, as funds become available, properties and/or easements the full length of the Gorge, ultimately totalling several thousand acres in public ownership.

Part of the grand plan is a trail from one end to the other, sometimes at river level, sometimes on the walls, sometimes on the rim. By following old woods roads and fishermen's paths and busting a certain amount of brush a determined hiker very possibly could manage the entire distance now.

In late summer and early fall, when Tacoma is drinking so much of the Green there is only enough water left in the river to float the fish, much longer hikes can be taken than are described here. Indeed, since the river can then sometimes be easily forded at some points, by getting wet feet (and perhaps knees) a water-level route conceivably could be walked the full 12 miles.

The trips herein are the merest introduction to glories of the Gorge. They are, first off, limited to those possible during the high-water season of (roughly) winter and spring. Second, only described are hikes in the official trail systems or on undeveloped but safe routes open to the public. By no means are all the secrets of the region revealed; any wily fisherman-trespasser would consider this the most meager of primers.

FLAMING GEYSER RECREATION AREA (MAP-PAGE 197)

At the downstream end of the gorge, where the bluffs, though still high and steep, retreat from the river, which thereafter flows over a floodplain ½ mile wide, is the site of an old resort now a state park with a full-fledged trail system.

East of Auburn, just before Highway 18 crosses the Green River, exit onto Auburn-Black Diamond Road and from that almost immediately exit right onto Green Valley Road. Drive 7 miles east to a Y and go right to the bridge over the river to the park. (Or, stay on the Auburn-Black Diamond Road to the Black Diamond-Enumclaw Road, follow it to 1 mile south of Black Diamond, turn west at the "Flaming Geyser" sign, and drive a scant 3 miles past Kummer to the bridge.) Parking is available at the park gates but the hikes are described here from a start at the far end of the park, 1¼ miles from the gate, elevation 225 feet.

Perimeter Loop, Hillside Trail and Riverbank Trail

Walk upriver from the picnic area parking lot past a series of concrete fish ponds. At the fence corner turn right up Christy Creek. Pass a pool bubbling with gas, the flow from a pipe ignited (sometimes) to form a flame 6-12 inches high. In 1911 a test hole probing coal seams was drilled 1403 feet down. At 900-1000 feet were showings of methane gas. In early days of the former private resort the "Geyser" was flaming many feet in the air; now it's pretty well pooped out.

Continue over a bridge and up the creek in mossy-ferny maple woods, the trail dividing and uniting, passing a bridge and stub trail to the gray mud of Bubbling Geyser. Up a short set of stairs and then again upstream, the main trail recrosses the creek and ascends the bluff and begins a long upsy-downsy contour along the sidehill in a green tangle of maple and cedar and alder and lichen and moss. Views (screened) down to the river. Sidepaths offer secluded nooks for lunch or rest or small adventures suitable for small folk. The way at length drops to the floodplain and road, the trail now a mowed strip (or strips) in pasture grass. Cross the road and walk out in the field to the park entry bridge. Turn right and follow the riverbank upstream to the picnic area, by sandy beaches, through patches of woods, meeting ducks and water ouzels, gulls and herons, and kayakers landing after voyages down the gorge.

Loop trip 3 miles, allow 2 hours
High point 425 feet, elevation gain 200 feet
All year

Gorge Outlet

Beginning as before, past the fence corner cross Christy Creek to a Y. Go straight on the right fork (the left quickly ends at the river) and then left (the right goes to the rim) up the old road-now-trail, climbing 100 feet above the river, contouring the sidehill, then dropping to a sandy flat in fine woods. The width of the floodplain dwindles to zero, the walls crowd the river, and as the trail enters the very gorge it ends. Admire the 100-foot cliff of stratified rock, the river cutting the base. In low water a hiker can round the corner and proceed into the gorge.

Round trip 1½ miles, allow 1 hour
High point 325 feet, elevation gain 200 feet

Green River in Flaming Geyser State Park

Gorge Rim

Beginning as before, at the Y just past Christy Creek go straight on the right fork, then immediately right again on a lesser road-trail which ascends to touch the Christy Creek trail and then veers left, climbing to the bluff top at 525 feet.

The inexperienced hiker should turn back here (or not start up at all). Canny navigators can proceed upvalley on woods roads along and near the gorge rim, consulting the map often, guessing right at the myriad junctions, backtracking when the guesses are wrong. This is all second-growth forest, lacking the lushness of the gorge depths, which can, however, be looked down into from a number of vantage points. Moreover, by persistent snooping one can find at least two paths slippery-sliding down into the wild gorge, visiting spots otherwise known only to kayakers.

In 3 easy-walking (if sometimes bewildered) miles the roads connect with the route to the river from the Black Diamond Bridge (which see).

Round trip 6 miles, allow 4 hours (or more for getting lost)
High point 525 feet, elevation gain 500 feet, not counting sidetrips down to river

Across the River and Into the Trees

Half the park is across the river, where trails are only now being developed from old mining and logging roads. If wild nature is a major attraction of the gorge area, so are memories of a long human past — mysterious ancient water pipes, collapsed buildings, roads dating from different eras, grades of logging railroads, and the like. Including old homesteads reverting to nature, as here.

To reach this part of the park, recross the river on the entry road, turn right, and in a scant ½ mile up the hill toward Kummer turn right off the Green Valley Road onto SE 354 Street. Descend to parking area on the valley floor, elevation 200 feet.

Pass the barn and keep left, crossing the green floodplain at the foot of the bluff. In ¼ mile pass a road-trail up the hillside; this is the exit of the loop trail noted below. At ½ mile are an old orchard and Y. Take the road-path straight ahead and downhill into woods. In a short bit is a Y. The right fork goes ¼ mile through forest to the river and a sandy beach for kiddies to safely wade, and a luscious pool of limeade for anybody to deliriously swim; a trail is planned downstream along the bank 1 mile, looping back to the parking area. The left fork goes a similar short way past a sagging structure and interesting coal-mine garbage to the river; a trail is planned upstream to the outlet of the gorge.

For the complete tour (as of late 1981), return to the many-fork junction in the orchard and take the path uphill, bending leftward and sidehilling downvalley, then dropping steeply to the entry road, reached ¼ mile from the parking area.

Complete (1981) tour 4 miles, allow 3 hours
High point 400 feet, elevation gain 200 feet

BLACK DIAMOND BRIDGE (MAP-PAGE 201)

The view of the gorge the best-known to the most people is that from the Black Diamond (or Kummer) Bridge. Though not officially developed, long-used walking routes exist. WARNING: Caving-in mine shafts make this one of the most dangerous areas of the gorge.

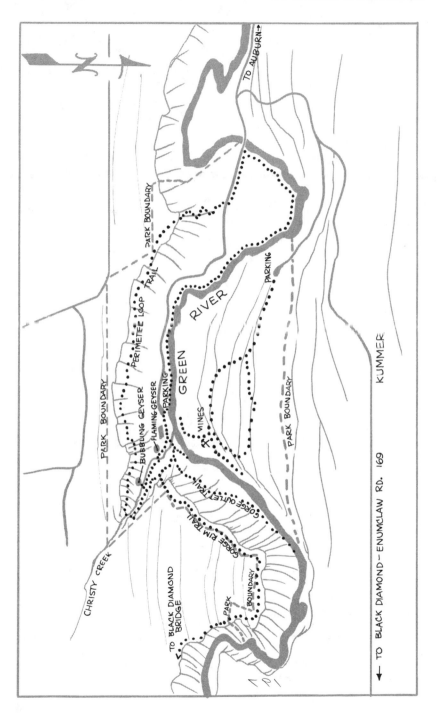

Green River Gorge near Black Diamond Bridge

(Note: South from the bridge is a Department of Natural Resources campground signed "Green River Gorge Camp and Picnic Area." This is a splendid forest with a dandy ¾-mile nature trail but has no connection to the gorge.)

Drive the Black Diamond-Enumclaw Road, Highway 169, south from Black Diamond 2½ miles to the bridge. Cross and start uphill and in ½ mile spot an unmarked woods road to the right. Drive it a long ¼ mile to a Y and park, elevation 557 feet.

Walk the right fork, by a gate, ¼ mile to the edge of a vast, growing-over gravel mine. By a concrete foundation, turn right on a grassy road into the woods. Soon pass greenery-swallowed relics of a coal mine at the end of a powerline. After a vista down to the river and upstream to the bridge, descend steeply to the river level and a Y. The left goes downstream a bit to end at a pile of fallen-down timbers of a mine structure. The right proceeds upstream on a lovely alder-cedar flat, becoming a rude fishermen's water-side route. Nearly

½ mile up the river, close to the bridge, is the high-water end of walking; at low water the route can be extended on and on along gravel bars.

Round trip 2 miles, allow 1½ hours
High point 557 feet, elevation gain 300 feet
All year

Driving by, one almost always sees cars parked on the shoulder north of the bridge. This is because a protected sidewalk on the bridge offers thrilling views of the vasty deeps. And also because a path from the bridge dives to the river, where it goes downstream about ½ mile and upstream to the foot of an impressive sandstone cliff. And in low water much farther, of course.

HANGING GARDENS (CEDAR GROVE POINT) (MAP-PAGE 201)
This block of public land extends along nearly 3 miles of the river on the north side, half that on the south. One short south-side walk is suggested to sample this large, presently-undeveloped area.

Drive Highway 169 south from the Black Diamond Bridge 1½ miles and turn east on the Enumclaw-Franklin Road. Curving north, at 2¼ miles, just past a big old borrowpit, note a meager road crossing, the left segment blocked by a deep ditch, a feeble defense against razzers. Park here, elevation 680 feet.

Walk the road into the woods, shortly reaching the chainlink fence of the Black Diamond Watershed. Follow the fence to where it turns right; at a Y there, take the right fork down into lush mixed forest. The road soon yields to a trail plummeting down the bluff, following the crest of a finger ridge around which the river makes a sharp intrenched-meander bend. The point is distinguished by a noble grove of big cedar trees. It also features a sandy beach at the tip directly across from the Hanging Gardens, a vertical wall from which jut ledges sprouting shrubby trees and (in season) gaudy splashes of flowers—a phenomenon not unusual in the gorge but rather especially nice here.

Round trip 1½ miles, allow 1 hour
High point 680 feet, elevation gain 250 feet
All year

GREEN RIVER GORGE RESORT (MAP-PAGE 201)
Adjoining the public Hanging Gardens area is the private Green River Gorge Resort, operated for more than half a century, offering picnicking, car-camping, walk-in camping beside the river, and trails. A fee (as of 1981, $2 for adults and less for others, a yearly pass $10) is charged for entrance to the trails. The fee is modest considering the way the operators are industriously and imaginatively enlarging the system of trails and campsites. Here, in the quintessential gorge of close-together sandstone walls, caves and clefts, buttresses and potholes, green pools and green wall-hangings, is the quintessential gorge trail, under and over waterfalls, close under and spookily over cliffs, into dark, green, dank corners.

From Highway 169 in Black Diamond turn east on the road signed "Green River Gorge" and drive 4 miles to the site of the old town of Franklin and the Franklin Bridge. (Alternatively, from Highway 169 at 1½ miles south of the Black Diamond Bridge take the Enumclaw-Franklin Road 4 miles to the bridge.) Park near the inn, elevation 580 feet.

Waterfalls into Green River at Green River Gorge Resort

Built in 1914, the bridge is signed "one legal load limit at a time," which adds interest to walking out for the gasper view down. For a similarly vertiginous perspective, enter the Duck Ponds area, find the Gorge Viewpoint Trail, and walk it uphill a short bit to a perilous-feeling overlook.

After dropping the trail fee in a box provided at the inn, descend the trail to a Y. To begin with the downstream route, turn left down a staircase-path over the brink of a waterfall to the river. There's too much to see to go fast and that's good; speed kills. Passing through dark clefts between huge mossy-green boulders, over slippery slabs by churning green pools of The Chute, under fern-and-moss cliffs where in season hikers can get a free shower from Rainbow Falls, the trail leads eventually, by a switchback up to the camp known as Hippieville (other camps of the Resort are Inner Earth and Tutville—ask the owners why) to the Smoking Fields, where noxious gases issue from dangerous old coal mines that smolder on.

To go upstream from the Y, turn right, in ¼ mile descending a staircase to walk-in camps on a forest flat by the river. This is a loop trail—but only at low water because at high water a stretch of several hundred feet requires knee-deep wading. At seasons when the trail so enters deep water, turn back to the camp area and take a straight-up path to the gorge rim, reached in a picnic area. From the upstream end of this area find the other end of the loop trail and descend spectacularly on staircases to the river and a T. The left fork goes downstream (the loop way) to a high-water end at a wonderful great cave. The right fork, a delight every step, proceeds to exposed coal seams and—it is claimed—all the way to the Cinnabar Mine.

Complete roundtrip all trails (1981) 6-8 miles, allow 4-6 hours
High point 580 feet, elevation gain 500 feet or 1000 or more
All year

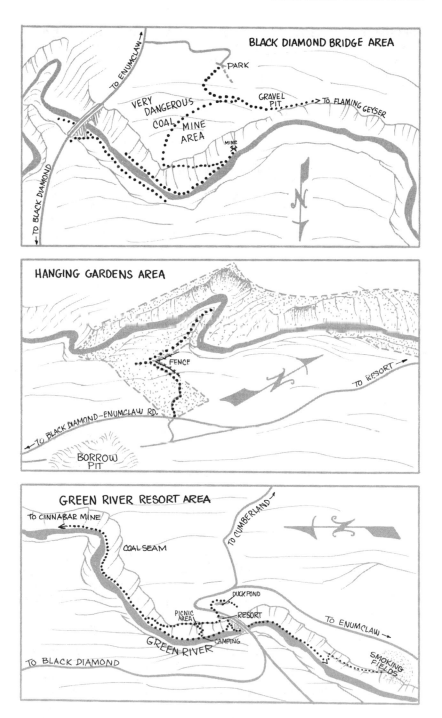

JELLUM SITE (BIG BOULDERS AND CINNABAR MINE) (MAP-PAGE 203)

Two undeveloped park areas are called the "Jellum Site." One is a magnificent spot for the special gorge sport of creeping through cracks between huge mossy boulders. The other is notable for relics of the ancient cinnabar (mercury) mine.

From the junction just uphill and east from Green River Gorge Resort, drive east on Green River Gorge Road ½ mile. At the top of a rise spot a woods road left barred by a white gate. Park here, 789 feet.

Walk the road (in private property but on a public easement) over a plateau in nice fir forest to a Y in a scant 1 mile.

For the bouldery place, go right a short bit to the bluff rim, down which the road sidehills to a broad bench, in ½ mile from the Y ending in a fir-grove camp, once the site of some complicated activity (mine-related?). From the bench a trail goes over the brink, instantly splitting in two pieces, left and right, the two ends of a loop demanding to be hiked in its entirety. It is, however, the left fork that leads directly to The Place, featuring one enormous boulder that has atop it 18-inch hemlocks whose roots reach 25 feet down the rock to find nutritious earth. Not so much a trail as a clambering route, the way proceeds downstream, dodging through clefts, passing under a great overhang sheltering a ramshackle cabin, crossing sandy beaches, to a high-water end ½ mile from Camp Flat.

Round trip 4 miles, allow 3 hours
High point 789 feet, elevation gain 200 feet
All year

For the mine, go left at the Y to ruins of an old shack on a jutting point, then follow the switchbacking road-trail down to mine garbage and timbers. From here a path drops to the mine mouth (collapsed) and the waste rock sloping to the river. Mine artifacts and cinnabar ore mixed with coal are interesting, and the bouldery river, and the forest, displaying one 8-foot cedar. But the scene for soft summer days is the great sprawl of sand dipping into the slow flow of river, a place that demands taking off shoes and rolling up pants and wading—if not taking it all off and thrashing around, crying "Evoe!"

Round trip from the Y 1 mile, allow 1 hour

Palmer Recreation Area (Map-page 203)

The Flaming Geyser Recreation Area celebrates the exit of Green River Gorge; the Palmer Recreation Area does so for the entrance, where the river issues from the Cascade front, passes the old coal-mining hamlet of Palmer, and plunges into its finest moments.

From the junction east of Green River Gorge Resort, drive Green River Gorge Road 2 miles to Cumberland (more old coal history here), turn north on Enumclaw-Cumberland-Kanaskat Road (history everywhere) a long 2 miles to outskirts of Palmer and enter the park, elevation 880 feet.

During the latest survey in late 1981, loud beasts were chewing up trees and bushes, making roads, preparing for the 1982 opening of one of the hottest

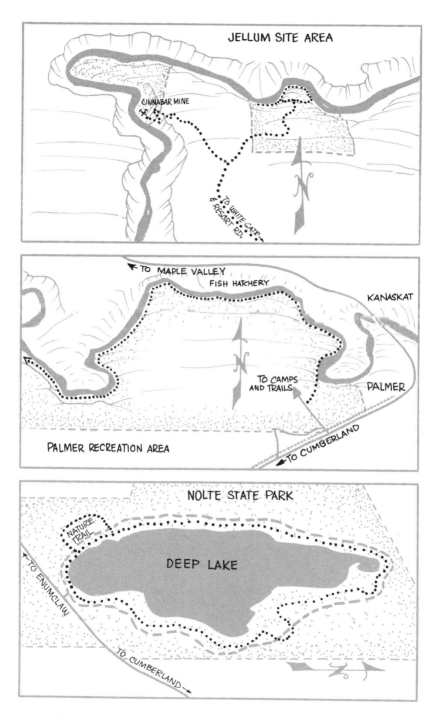

JELLUM SITE AREA

CINNABAR MINE

TO WHITE GATE RESORT RD.

N

TO MAPLE VALLEY
FISH HATCHERY

KANASKAT

TO CAMPS
AND TRAILS

PALMER

N

PALMER RECREATION AREA

TO CUMBERLAND

NOLTE STATE PARK

NATURE TRAIL

TO ENUMCLAW

DEEP LAKE

TO CUMBERLAND

N

outdoor recreation spots in the region. The initial batch of 50 campsites (another 100 planned) and 50 picnic sites would ensure that. But the river trail is what will enthrall the throngs.

Because the late-1981 revision is awkwardly timed, the surveyor can only say that within this park the walker will find, in 1982: the non-gorge Green River meandering around a large jut of floodplain-terrace, where amid willows and cottonwoods and ducks the surveyor first met a blossoming Easter lily; the start-of-gorge Green bending into a waterlane walled on one side (only) by cliff; a virgin forest of cedars up to 6 feet in diameter and firs and hemlocks not much less; the Gorge Entry, walls of rock and green on both sides of the Green.

Roundtrip of all trails probably 6-8 miles, allow 4-6 hours
High point 880 feet, elevation gain 600-odd feet
All year

NOLTE STATE PARK (DEEP LAKE) (MAP-PAGE 203)

Not in the gorge but nearby is 39-acre Deep Lake, owned by the Nolte family since 1883, operated as a private resort since 1913, and on her death in the late 1960s willed to the public by Minnie Nolte. Because during olden-day logging only the cream (the huge cedars) was skimmed, the forest of Douglas firs up to 6 feet in diameter feels virgin, giving a pristine quality to the quiet (no motorboats allowed) waters they ring.

From Cumberland (see the Palmer hike above) drive south 1 mile to the park, elevation 770 feet.

The trail loops 1 mile around the lake, through the big firs, plus 5-foot cedars and 3-foot cottonwoods, crosses the inlet, Deep Creek, passing a number of paths to the shore.

Loop and sidetrips 1½ miles, allow 1 hour
High point 770 feet, no elevation gain
All year

Mount McDonald (Map-page 205)

A supreme vantage for studying the geography of Puget Sound country. From the Cascade front between the Forbidden Valleys of the Cedar and Green Rivers, look across the upland sliced by the Green River Gorge to the Osceola Mudflow and The Mountain from which it gushed 5000 years ago. Look to the peninsula thrust of the Issaquah Alps touching shores of Lake Washington. See Seattle and the Olympics and smoke plumes rising from the pall customarily hiding Tacoma.

Drive Highway 169 south from Maple Valley 3 miles and turn east on SE 272 Street, signed "Ravensdale." In 2 miles is Georgetown, a grocery store, and a junction with the Hobart-Landsburg Road (an alternate access from I-90 via Issaquah). Continue straight east 1 mile to a Y and turn right on a road signed "Kanaskat." Proceed 3 miles, passing Lake Retreat and a Bonneville switching station (with a view of McDonald) to a dangerous Y. The right fork rises to a bridge over railroad tracks. Go left (straight) and in ¾ mile, at a deadend driveway signed "SE Courtney," park on the highway shoulder,

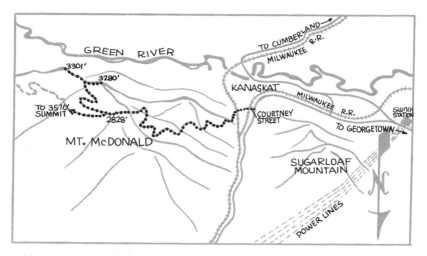

taking care not to block access to driveway or mailboxes. Elevation, 874 feet.

Walk up Courtney Street through the passel of barking dogs past where the railroad tracks were until the late 1970s. Turn left on a woods road to a gate, rarely open but bypassed by an outlaw track that lets four-wheelers as well as the motorcycles illegally razz.

The road climbs steadily in mixed forest, lesser spurs going off left and right. In ½ mile a window opens to pastures below and out to the Olympics and Rainier. At 1 mile is a waterfall-creek. As the road twists and turns around the mountain, the forest changes to young conifers, mostly hemlocks, and views commence over treetops and through them. At 3 miles, 2828 feet, is a Y where both forks are major. Go right, climbing. The views on this trip are cafeteria-like — something of this here, a bit of that there, never everything all at once. In this stretch are the best views north, down to the Cedar River and out to Taylor and Tiger and Squak and Cougar, as well as to Rattlesnake and Si, Baker and Index and Three Fingers.

In a final 1 mile, with a couple more switchbacks, the road reaches an open plateau atop McDonald Point, elevation 3280 feet. Here, formerly the site of a fire lookout, is a great monster of a TV repeater powered by a noisy diesel generator. Avoid the fumes and enjoy the grand view off the edge of the scarp. Then, for a variation, follow a sketchy road ¼ mile through small silver firs and western hemlocks to a 3301-foot point. See huge Rainier and distant St. Helens and nearby Grass. See the Enumclaw plain and silvery meanders of the Green River and hear the trains blow, boys, hear the trains blow. If you're lucky.

Round trip 8 miles, allow 7 hours
High point 3301 feet, elevation gain 2400 feet
February-December

From Junction 2828, the left (straight ahead) fork goes on and on. The 3570-foot summit of McDonald ought to be accessible with some 6 more round-trip miles.

Fogbound Grass Mountain

WHITE RIVER

Something scary here. Arriving on the lower White utterly ignorant of the region, a perceptive visitor quickly—and nervously—would note the difference between this river and those to the north. The black sands, the black and red boulders. That's lava rock. There's a volcano upstream. And the murky water, the wide gravel bed with an interweaving of channels old and new. That's rock milk and channel-braiding. There's a glacier upstream. A dangerous combination, a glacier and a volcano.

Indeed. Tell it to The People who were peacefully going about their business 5000 years ago when the steam bomb exploded 30 miles away on The Mountain, melting thousands of tons of snow and ice, sending down the valley to Puget Sound a roaring slurry of muck, perhaps 2.5 billion cubic yards of it. The Osceola Mudflow. Leaving in the lowlands a deposit up to 70 feet thick. A once-in-a-dozen-eons rarity? No. Rainier has spewed countless such "lahars"; just 600 years ago the Electron Mudflow rumbled down the Puyallup to saltwater. Come the next big show and real estate in Enumclaw, Buckley, Kent, Auburn, Sumner, and Puyallup—all of whose sites were buried by the Osceola—won't be worth a nickel.

If man has performed no single so dramatic a stunt of river manipulation, he's puttered for decades, tinkering this way and that with the White. Long ago the farmers, weary of the river's habit of periodically swapping outlets, sometimes flowing north in the Big Valley to join the Green and empty into Seattle's Elliott Bay, sometimes south in the Big Valley to the Puyallup and Tacoma's Commencement Bay, called in the engineers to build dikes to fix it in a southward course. At the point of diversion, where it exits from the narrower (true) White Valley into the Big Valley, the river changes name, golly knows why, to the Stuck.

After a disastrous flood of the 1930s wreaked havoc in the Big Valley and demonstrated the shortcomings of Commencement Bay for industrial development, the Mud Mountain Dam was built above Enumclaw; the river is no longer permitted to flood and on occasion is reservoirized upstream from the dam, whose fate in the next Osceola is a subject of amused speculation by Luddites.

Last, Puget Power devised a scheme to put the White to work, at Buckley diverting water through a flume to a reservoir, Lake Tapps, thence into turbines at Deiringer and a return to the White (Stuck) in the Big Valley. As a consequence, when everybody is cooking supper and taking a shower and watching TV and making aluminum all at once the White-Stuck between Buckley and Deiringer dwindles to the minimum legally required for the comfort and convenience of fish.

The White thus is a tame and useful river—until the next Osceola. But it doesn't feel tame. None of these tinkerings diminish its excitement for the hiker. Especially the one who keeps an ear cocked, alert for dull distant booms up that-a-way.

The lowest segment of the province, the Stuck River in the Big Valley, was but cursorily surveyed for this book. Miles and miles of gravel mining and boxes in a row were disheartening. Yet the dikes, open all winter, close to the city, are popular with locals and ought not to be ignored.

The detailed survey began at Pacific, on the edge of the Big Valley at the mouth of the White Valley—and discovered a wonder. Here at virtual sealevel, hikable all year, on Metro buslines in southern neighborhoods of Puget Sound City, is wildness. For 15-odd miles upstream the plain above the river canyon is thoroughly civilized; down in the canyon, on alluvial terraces and gravel bars beneath steep bluffs, are river and woods and solitude, a finger of wilderness thrusting far out from The Mountain to the city.

Where the White debouches from the mountain front to its canyon sliced in the Osceola plain there ought to be established a Cascade Gateway Recreation Area, centered at Enumclaw, to serve the masses of Puget Sound City living an hour and less away. (Other such Cascade Gateway Recreation Areas, centered at North Bend and Mount Index, are suggested in **Footsore 2.**) As the northernmost of Rainier's great rivers the White is the shortest route for the most people to the national park. But many a hiker would be pleased not to contribute to the overcrowding and boot-battering of the park, would be happy to take exercise much nearer home, at elevations from under 1000 feet, open all year, to high views at 3000 feet, open (with some snowline-probing) nearly all year. Buses currently do not usefully serve trailheads but development of the Recreation Area could correct that.

Though partly on state lands and partly on those of the U.S. Army Corps of Engineers, and farther up the valley in national forest, a major portion of the Recreation Area would be on the White River Tree Mine of Weyerhaeuser Company. On the north side of the valley is a continuous ridge which as it moves east is successively called Boise Ridge, Grass Mountain, Huckleberry Mountain, and Dalles Ridge. On the south side are outer buttresses of Rainier and the tributary valleys of the Clearwater, West Fork White, and Huckleberry Creek. In this intensively-exploited country, plantations ranging in date from the 1930s to a few minutes ago, the clearcutting proceeding now to elevations above 4000 feet, are hundreds of miles of superb, little-driven footroads. Down low, hikable except in dead winter, are green tunnels in tall second-growth forests. Higher are excellent snowline-probers in younger trees. Highest are top-of-the-world freshly-scalped ridges with views from here to forever, always dominated by the immense white heap.

NOTE: The supreme high-elevation mountain-front viewpoint of the White River, the Three Sisters, is not discussed here—because for a long time the surveyor couldn't figure how to get there. Persistence and virtue ultimately triumphed and he found two ways, both described in **Footsore 4.**

Farther up the valley, deeper in the mountain icebox and thus with a shorter season, are virgin forests. Prefaced at the mountain front on Corps of Engineers land above Mud Mountain Dam, in Federation Forest State Park and the Greenwater River are truly religious experiences for fans of the hamadryads.

Finally, though the book was not meant to go that far (the drive from many parts of Puget Sound City is closer to 2 hours than 1), and elevations are getting high (2400 feet minimum), it was found impossible to chop off the survey short of Camp Sheppard, hub of a stupendous Scout-constructed trail system. Only the lowest paths are sampled here; the highest lead to the Pacific Crest Trail and the Wonderland Trail. A great way to conclude a book.

USGS maps: Lake Tapps, Auburn, Sumner, Buckley, Enumclaw, Cumberland, Greenwater, Lester

For a free copy of a map of the company's road system on the White River Tree

White River near Enumclaw

Farm, write Weyerhaeuser Company, Box W, Snoqualmie, WA 98065. Before setting forth on a trip that will pass a gate on a Weyerhaeuser road, call (on a weekday) the company office, in Snoqualmie, 888-2511.

White-Stuck River (Map-page 211)

Here, where the White River begins to be called by some (not all) the Stuck, it also changes in other ways, emerging from the comparatively narrow valley appropriate to a mountain river onto broad flats of the Big Valley, flowing from its wild-seeming braided channels into a bed channelized by dikes and extensively mined for gravel.

Two walks can be made through this White-Stuck transition zone. On the south side of the river is a much-driven gravel dike-road, garbage-scabby but easy; some measure of peace can be obtained by (1) choosing a quiet winter weekday morning, and/or (2) as much as possible, leaving the dike to walk on gravel bars at water's edge. On the north side of the river is the Sunday walk, cleaner, machine noise from the far side masked by river babbling, and past the first stretch perfectly wheelfree, but before long more a scramble than a walk.

From Auburn drive south on Auburn Way towards Buckley. Exit onto R Street and continue about 1 mile to the bridge over the Stuck-White. For the south-side hike, turn right just beyond the bridge on Stuck River Drive (gravel) and park, elevation 100 feet.

Walk the dike-road along the river, by riprap of columnar basalt, or drop to the black-sand and volcanic-rock bars. This is above the limit of gravel mining and the stream takes on the normal appearance of a glacial river at low water. (Most of the river most of the time is diverted through Lake Tapps for power production by Puget Power; in 1976, one sunny day when the river was abruptly "turned on" without notice, two children were drowned; watch out for unannounced "walls of water.") Soon the Big Valley is left, portal bluffs passed, the true White Valley entered. Ducks swim, fish jump, kingfishers dive. How far to go? The dike-road was surveyed 3 miles on a weekday afternoon and found good. Then school let out and the motorcycles arrived.

For the north-side hike don't cross the R Street bridge; just before it, turn right on 37 Way SE and in ¼ mile park by the river on the dead-end stub of 36 Street SE.

Walk the cable-barred dike-road upstream, passing the former state game farm, now undeveloped public park. Try to figure out where the White used to turn north up the Big Valley to join the Green River. In ¼ mile reach the bluff and enter the true White Valley. In another ¼ mile the dike ends and so do the wheels and the fun begins. From here upstream the way is strictly for pedestrians—on river bars, along the toe of the wildwood bluff, and where it is vertical cliffs of clay, gravel, and till, perhaps up to the knees in the river. Some problems may not be soluble by conservative hikers—or in high water by any sane hikers. How far to go? The way was surveyed a dozen miles upstream (see White River Bottom)—some of it doubtless too strenuous for most tastes. About 1-2 miles probably are sufficient entertainment for a Sunday afternoon.

Round trip 2-6 miles, allow 1-4 hours
High point 200 feet, elevation gain 100 feet
All year
Bus: Metro 150 south from Auburn on R Street to 29 Street, walk 8 blocks
** to the bridge**

White River Bottom (Map-page 211)

One would never guess, driving through farms of the Osceola Mudflow plain, that a stone's throw distant, down the 125-250-foot bluffs at the edge of the plain is a river bottom where the human presence is virtually unfelt. Old and very old woods roads wander this way and that, and fishermen's paths seek riverbanks, and gypos cut alder and river-rafted cedar logs, and here and there are small pastures and glimpses of houses on the brink of the bluff. But most of the time, down there in the broad bottom up to 1 mile wide, amid braided, shifting channels, marshy sloughs, tanglewoods, and beaver ponds, one could imagine the year to be 1850—or 1650.

Getting down to the river through the belt of residential land along the rim of the bluff may require a bit of poking about. For the access used on the surveys of 1977 and late 1981, drive Highway 164, the Auburn-Enumclaw Road, to 4 miles west of Enumclaw and turn south on 196 Avenue SE to the bluff edge, where the road bends east and is signed SE 456 Way. In a scant 2 miles from Highway 164 spot a mucky road that drops abruptly westward from the rim. (If you hit 212 Avenue SE, you've gone a bit too far east; back up.) In a street machine, park here, elevation 640 feet.

Otherwise (that is, in a beetle), drive carefully down the bluff to the bottom, to

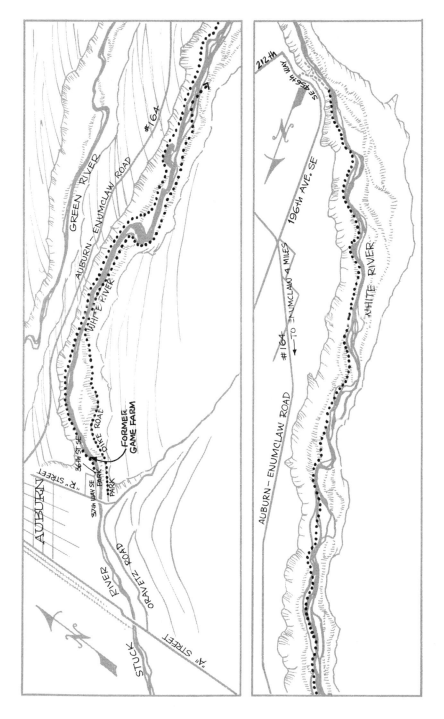

a Y. The left fork, upstream, was surveyed only a short distance but seemed to promise all manner of interesting explorations. The right fork proceeds downstream, goes out to the river and eventually leaves motorcycles behind and becomes trail, brush, gravel, and etcetera.

The route beyond here cannot be described usefully; the maze of paths would only be made the more confusing and the river keeps changing all the time so that gravel bars are now dry, now underwater. However, even an inexperienced hiker can find machine-free solitude by carefully picking a way on woods roads, paths, and gravel, now near the bluff, now near the river, now far from both. A fine encounter with the river comes in 1 long mile from the start. In another 4 or so miles (not streamflow or crowfly but footplod) the river cuts the base of a gravel-clay bluff, possible to skirt at low water but one of many logical turnabouts for a hike. The survey continued downstream to the White-Stuck River (which see), constantly rewarding but complicated by brush and barbed wire.

Round trip 2-10 miles, allow 2-8 hours
High point 640 feet, elevation gain 400 feet
All year

Mount Pete (Map-page 212)

What accounts for the "Enumclaw Blobs," the miniature mountains pimpling the pastured plain? Hearts of hard basalt explain their steepness; the Osceola Mudflow provided the surrounding flatness. What accounts for the survival on the biggest of the blobs, Mount Pete (more officially known as Pinnacle Peak), of a grand stand of virgin forest, a veritable wildland arboretum? Well, in 1979 the state DNR proposed to log it, and one would have thought from the instant uproar the proposal was to install Golden Arches in the Garden of Eden. Somebody loves ol' Pete. Lots of bodies. And they know how to yell.

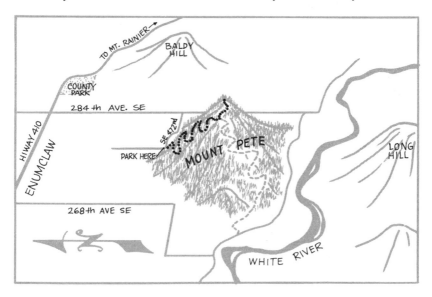

Columnar basalt near top of Mount Pete

Drive Highway 410 to the eastern outskirts of Enumclaw and at the Enumclaw Park swimming pool turn south on 284 Avenue SE. Follow it 1½ miles and turn west (right) on SE 472. In ½ mile, at a sharp bend right, park on the shoulder by the obvious trailhead, elevation 770 feet.

The trail is very steep and can be slippery but is wide and well-beaten. Beginning in lush undergrowth of a moist, mixed, second-growth forest with at least four varieties of ferns and lots of frogs, the way quickly ascends to startling big Douglas firs, up to 4 feet thick, plus a full assortment of other good green things suitable for a virgin forest. In ¾ mile the path joins the old road built to serve the lookout tower, removed in the mid-1960s. Little-driven even by sports and now narrowing to a trail, in ¼ mile the road, after passing the finest of many displays of columnar basalt, curves around to an end close under the summit, 1801 feet.

With the tower gone and the trees a-growing, the panorama ain't the 360-degree circle of yore but is a still splendid 200 degrees. Only small windows offer looks at beautiful downtown Enumclaw and other points west but on the east side are vistas that, pieced together, extend from the Issaquah Alps to McDonald, Boise Ridge, Grass—and Rainier, with the Clearwater River valley and Three Sisters prominent. And a voyeur's view down to cows and chickens at the foot of the peak. In mind's eye one can see the Osceola Mudflow surging down the White River valley, dividing to sweep around both sides of Baldy and Pete and overwhelm camps of The People. (Is the racial memory responsible for the name, "Enumclaw," which means "place of the evil spirits"?)

Round trip 2 miles, allow 3 hours
High point 1801 feet, elevation gain 1030 feet
All year

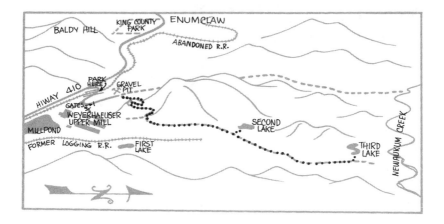

Second Lake (Map-page 214)

A pleasant stroll along an abandoned "motor nature trail" on a hillock above the Weyerhaeuser Upper Mill, then through fields and forests to a quiet little lake in a secluded forest nook.

Drive Highway 410 east from Enumclaw County Park 1 long mile and turn left at the sign, "Weyerhaeuser White River Operations." Cross the abandoned railroad and in ⅛ mile come to a triple junction. Straight ahead is the "Office." Sharp left is "No Admittance." Even sharper left is a narrow gravel road to a gate inhospitably signed "No Parking." So, back up, maybe to the railroad tracks. The Weyerhaeuser employees who designed the "motor nature trail" are long gone, and so is the company's geniality. Park where you can, elevation about 1100 feet.

Walk the narrow motor nature trail, switchbacking sharp right from an old gravel pit and winding up the knoll, passing signs identifying tree species, to the 1280-foot summit, and descending to a T. The right leads to the mill; go left in fields, by a marsh, to woods, and shortly to Second Lake. Paths drop to the peat shore, the lilypads and skunk cabbage, of the small lake set in an outlet-lacking bowl at 1100 feet, ringed by low forested ridges.

Some ¾ mile north of Second Lake is Third Lake, actually a marsh.

The road straight ahead from the gravel pit is narrow and mucky, a fine footroad. It goes down and up, past a nameless inhabited lake and uninhabited marshes, some 2 miles to Newaukum Creek.

Round trip to Second Lake 3 miles, allow 2 hours
High point 1280 feet, elevation gain 400 feet
All year

Boise Ridge (Map-page 217)

Atop the abrupt scarp of Boise Ridge are airplane-wing looks down to Enumclaw and farms around, with naught but the murk from Tacoma to block views over the plain to Puget Sound and the Olympics.

Drive to Cumberland by any of several routes. One simple way is to drive

Highway 169 to 4 miles south of Black Diamond and turn east on the Enumclaw-Franklin Road, following it under various names to Cumberland, there
intersecting the Enumclaw-Cumberland-Kanaskat Road. On the latter road at
the north edge of Cumberland turn east on SE Kuzak Road. Twisting and
turning through the fascinating glacier-complicated drainages of Deep and
Coal Creeks, the road goes 2¼ miles to a T with the big wide Green River
Mainline. Turn right on this major log-haul road (to the Weyerhaeuser mill) and
proceed south 5 miles to road 5307. Turn left and drive ¼ mile to a gate and
park. Do not drive on—weekends the gate is closed so you can't and
weekdays log trucks are barreling out in a steady stream. Elevation, 1550 feet.

With the leisurely elevation-gaining rate of the 1902 logging railroad whose
grade it follows, the broad road runs south through a young plantation, passing
a sideroad left, into second-growth on the steep scarp, marked with basalt
walls. Views to Enumclaw and the Weyerhaeuser mill at about 1 mile are left
behind as the road swings around the south end of Boise Ridge into the valley
of Boise Creek. At 1850 feet, 1½ miles, is a decision. The main road straight
ahead is the long but self-evident way to the summit. The sideroad left, 5307-2,
is much shorter but not recommended for inexperienced wilderness navigators. Both are splendid walks.

The long way: Continue sidehilling up Boise Creek, crossing two tributaries
and passing sideroads down to the valley bottom, emerging into the universal
clearcut that soon will finish denuding the whole of Boise Ridge and, across the
valley, Grass Mountain's Woot Peak. In wide views of naked hills and Rainier,
the way climbs steeply beyond the end of the old railroad, attaining the ridge
crest at 2950 feet, 3 miles from Decision Junction.

Look down to basalt-hearted hillocks dotting the green plain of the Osceola
Mudflow, to houses and barns, cars and cows, and into the dimness where lies
Tacoma, the Invisible City. On a crystalline winter day, look out to Bald Hills
and Black Hills and Olympics, Lake Tapps and Vashon Island, and downtown
Seattle.

View from Boise Ridge

The 3080-foot summit of Boise Ridge, ½ mile south, was still forested and viewless in late 1981 but that will change. Whether in happy trees or sad stumps, the trip can proceed to a loop, exiting via the trail of the short way.

The short way: Ascend road 5307-2 to a creek crossing at 2200 feet, ½ mile. Now, look sharp. At the next bend some 500 feet up the road (and about the same short of its 1977 end) watch on the cutbank left for a blazed tree next to a stump with a rusty cable wrapped around. By it, follow a meager cat road up the bank and the short bit to the forest edge. Spot a 12-inch fir with two large weathered blazes. Step into the woods (trust me) and soon discern unmistakable tread of an old old trail, unmaintained and virtually unused but quite good and still easy for an experienced pathfinder to follow. The trail goes straight up the fall-line of the slope on a 1902 log skidway. Attaining a subsidiary ridge at about 2600 feet, it goes near the crest, entering virgin forest, contouring to a saddle in the main ridge at 2870 feet. Here the route turns right, following blazes made in 1977 along the scarp edge to a natural (not made by logging) viewpoint at 2930 feet. A litter of shakes and rotting logs remains of a Boy Scout shelter, 1½ miles from Decision Junction. The summit is ¼ mile away.

As logging proceeds this trail will be progressively snipped off bit by bit but any remainder will be found by proceeding directly uphill from road 5307-2. The roads that replace the trail will continue to be the short way to the summit.

Long round trip 9 miles, allow 6 hours
Short round trip 6 miles, allow 4 hours
High point (both) 2950, elevation gain 1400 feet
April-November

Grass Mountain — West Peak (Map-page 217)

Little lower than the Main Peak (which see), the West Peak of Grass Mountain is far enough removed to be a whole different thing. It shares Rainier, of course, the monster heap of snow across the White River valley. With this it combines a broad panorama of the Puget Sound lowlands which commence just a couple miles away beyond the abrupt Cascade scarp.

Drive to Cumberland and the Green River Mainline (see Boise Ridge). Turn right on the Mainline a short bit to cross Coal Creek. Just beyond, turn left on (unsigned) road 5400, the gate usually open. Steeply ascend the good but narrow road above South Fork Coal Creek, switchbacking, avoiding lesser sideroads.

The question is, where to stop driving and start walking? The sports (fortunately in small numbers) go clear to the summit, but they of course get neither healthful exercise nor the full flavor of the beer. Two versions of the trip are suggested, one long, one short. For the long of it, park in a ridgecrest saddle at 2550 feet, 3 miles from the Mainline.

The route is partly in fresh clearcuts, partly in plantations of various dates back to the 1960s, and if you get there soon enough, partly in cool virgin forest with nice creeks. A short way from the saddle is a Y; go right, uphill, in a clearcut with views across the East Fork Coal Creek to the northernmost peak of Grass, 3521 feet. At a 2800-foot saddle the road crosses over to the South Fork Coal Creek side of the mountain and traverses slopes of Peak 3921, newly scalped and a superb bald viewpoint. As lesser roads go left and right stay straight.

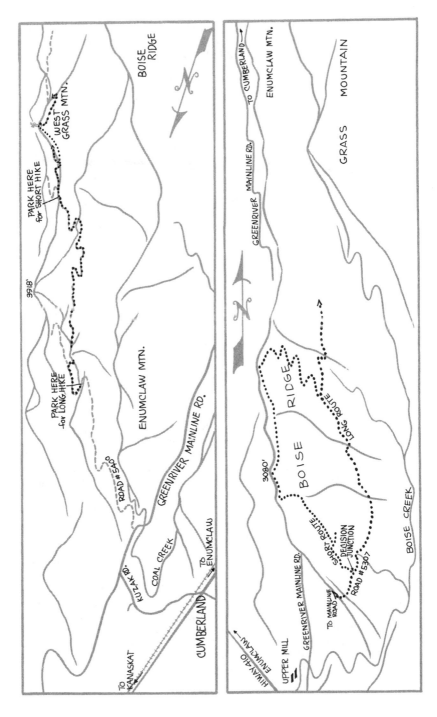

At 3200 feet, just past a big view west to Enumclaw Mountain and Boise Ridge and out to Enumclaw, a shoulder of a divide spur is crossed from Coal Creek to Boise Creek drainage. Passing more sideroads, the main road now descends moderately to a long wide saddle in the main crest of Grass, bottoming at 3050 feet, 3½ miles from Saddle 2550. Charley Creek is below to the left, Boise Creek to the right, and straight ahead rises the West Peak in all its naked glory topped by an enormous thingamajig. For the short hike, park here.

Go directly across the saddle, avoiding sideroads left and right, to the foot of Grass and a Y; go right. In a few yards a sideroad switchbacks right; go straight. Dodging deadend spurs, switchback to a 3550-foot saddle in a spur ridge, the view now extending to the Main Peak.

From this saddle the service road to the summit thingamajig takes a round-about route. Instead turn right up lesser roads and cat tracks that ascend the crest to the summit, a tad under 4000 feet, at 1½ miles from Saddle 3050.

Goggle at the Enormous Thingamajig; it appears to be the Bell System relay to Mars. Then look down Scatter Creek to the White River and across to the White-Clearwater-Prairie-Carbon sector of Rainier. And, of course, The Mountain. Look along the bald ridge to the Main Peak of Grass and north down Charley Creek to the Green River and out to McDonald Mountain and Cascades as distant as Baker. And look west past Boise Ridge to Enumclaw and farms and cities and smog and saltwater and Olympics.

Round trip 3 or 10 miles, allow 3 or 7 hours
High point 4000 feet, elevation gain 1000 or 1900 feet
May-November

White River Rim Trail (Map-page 219)

When listing the longest and finest low-elevation walks close to Puget Sound City, don't forget the Rim Trail dedicated by the U.S. Army Corps of Engineers in 1976. For pedestrians only, no noise permitted except of river and wind and birds, it samples a wide variety of forest types, from swampy stands of cedar and spruce to dry slopes of big old Douglas fir and hemlock to second-growth alder-maple-salmonberry. In spring the shadows turn a person's skin green. In autumn the vine maple inflames the eyes.

Drive Highway 410 east from Enumclaw to the sign announcing Mud Mountain Dam and Recreation Area and turn right 2 miles to the picnic ground-children's play area. Turn left at the sign, "Vista Point," to the trailhead parking, elevation 1300 feet.

(Before or after the long hike, proceed to the Vista Point to do the ⅓-mile trail. At the top is a staggering view of the dam that was begun in 1939 and completed in 1953. It rises 425 feet above bedrock, one of the world's highest earth-core-and-rockfill dams. Built to control floods, the dam has a reservoir that, when filled, is a lake 5½ miles long, covering 1200 acres. But the upper portions of the reservoir area are normally not filled and most of most years there is no reservoir at all; except for a stretch above the dam the White River usually appears wild and free. At the bottom of the Vista Trail is a view that in flood time can send a person reeling.)

The Rim Trail, partly on old woods roads and service roads, mainly on built

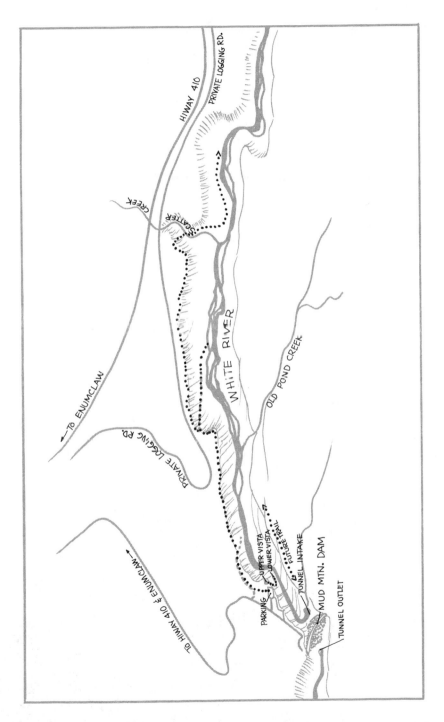

path, is well-marked, but mostly in one direction; the walker does well to mentally note the many junctions to avoid mistakes on the return. But then, the mistakes are pleasant strolling too, in the spirit of the correct trail, which is in no hurry to get anywhere, seeks only to give the fullest experience of forests and ravines and views, omitting none of the good stuff.

Not far from the trailhead a service road plunges to the river, a nice sidetrip — as is another service road farther along. The trail descends from one alluvial terrace to a lower one, all swampy ook and skunk cabbage traversed by cedar bridges and puncheon. The way comes out on the brink of this lower terrace — hold onto the kids and tighten up on the dog's leash, because the brink overhangs. Gaze giddily down to the White River (or in season, a brown lake), downstream to Mud Mountain Dam, and straight up to the tower on the summit of Three Sisters 3.

More forests, more views, more sidetrips (many of those sidetrails are the work of elk, commonly met by hikers here). At 4 miles the way drops to Scatter Creek and ends.

Catastrophically destabilized by Weyerhaeuser clearcutting of its headwaters, Scatter Creek now has a gravel fan as broad and naked as if it flowed from a glacier. Where it joins the White River a hiker can be so overwhelmed by water noise, so insulated from machine noise, that the year might well be 1776 — or 1066.

The bars of black volcanic sand and lava boulders can be followed another couple miles of "reservoir park" to the vicinity of Mount Philip. Backpackers

White River from Mount Philip

who want to camp where they please and build great big "John Muir fires" can do so, no permit required.

Round trip to Scatter Creek 8 miles, allow 5 hours
High point 1360 feet, elevation gain 400 feet
All year

In Corps files, awaiting a wealthier future, is a plan for a trail across Mud Mountain Dam and up the other side of the river. From there a route readily could be provided to the top of Three Sisters 3 (see **Footsore 4**).

Mount Philip (Map-page 223)

A little trail but not to be belittled, ideal as it is for short walks and short-legged walkers. A sizeable reward for a small effort: a rock garden on a surprising cliff, views down to braided channels of the White River (at the upper end of the Army Engineers' White River "Park"), the tributary valley of the Clearwater, and footings of Rainier—though The Mountain itself is hidden.

Drive Highway 410 east 3½ miles from the turnoff to Mud Mountain Dam. On the left (north) side of the highway spot a woods road making a reverse turn downvalley. A sign (usually) says, "Hiking Trail to Vista Point ½ mile Weyerhaeuser Company." Park here, elevation 1450 feet.

Cross the highway and drop a bit to a narrow road and find another trail sign (probably) pointing into the forest.

Passing big old stumps in an alder bottom, in a short bit the path reaches a Y; go right, as suggested by a post with an arrow. The trail switchbacks up through choked second-growth dating from the logging in 1931, breaking out in the open atop the cliff, a dandy spot for a picnic.

The company forester who built the trail for public pleasure named this little peak for John Philip Weyerhaeuser, former president of the firm.

Round trip 1 mile, allow 1 hour
High point 1700 feet, elevation gain 300 feet
February-December

Stink Lake (Map-page 223)

A moody walk, much of the way claustrophobic in dense young forest; the views out, when they come, jar the hiker's reverie, which judging from the low beer-can count would ordinarily not be disturbed by razzers. Do it as a loop, saving the best for last.

Drive Highway 410 to the Mount Philip (which see) parking area, elevation 1450 feet.

Walk the closed-gate (usually) woods road, gradually veering from the highway, passing an old railroad trestle whose stringers serve as out-in-the-middle-of-the-air nurse-logs for hemlocks. In ½ mile hit a more-used road from the west; turn right (east) on it, ascending upvalley. Pass obviously lesser spurs and in another 1¼ miles, after a switchback left, come to a Y; turn right on the little-used less-good road which drops to a mudhole, then ascends to cross a leftward-flowing headwater branch of Scatter Creek. The way is now up, in ¼ mile hitting another poor road; turn right. A bit later, at a Y, again go right, soon crossing a rightward-flowing creek and now, on the flat, following an old railroad grade northeasterly. In 1 mile from the Y, 3 miles from the highway, the "goal" is attained. Sort of. The road passes first a marshy pond littered with debris of beaver logging and then a window out to debris of human logging. By poking around in the woods one can get near—but not to—shores of the "lake," really a collection of marshy potholes in a little basin, 2300 feet. The stink apparently is from gasses of decomposing vegetation—nostrils occasionally catch a whiff of rotten eggs.

Now for the fun return. Back at the beaver pond spot a boot-beaten path downhill. The way descends near the Stink Lake headwater of Clay Creek, then trends away from it, drops off a scarp into the creek valley, sidehills on an old roadbed, and at ¾ mile from the beaver pond hits a logging-railroad grade abandoned in 1950—one of the last such lines to operate in the state. Turning right (west) on the grade, the trail passes close by a Second Wave clearcut of the early 1970s; go out on it for clear views of big white Rainier and the White River valley. The grade-trail passes under an imposing vertical lava cliff, then a waterfall showering off an overhang and then (the best part for history buffs) a nearly-intact and splendid trestle bypassing the wall. Gradually the trail turns into an old road. Watch for famed Goodwater Spring, reputed by locals to have the best flavor in the country. The path returns to the highway a few yards from the parking place.

Loop trip 6 miles, allow 4 hours
High point 2300 feet, elevation gain 850 feet
March-November

Clearwater Vista: Jensen Point (Map-page 225)

A long walk through a green tunnel of second-growth forest on a narrow, little-used road, in its lower reaches mostly an old railroad grade. Creeks enliven the route, and remnants of old trestles, and elk tracks, and gaudy volcanic rocks, and windows out to Enumclaw farms this way and Rainier glaciers that way. At the end, two (not one) smashing views.

Drive Highway 410 past the Mud Mountain Dam turnoff 5¾ miles and turn right on a White River Tree Farm logging road signed "Bridge Camp Gate." (This gate is always open except during closures for extreme fire danger, most common in late summer.) Descend to cross the White River. At the junction on the wide flat beyond, turn right, downvalley, on great big high-speed road 6000. At a scant 2 miles from the highway spot on the left a narrow woods road, elevation 1380 feet.

Because the gate on the road is almost always locked, this walk is purely for long-leggitty beasties seeking a good stretch. The less-energetic would do best to take the next hike described in these pages. The lovely green tunnel ascends gently 2¾ miles to the Big Switchback at 2075 feet.

From the Switchback is a peek down to the Clearwater and up to Rainier. Windows become more frequent, with bitty views out to the Enumclaw plain and the Olympics, to Pete and Philip and Grass. At 1½ miles from the Big Switchback is a Y; go right. In 2 miles more is a T with a newer road, 2900 feet. Here, some 6¼ miles from road 6000, 3½ from Big Switchback, is a choice. If

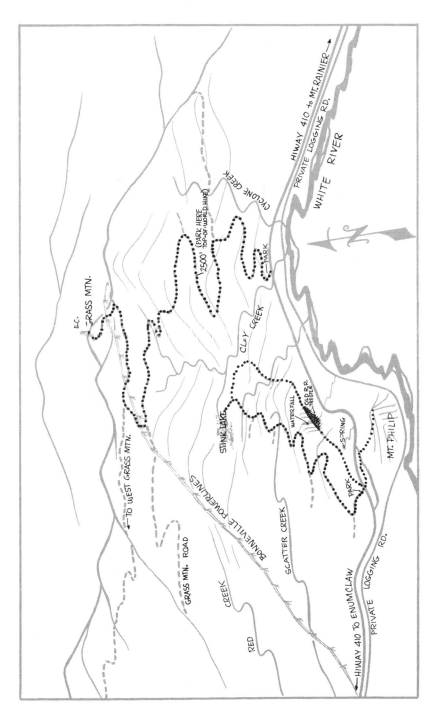

HIWAY 410 to MT.RAINIER →

PRIVATE LOGGING RD.

WHITE RIVER

CYCLONE CREEK

2500' (PARK HERE
TOP-OF-WORLD HIKE)

PARK

CLAY CREEK

G.C.
GRASS MTN.

OLD R.R.
TRESTLE

WATERFALL

STINK LAKE

SPRING

MT. PHILIP

PARK

TO WEST GRASS MTN.

BONNEVILLE POWERLINES

GRASS MTN. ROAD

SCATTER CREEK

RED CREEK

HIWAY 410 TO ENUMCLAW

PRIVATE LOGGING RD.

223

pooping out, turn right ⅓ mile to a recent clearcut with worthy views. For the full treatment turn left and proceed ¾ mile to the first Smashing View, from a leveled-off stretch of the ridge crest at 3100 feet, down to the White River and across to the full length of Grass Mountain with its awesome clearcuts and brown-slash road network. Second-growth mostly screens the view from the other side of the crest so continue 1 mile to a 1975 clearcut and down the second of two sideroads ¼ mile to the jutting prow of 3200-foot Jensen Point and the second Smashing View.

Look across Jensen Creek and Mineral Creek to enormous brown clearcuts surrounding Noble Naked Knob and beyond to still-green headwaters of the Clearwater, least-known of Rainier's rivers because it doesn't quite start from The Mountain proper. Look past Hurricane Gap and Bearhead to the big ice cream cone, every detail close and clear from Curtis Ridge to Willis Wall to Liberty Ridge to Ptarmigan Ridge to the Mowich Face. Also see, across the Clearwater, 4960-foot Three Sisters, whose ascent is described in **Footsore 4**.

Round trip 16 miles, allow 10 hours
High point 3300 feet, elevation gain 1900 feet
May-November

Clearwater Vista: Noble Naked Knob (Map-page 225)

In striking contrast to the long gradual ascent on old railroad grade through a green tunnel to Jensen Point, this is a short steep climb on modern truck roads through recent clearcuts to Noble Naked Knob, a scalped knoll on a point of a ridge thrust far out into valley air, commanding a view up and down the Clearwater. Look there and see cow-grazed pastures of the Enumclaw plain. Look there and, if The Mountain is in the mood, watch silent avalanches slide in slow-motion down Willis Wall.

Drive road 6000 (see Jensen Point) up the narrowing Clearwater valley, crossing Jensen and Mineral Creeks. At 5½ miles from the highway is a Y, both forks gated. Whether or not the gate is open, park here, elevation 1520.

Take the left fork, road 6015, entering Byron Creek valley and steeply climbing beside the tumbling waters, passing from tall second-growth of the 1940s-50s to still-shrublike plantations of the 1960s. In ¾ mile cross Byron Creek to a Y at 2050 feet. Go left, recrossing the creek (and vowing to linger here on the descent, beside the white froth rushing down slabs from pool to pool) and switchbacking up the open ridge slopes. Pass a sideroad up the valley and continue to a promontory at 2400 feet. Wow. Tarry to goggle at the views, but not long because this is only the beginning. The road now swings into indecently-exposed Mineral Creek valley and ascends to a Y on the ridge crest. Turn right the short bit along the crest to the 2900-foot summit of Noble Naked Knob.

Zounds. Up there beyond the still-wild headwaters of the Clearwater, beyond Hurricane Gap and Bearhead, stands The Mountain. And down there in the smog out the White River are Boise Ridge, fields of Enumclaw, and the Olympics. And all around are valleys and ridges stripped of trees in the 1970s, the seedlings still small (or not yet planted, since the logging continues). A maze of yellow-white roads, switchbacking and contouring and wiggling

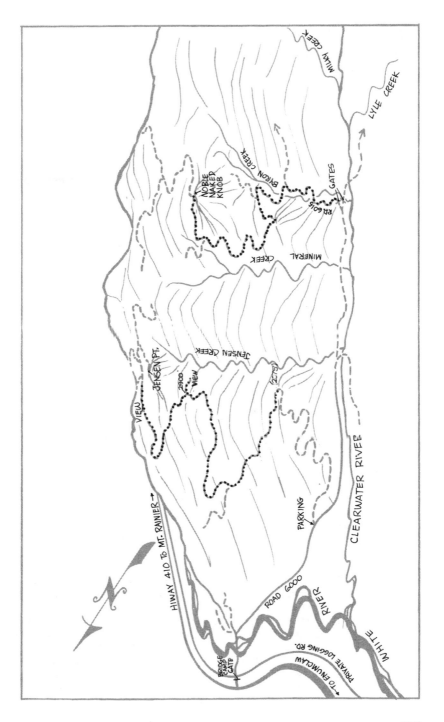

around, inscribes the red-brown slopes littered with bleached sticks.

It's enough. But there's more. Another 2 gently-climbing miles up the ridge road, views ever-growing, is the head of Mineral Creek and the foot of the final ridge, in a saddle at 3750 feet. And the bald summit of the ridge, 4560 feet, may very well urgently call those with sufficient energy.

Round trip to Knob 5 miles, allow 3 hours
High point 2900 feet, elevation gain 1400 feet
May-November

Having done this and the previous trip and thus been introduced to the White River Tree Farm slopes of Rainier, a hiker can devise dozens more walks on his own, no need for a guidebook. Buy the appropriate USGS maps, write Weyerhaeuser (see chapter introduction) for a map of company roads, and go exploring.

For example, at the 2050-foot crossing of Byron Creek, go right instead of left, ascending to the ridge between Byron and Milky Creeks.

At the gates at 1520 feet, take the right fork, road 6000, cross the Clearwater, and climb the ridges around Lyle Creek that are so prominent from Noble Naked Knob.

At 1½ miles back down the valley from the gates, 4 miles from the highway, take road 6050 across the Clearwater and find miles and miles of high routes in Canyon Creek and Three Sisters country. (See **Footsore 4**.)

Just after crossing the White River, turn left, upvalley, to the logging roads of Camp Creek and Rocky Run.

Keep going to the West Fork White River, with road systems ascending high on both sides.

Grass Mountain—Main Peak (Map-page 223)

Grass Mountain is some 15 miles long, rising from the Green River at the Cascade front and extending far into the range, for most of its length forming the north side of the White River Valley. The only reason it's not longer is that at a certain point, for no apparent reason, the map gets tired of Grass and starts calling the ridge Huckleberry Mountain. This much mountain obviously provides material for any number of hikes, mostly in the stark landscapes of recent clearcutting, the views beginning early and growing and growing as elevation is gained. As representative examples on the highest or Main Peak, two hikes on the same route, one low, the other high, will be described. (For another summit see Grass Mountain—West Peak.)

Drive Highway 410 east 6 miles from the turnoff to Mud Mountain Dam. Just after crossing Clay Creek (unsigned), note on the left a logging road making a reverse turn and climbing to a power transformer. For the first (lower) hike park near the highway, elevation 1500 feet.

Bad enough to scare off family sedans but not bad enough to much interest sport-drivers who in any event have thousands of miles of roads to razz hereabouts, the narrow, rough, steep road ascends Clay Creek valley, at ¾ mile, 1900 feet, swinging under a basalt cliff to splendid views down to the highway, Stink Lake, Philip, and Rainier. Now on a flat railroad grade in second-growth from the 1930s, the road contours east 1 mile to the edge of

Fog streaming over a shoulder of Grass Mountain

Cyclone Creek valley. Bending left, in ½ mile it comes to a Y, the right dropping to the creek; go left, climbing to a railroad grade that contours west at 2300 feet a scant 1 mile, then switchbacks east onto another flat grade for ½ mile to a series of view windows. Here, at 2500 feet, 3¾ miles from the highway, is a satisfying turnaround. (But if snow is deep, a party may well be satisfied with the viewpoint at 1900 feet.)

Round trip 7½ miles, allow 5 hours
High point 2500 feet, elevation gain 1000 feet
February-December

For the second (top-of-the-world) hike, drive to the windows at 2500 feet; otherwise it's a very long trip. Park here, where the road crosses a cutbank of rotten lava rubble-dirt on a steep sidehill and could be car-endangering.

Just past the dirt bank the road makes another switchback, west, and ascends to a T at 2650 feet. The right fork drops to Cyclone Creek; turn left on another railroad grade that goes on and on — and on — swinging into a number of creeklets feeding Clay Creek, each with its ghosts of old trestles. Windows open on Rainier. And now from nice young forest begin views to the scalped ridges of Grass.

Approaching a Bonneville powerline which crosses Grass from the Green to the White, out in a flat of recent alder-logging on state land, pass a sideroad right to the powerline. Now climbing, pass a gravel pit and at 2¾ miles, 3100 feet, meet the Grass Mountain Road (see below) at a point some 10 miles from Highway 410.

Turn right on the wider road (much-driven, more's the pity, by sports) and settle down to grind out altitude. During the first ½ mile keep right at two Ys; from then on simply forge ahead, passing many obviously deadending spurs. The road starts up across the steep final slopes of the mountain, clearcut in the 1960s, the new plantation a sprinkling of small shrubs. Views become continuous and overwhelming. At 4000 feet is a saddle; now there are views down to the basin of Lynn Lake and north to the Green River. The road ascends the ridge crest, on top of the stripped-naked world, to the summit at 4382 feet, 4¾ miles.

What a world! Out the White River to Enumclaw, Puget Sound, Seattle, the Olympics. Across the Forbidden Valley of the Green River to McDonald, Issaquah Alps, Si, Baker, Glacier, and beyond the Cascade Crest to Stuart. Let's see, there must be something else. Oh yes, The Mountain. Pow.

The summit is decorated by the usual batch of over-communication towers.

Round trip 9½ miles, allow 6 hours
High point 4382 feet, elevation gain 1900 feet
May-November

Grass can get to be a habit. Having attained this highest peak, one may aspire to only slightly lesser highs east and west.

From the (unsigned) Grass Mountain Road, departing from Highway 410 about ⅓ mile past the turnoff to Mud Mountain Dam, one can drive for miles, gaining access to western portions of Grass—and also the Main Peak, as described above. Indeed, for explorations of the peaks and basins neighboring Main Peak one does best to use this approach, saving time for the high rambles.

Up the White River valley from the Clay Creek logging road described here, several other roads take off before Federation Forest State Park is reached; all can be used for walks or drive-walks to eastern summits of Grass, some of which are still green.

Federation Forest State Park (Map-page 229)

A half-century ago leaders of the Washington State Federation of Women's Clubs realized there soon would be no low-elevation virgin forests of big trees except those protected in parks. Their efforts led to acquisition of this 612-acre preserve, part of it aptly called "Land of the Giants." Plantings by the Interpretive Center, plus identifying signs on the nature trails, provide a fine classroom in which to learn the native shrubs and trees, including centuries-old Douglas fir, western red cedar, western hemlock, grand fir, Sitka spruce (uncommon this far from the ocean), yew, and more.

Drive Highway 410 east from Enumclaw 17 miles to the Interpretive Center and parking area, elevation 1650 feet. Here begin the two Fred Cleator Interpretive Trails, both loops, the West Trail just short of 1 mile, the East under ½ mile. Together they introduce five distinct forest communities on a broad river terrace perched some 30 feet above the present level of the White River.

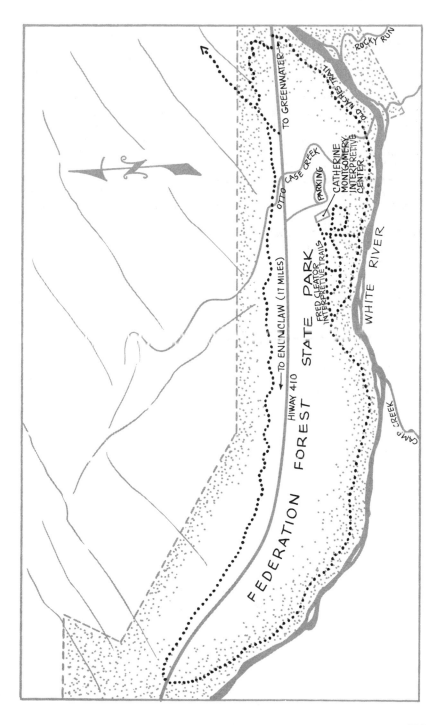

Also preserved is a section of the Naches Wagon Road, or Naches Trail, over which the Longmire party came from the east in 1853.

Begin with a tour of the Center, if open; if not, study the plantings around it, all identified with tags, a living textbook. Then walk the interpretive trails, totalling some 2 miles.

Now properly warmed up, take the loop trail, 5 miles in length, that tours the whole park from one end to the other on both sides of the highway. Start at the Interpretive Center and follow the path as it winds along the bench with views of the White River, dips into tall trees, crosses springs and marshes to the far west end of the park. Then cross to the north side of Highway 410 and loop back to the Interpretive Center.

Finally, the broad gravel swath of the glacier-fed White River is close at hand; hikers weary of ogling and gasping at forest giants can burst free from green twilight into bright day and wander the braided channels for miles.

Round trip 1-12 miles, allow 1-10 hours
High point 2000 feet, minor elevation gain
February-December

Greenwater River (Map-page 230)

The lovely little Meeker (Greenwater) Lakes. The groves of Douglas fir up to 5 feet in diameter, the more astounding after the long drive through miles of skinned valley. The basalt walls, moss-green and fern-decorated and water-fall-ribboned. And the river, now in greenwater pools lapping cliffs, now tumbling down bouldery gorges. What a superb entry to the proposed Cougar Lakes (or William O. Douglas?) Wilderness! Surely such grandeur, and the national interest in its protection, cannot be casually dismissed. Wrong. Expect

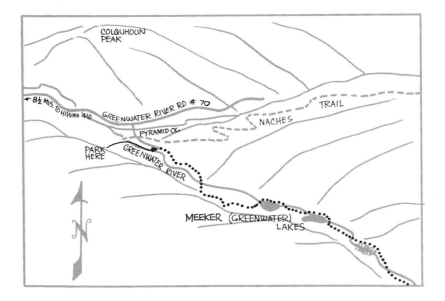

Greenwater River trail

on this hike to be transported by the beauty. But also expect to become very angry at the beast.

Drive Highway 410 east 2 miles from the hamlet of Greenwater and turn left on Road 70. Follow this high-speed logging freeway 8½ miles through numbing stumpland to the concrete bridge over the Greenwater. Several hundred feet beyond, turn right on Road 8028 to a plank bridge over Pyramid Creek. Pass a gravel gully ascending left—the historic Naches Pass Trail. Recalling what the heirs of the pioneer wagon train did when they got to Puget Sound, the Forest Service has provided a fitting memorial by letting their "Trail" become the pigpen of four-wheelers who sincerely believe that rassling a couple tons of machinery over a hill rates a merit badge. At ⅛ mile from Road 70, when 8028 proceeds left up the valley wall, park at the head of Trail 1176, elevation 2450 feet.

Walk a logging spur through the brush to the forest edge and the trail, made road-wide by motorcycles. **This** crime can't be laid at the door of the Forest Service. Try Weyerhaeuser, who lets the razzers run free.

Enter the forest cathedral. On the survey day in 1977 the mood instantly became deeply religious, in the green peace of ancient plants whose very existence, much less size and age, nigh surpasses human understanding, so puny and brief we are. It was Heaven. On the return survey late in 1981 chainsaws were whining, trees crashing, logging trucks rumbling on both walls of the valley, close beside the narrow lane permitted the river and trail by the heirs of the nefarious Northern Pacific Land Grant. Hell.

A devout walker should say prayers for the souls (if any) of the comptrollers who perform what in this company is called "forestry." And try not to look up and out from the forest dark. Focus in.

Admire the trees. Pause to count rings on fallen specimens sawn through to clear the trail. Beyond the first of the lovely green basalt walls, ¾ mile from the trailhead, is the first of the many picturesque footlog-bridges over the river.

At 1½ miles, 2800 feet, is the first lake; the best part is the green pool at the outlet, crossed by the second bridge at the foot of a ferny wall. Twice more the river is crossed in the ½ mile to the second lake. Above its inlet, in a glorious cedar flat, big trees standing beside a tall basalt wall, are two nearly end-to-end footlogs—over Meadow Creek and over the Green-water. In ¾ mile more, 2¾ miles from the car, 2950 feet, the trail crosses the outlet of the third "lake"—now a large alder marsh. Here, beneath a cliff of cordwood-stacked columnar basalt, beside a deep sand-bottomed pool that in season must stir thoughts of swimming, is a logical stopping place. But the trail goes on and so does the wilderness, unless Weyerhaeuser has beaten you to it.

Round trip 5½ miles, allow 4 hours
High point 2950 feet, elevation gain 500 feet
May-November

Snoquera Flats—Camp Sheppard (Map-page 233)

Along the Chinook Pass Highway on the approach to Mount Rainier lies the Mather Memorial Strip, dedicated to the first director of the National Park Service. In the portion outside the park, in Mt. Baker-Snoqualmie National Forest, the Forest Service is pledged to preserving the visual integrity of the White River valley as seen from the highway. Thus the valley floor and walls will remain forested—and beautifully so.

In this strip, on a flat alluvial terrace, during early New Deal days was located a camp of the ERA, older-folks version of the CCC, occupying a former campsite of the 1890s trail to the Starbo Mine on slopes of Rainier. From Snoqualmie minus almie plus ERA came the names, Snoquera Creek, Falls, Palisades, Flats, and Camp Snoquera, later renamed Camp Sheppard.

The site is now leased to the Chief Seattle Council of the Scouts of America. Under direction of Camp Ranger Max Eckenburg and support Ranger Ivan Kay, in the past dozen years the Scouts based at the camp have built 23 miles of trail, with another 29 miles on the master plan. The system ties into both the Pacific Crest Trail and the Wonderland Trail so the camp is a base for hikes in all directions. However, coverage in this book is restricted to trails in the immediate vicinity of camp, on and near Snoquera Flats.

"That's great for Scouts," you say, "But what about us?" When Ranger Max was asked if the trails might be used by the general public, he responded, "That's who they're for!"

Drive Highway 410 east 11 miles from the hamlet of Greenwater to the sign, "Camp Sheppard," and turn left into the large, marked parking area and picnic ground, elevation 2400 feet.

For openers take the Moss Lake Nature Trail. From the parking lot a path

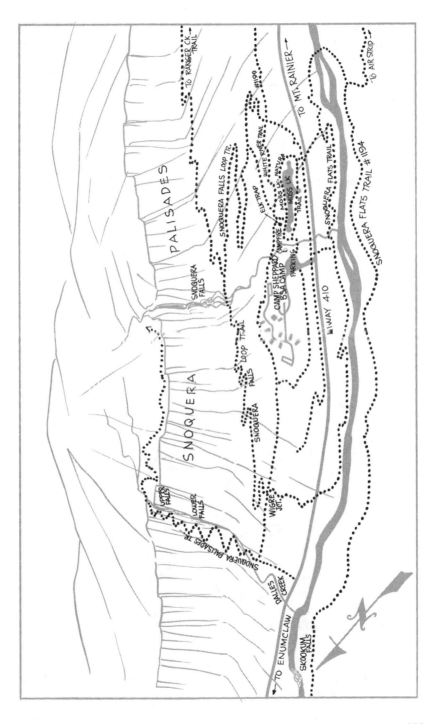

leading toward the valley wall comes in a scant ¼ mile to Campfire Circle in a stunning grove of forest giants. Here is the start-end of the nature trail loop of some ¾ mile. The way circles the marsh bottom of the "lake," whose amazing display of many varieties of moss usually climaxes in July. Moss and frogs here—and up there, on the valley wall, huge trees.

Back at the Campfire Circle, proceed on a trail to the inner camp. The public is welcomed; see where and how the Scouts live.

Back at the parking lot, walk the entrance road to near the highway and turn left on a paralleling trail. In a scant ¼ mile it leads to a highway crossing and on the other side to a Y. The left is to Skookum Flats across the White River; go right, downstream, on the Snoquera Flats Trail. In ½ mile is a Y. The left (straight ahead) fork proceeds along the river (and eventually, by taking appropriate right turns, back to camp in about 2 miles); for a shorter trip go right, in a scant ¼ mile recrossing the highway and returning to the parking lot.

Introductory round trips 3 miles, allow 2 hours
High point 2400 feet, minor elevation gain
April-December

Snoquera Falls

Snoquera Falls Loop (Map-page 233)

Big-tree virgin forests. Intimidating looks up-up-up lava precipices of The Palisades of Dalles Ridge. Views down to the White River, whose greenery completely hides the highway. May is the best time to see the falls—in that season the meltwater-swollen torrent plunges into a 30-foot-deep heap of avalanche snow and spray clouds drench hikers. But the display of icicles hundreds of feet high is worth an early-winter visit.

Drive to the Camp Sheppard (which see) parking lot, 2400 feet. From there take the trail pointing at The Palisades—and up on that 500-foot near-overhang of a cliff see the thin ribbon of Snoquera Falls pluming down—or in spring see the Niagara flooding down—or at the right hour of a fall day see the mists windblown in a wavering rainbow. Walk to the start-end of the Moss Lake Nature Trail by the Campfire Circle; just beyond, intersect a road-wide trail. Turn right, uphill, to an elk trap maintained for research purposes. Here, ¼ mile from the parking lot, is the junction of a whole mess of trails, all clearly signed. Note the one going uphill right, signed "Snoquera Falls Loop Trail 1167, Snoquera Falls 1½"—that will be the route of the return.

Go left on White River Trail 1199, signed "Camp Sheppard ¼, Snoquera Loop Junction ¾." (The reason for doing the loop this way rather than the other is because it sneaks up on the falls, keeping the surprise to the last minute.) Proceed carefully through a profusion of crisscrossing paths to and from camp, whose roads and buildings are passed. At all unsigned junctions forge straight ahead. At all signed junctions stick with "Snoquera Loop." Passing mysterious open swaths on the hillside (they're for innertube sliding in snowtime), leave camp and proceed in continuously superb forest, in green twilight, on and near the valley floor. In ¾ mile from Elk Trap Junction is Wigre Junction, so called for a Scout leader who suffered an injury while building trail.

Turn right, again following the "Snoquera Loop" sign, and switchback up to the foot of the cliffs. Now the trail more or less contours, often close enough to the wall to reach out and put hands on. Look up the thrilling precipice. See the gorgeous fern-moss walls. See the monster Douglas firs growing from the rockslides—and marvel that they've survived the centuries of battering and gouging by falling rocks which have left every trunk a mass of impact wounds—and these superimposed on burn scars from repeated fires over the ages.

Hark. What is that sound? Why does the earth tremble? What mystery is creating these clouds drifting through the forest? Turn a lava corner—and there are the falls! (This is an example of how the Sheppard trails are designed—not to get from here to there in a rush but to squeeze the maximum excitement from the country.) Even in season when the falls aren't falling, well may one cower, gazing up the beetling black walls. They do not have a permanent look. One imagines more substantial and fearful falls than mere water.

The loop trail now starts down, passing an unsigned junction and a signed one, and returning in constant grand forest to Elk Trap Junction.

Round trip 4½ miles, allow 3 hours
High point 3100 feet, elevation gain 700 feet
May-November

Snoquera Palisades (Map-page 233)

Having looked up-up-up the Palisades from the bottom, ascend a spooky little gorge via an impossible route and look down-down-down from the top.

At Wigre Junction (see Snoquera Falls Loop) continue straight ahead downvalley on trail signed "Dalles Creek Trail Jct ¼ mile." In that ¼ mile (1½ miles from the parking lot) reach a junction at the dropoff to Dalles Creek. Switchback right, uphill, on Snoquera Palisades Loop Trail 1198. Switchback into the gorge and cross the creek in its dark, lush, big-tree depths, a place that in twilight is full of the oogalies that pad silently along behind lone hikers.

When Max and Ivan declared the Scouts were going to build a trail up this gorge, some Forest Service engineers burst into hysterical laughter. And truly, it's such a place as no trail has a right to be. Under drippy black-and-green-mossy Palisades walls, by pillars and clefts in the lava, amid big cedars anchored to rock, the trail switchbacks by a short spur to Lower Dalles Falls. Now, trapped in its idiot resolve to ascend this dank dark slot, the path writhes and wiggles between fern-garden cliffs and solemn great trees, trying to escape. The route is never dangerous, though looking up and down the switchbacks may give hikers the vertigo. Then, after some 30 switchbacks in ½ mile, the trail passes the Upper Falls, most of the year a small trickle, and incredibly breaks free of the gorge onto a forest shelf above the Palisades.

Now on gentle slopes, the trail turns southerly, traverses into a nice valley of a more relaxing Dalles Creek just below another falls hiding upstream in a little canyon. One has the suspicion that vast amounts of air are close by—and at 3350 feet the way emerges from trees onto the bald brink of a promontory. Be careful! Don't run to the edge! Cautiously step out on the viewpoint, look to nearby higher Palisades in stark profile, look down to forests of the valley, up to the 5270-foot summit of Sun Top.

Continue on, leaving the brink for more forest, ascend to the edge of the little Dalles Creek canyon just passed, then switchback out near the edge of the Palisades. At the turn of another switchback take the short sidepath to Point of Springs, a thrilling viewpoint with the added embellishment of ice-cold springs. Return to the main trail and continue into a pole forest of an old burn and break out on the bald brink of North Snoquera Point, 4000 feet, 4 miles from the parking lot. This brink is not so giddy and invites cautious poking around in the rock garden of herbs and shrubs. Look down to Camp Sheppard, 1600 feet directly below; to leap off would seemingly risk being skewered by the camp flagpole. To previous views now are added Rainier.

Continue if you wish to a bridge over Snoquera Creek or onward to South Snoquera Point, 4800 feet.

Round trip 8 miles, allow 5 hours
High point 4000 feet, elevation gain 1600 feet
June-November

Skookum Flats (Map-page 233)

Machines speed along the highway on one side of the White River. On the other side, in big old trees of Mather Memorial Strip, between lava cliffs and river gravels, hikers can forget there are machines in the world.

From the 2400-foot parking lot at Camp Sheppard (which see) walk toward the highway on the entry road, find a trail paralleling the highway, and follow it

White River valley from Snoquera Palisades viewpoint

upvalley a scant ¼ mile. At a sign pointing right to Skookum Flat Trail and Buck Creek Trail, cross the highway, jog left a hundred feet, and take the Buck Creek trail dropping into woods to the White River trail. Follow this upstream ½ mile to a footbridge, perfectly safe but likely to give acrophobes a thrill. On the far side, 1 mile from Sheppard, is a junction with the Skookum Flat Trail.

The trail upstream makes a pleasant 1¼-mile walk to the emergency airstrip. Downstream is the choice trip, however. Except at the very end, the 4½ miles to the Huckleberry Creek road are a constant delight, now on alluvial terraces, now beside the water, always in giant forest, here and there with looks across the valley to the Snoquera Palisades. At 2¼ miles from the junction are Skookum Falls, a satisfying turnaround. But just a bit farther are Skookum Springs Seeps, from whose 300 vertical feet of mossy basalt wall water droplets fall free. In any event, to avoid breaking the spell don't go all the way to the road; at 4 miles, when Dalles Campground is spotted across the river, turn back, thus avoiding the sight of logging, of which any user of this book can see a plenty on other trips.

The constant little ups and downs hardly raise a sweat. A bit of snow is a minor obstacle on the easy route—indeed, snow adds interest, since this unmachined side of the river is an animal highway and a hiker is likely to see tracks of coyote, bobcat, deer, rabbit, and a variety of little critters, raccoon-size, mouse-size, bird-size.

Round trip to Skookum Falls 6½ miles, allow 4 hours
High point 2500 feet, elevation gain 500 feet
March-December

INDEX